OECD ECONOMIC SURVEYS

1997-1998

SPAIN

ORGANISATION FOR ECONOMIC CO-OPERATION AND DEVELOPMENT

ORGANISATION FOR ECONOMIC CO-OPERATION AND DEVELOPMENT

Pursuant to Article 1 of the Convention signed in Paris on 14th December 1960, and which came into force on 30th September 1961, the Organisation for Economic Co-operation and Development (OECD) shall promote policies designed:

- to achieve the highest sustainable economic growth and employment and a rising standard of living in Member countries, while maintaining financial stability, and thus to contribute to the development of the world economy;
- to contribute to sound economic expansion in Member as well as non-member countries in the process of economic development; and
- to contribute to the expansion of world trade on a multilateral, non-discriminatory basis in accordance with international obligations.

The original Member countries of the OECD are Austria, Belgium, Canada, Denmark, France, Germany, Greece, Iceland, Ireland, Italy, Luxembourg, the Netherlands, Norway, Portugal, Spain, Sweden, Switzerland, Turkey, the United Kingdom and the United States. The following countries became Members subsequently through accession at the dates indicated hereafter: Japan (28th April 1964), Finland (28th January 1969), Australia (7th June 1971), New Zealand (29th May 1973), Mexico (18th May 1994), the Czech Republic (21st December 1995), Hungary (7th May 1996), Poland (22nd November 1996) and the Republic of Korea (12th December 1996). The Commission of the European Communities takes part in the work of the OECD (Article 13 of the OECD Convention).

Publié également en français

Table of contents

Boxes

Tables

Figures

BASIC STATISTICS OF SPAIN (1996)

THE LAND

Area (sq. km)	504 748	Major cities, 1991 census (thousand inhabitants)	
Cultivated area (sq. km)	187 530	Madrid	3 085
		Barcelona	1 681
		Valencia	777
		Seville	705
		Saragossa	622

THE PEOPLE

Population (thousands)	39 270	Civilian employment (thousands):	12 396
Number of inhabitants per sq. km	77.8	by sector (per cent of total):	
Net natural increase (thousands)	15	Agriculture	8.7
Net migration (thousands)	42	Industry	20.2
		Construction	9.5
		Services	61.7

PRODUCTION

Gross domestic product, GDP (billion pesetas)	73 661	GDP at factor cost by origin (per cent of total):	
GDP per head (US$)	14 788	Agriculture	3.7
Gross fixed investment		Industry	24.9
Per cent of GDP	20.2	Construction	8.3
Per head (US$)	2 989	Services	63.1

THE GOVERNMENT

Public consumption (per cent of GDP)	16.5	Composition of Parliament (number of seats):	350
Fixed investment (per cent of gross fixed capital		Popular Party (PP)	156
formation)	14.6	Spanish Labour Socialist Party (PSOE)	141
Government revenue (per cent of GDP)	39.1	Izquierda Unida	21
General government deficit (per cent of GDP)	4.5	Convergence and Union (CIU)	16
		Basque Nationalist Party (PNV)	5
		Canarian Union (CC)	4
		Herri Batasuna	2
		Other	5

Last general elections: March 1996

FOREIGN TRADE

Exports of goods and services:		Imports of goods and services:	
(billion US$)	148.1	(billion US$)	143.0
(per cent of GDP)	25.5	(per cent of GDP)	24.6
Exports as a per cent of total merchandise		Imports as a per cent of total merchandise	
exports, customs basis:		imports, customs basis:	
Foodstuffs	12.7	Foodstuffs	7.2
Other consumer goods	28.2	Other consumer goods	17.0
Energy	2.4	Energy	9.2
Other intermediate goods	42.6	Other intermediate goods	49.6
Capital goods	14.1	Capital goods	17.0

THE CURRENCY

Monetary unit: Peseta		Currency units per US$, average	
		of daily figures:	
		Year 1997	146.4
		January 1998	153.9

Note: An international comparison of certain basic statistics is given in an Annex table.

This Survey is based on the Secretariat's study prepared for the annual review of Spain by the Economic and Development Review Committee on 15th January 1998.

•

After revisions in the light of discussions during the review, final approval of the Survey for publication was given by the Committee on 9th February 1998.

•

The previous Survey of Spain was issued in January 1996.

Assessment and recommendations

A strong economic performance provides a window of opportunity to tackle the sources of high unemployment

Spain is achieving its finest economic performance since the late 1980s. Growth is strong and broadly based, job creation rapid, inflation low, and the current account broadly in balance. Several forces have been acting. A major impetus came from visible progress in implementing sound policies, in particular fiscal consolidation. This helped to bring about a sharp reduction in interest rates as Spain's prospects for joining EMU from its inception were re-evaluated by financial markets. A nascent recovery in Spain's main trading partners also provided important support. These factors have been reinforcing and have raised consumer and business confidence to levels not observed for over a decade. The current economic setting provides a window of opportunity to attack several long-standing structural problems that afflict the Spanish economy, most strikingly an unemployment rate which – though now declining steadily – still exceeds 20 per cent. The approach of monetary union in Europe should increase the sense of urgency to implement further labour and product market reforms.

Output growth is among the fastest in the OECD

Economic activity has been accelerating rapidly since mid-1996. With the growth rate likely to have exceeded $3^{1}/_{4}$ per cent in 1997, Spain is now among the fastest growing economies in the OECD. External demand was the initial source of growth, as the competitiveness of Spanish

1

exports was broadly maintained and the buoyancy of Western hemisphere economies strengthened. Subsequently, domestic demand has been reinforcing the expansion as private investment and consumption were spurred by declining interest rates, rising disposable income, and improving confidence. Strong private sector activity has more than offset the demand effects of a significant fiscal consolidation, as the credible reduction in the deficit towards the Maastricht limit helped to reduce long-term interest rates by as much as 5 percentage points since 1995.

The strong economy has created jobs while inflation has fallen to a 30 year low

The strong economy has created many jobs, and pushed the unemployment rate to below 21 per cent in late 1997 compared with 23 per cent in late 1995. Though most of the new jobs created have been under permanent contracts, one in three employees still has a fixed-term contract of very short duration and low pay. The degree to which the labour market has tightened remains unclear. Starting in mid 1997, wage settlements have moderated significantly, reflecting lower inflation expectations; even so, real wages increased by more than productivity. Underlying inflation (which excludes energy and fresh food products), however, declined to 2 per cent at end 1997 – a 30 year low – helped by declining financial costs and subdued imported input prices. For the first time in many decades, inflation in 1997 was less than the rate of output growth. The good overall price performance, however, masks a diverging pattern between prices in sheltered sectors and those more exposed to competition, with the former increasing at a $3\frac{1}{2}$ per cent rate in late 1997.

Output growth is likely to remain strong

The short-term prospects for the continued recovery in output are very promising, with almost all forward looking indicators pointing to a strengthening recovery. The OECD Secretariat projects output growth to exceed $3\frac{1}{2}$ per cent in both 1998 and 1999. It could be stronger if a high household savings rate of 12½ per cent falls back toward historical norms, spurred by improved labour market conditions. On the other hand, growth could temporarily abate if the crises in Asia lower the economic growth of Spain's larger trading partners by more than currently assumed. The central projections point to a modest inflation rebound in 1998 and 1999 due to capacity constraints, cost pressures, and one-off factors. However, there is a risk of more intense wage demands, with a labour market with high structural unemployment providing an additional source of tension at a time when further large reductions in financial costs will not be forthcoming.

The rising prospects of achieving the Maastricht criteria led to a sharp decline in interest rates...

Macroeconomic policy during the past two years was geared towards satisfying the Maastricht Treaty criteria. An impressive 3½ per cent of GDP reduction in the general government budget deficit has been achieved, and Spain is likely to meet the 3 per cent limit for 1997. Fiscal consolidation during 1996-97 was mainly accomplished through deep cuts in discretionary expenditures, notably in personnel outlays as wages were frozen and hirings curtailed. Further adjustment was attained through a sizeable reduction in public investment which will be partly compensated by investment using new financing techniques, such as build-operate-transfer and the turnkey payment method, which delay payments to a project's completion. Transfers to some public enterprises were also moved off-budget, and will henceforth be covered by privatisation receipts and the surplus of profitable public enterprises. The remainder of the adjustment was the result of cyclical factors and the sharp decline in interest rates. The fiscal strategy avoided dependence on any significant measures to increase revenues, with the main exception of user fees.

... which initially facilitated the task of monetary policy

The sharp fall in inflation during 1996-97 permitted the Bank of Spain to relax a monetary policy stance that had been severely tightened in mid-1995. Following its independence in 1994, the Bank of Spain has earned a strong anti-inflationary reputation. Inflation has consistently been below the Bank's targets, which guided inflation and interest rates to meet comfortably the respective Maastricht criteria. A further easing of monetary conditions will likely take place with the approach of monetary union. Long-term interest rates have already broadly converged with those in Germany, and short-term rates should follow in the prelude to EMU. In the current economic conjuncture, however, there is a risk that such an additional monetary stimulus would occur in a situation where it is not warranted. With a gradual loss of monetary policy autonomy during 1998, fiscal policy will need to contribute significantly to restraining demand and hence maintaining inflation at low levels.

New challenges lie ahead as Spain prepares for entry into EMU

It is important to avoid a bout of excessive price and labour cost increases that exceed those of Spain's trading partners as this would erode Spain's currently strong competitive position and jeopardise employment prospects. Such developments would be more difficult to counteract in a situation where national monetary policy had ceased to exist. In order to meet the challenges facing the Spanish economy in EMU, the Government has prepared a new convergence programme covering the period 1998-2000. The programme aims to achieve some further fiscal adjustment, which would leave the general government deficit at 1.6 per cent of GDP by the year 2000. The main measures include, *inter alia*, a continued rationalisation of public employment, tax reform (including a reduction in taxes) and elements of pension reform. The other critical aspect of the programme is a set of prospective structural reforms which will be introduced so as to make the economy more flexible

4

and allow a smoother absorption of asymmetric shocks within EMU. These centre on policies which enhance competition in product and factor markets.

With a prospective relaxation of monetary policy...

Within this new programme, the 1998 Budget aims to reduce the general government budget deficit to 2.4 per cent of GDP. The bulk of the adjustment relies on cyclical factors and lower interest payments, but includes few structural measures other than the maintenance of hiring restrictions in the civil service. Moreover, following two years of fiscal restraint, the Budget takes advantage of the growth in revenues to raise spending on health, education, and active labour market policies as well as investment. Any unforeseen revenue is committed by the budget law to reduce the deficit. However, in view of the prospective monetary stimulus as well as a strong economy, it would be prudent to achieve a tighter fiscal policy stance.

... fiscal policy should show more ambition

With entry into EMU approaching, fiscal policy will need room to react to the economic conjuncture, as well as to meet Spain's commitments under the Stability and Growth Pact. Significant further fiscal adjustment will be necessary to attain a more comfortable position. OECD Secretariat estimates, presented in the body of the *Survey*, suggest that further structural improvement in addition to that contained in the convergence programme will be necessary to guard against exceeding the 3 per cent of GDP limit in the event of a large cyclical downturn. Such consolidation will also be necessary to attain a rapid reduction in a debt to GDP ratio of nearly 70 per cent.

... and it will need to focus on the entitlement programmes

In addition to cyclical considerations, structural factors, if left unchecked, will lead to a gradual deterioration in the fiscal situation. As in many other continental European countries, the ageing of the population will put pressure on the pay-as-you-go public pension system and the public health system. In addition, resources will soon be needed to meet several large payments, *inter alia*, those emanating from the new financing techniques for public investment which delayed their payment, and the potential write-off of government-guaranteed debt by loss-making public entities. The recent squeeze of discretionary expenditure is unlikely to be sustainable for much longer, and the Government is committed to raise the current level of public investment. Little fiscal adjustment will be forthcoming from the revenue side as the Government is also determined to reduce the tax burden. However, in tight fiscal times, tax reform should strive to reduce the distortionary effects of the system, balance a reduction of marginal rates with an elimination of tax expenditure, and leave average taxation broadly unchanged until a satisfactory fiscal position is achieved. In this framework, further fiscal consolidation has to come to grips with the largest and most intransigent items of the budget – the social entitlement programmes.

A fundamental reform is necessary in the public pension and health care systems

The 1997 reform of the public pension system, which implemented the agreement between social partners (the Toledo Pact), is a step toward addressing the fundamental problems facing the system. By practically doubling the pension base to the last 15 years of contributions, the generous replacement rate will be gradually curtailed, and by pushing back the pace with which pension rights are accumulated, the incentive to early retirement will be weakened. Nevertheless, the cumulated savings from the reform will – as is generally acknowledged – be far from sufficient to bring the future unfunded liabilities of the system under control. In view of the prospective rise in the old-age dependency ratio and the lack of a reserve fund, pension benefits are still too generous relative to contributions, and retirement (on average) occurs far too early, including

6

through the frequent use of invalidity pensions. Experience indicates that reforms can be implemented only gradually and therefore need to be introduced early. A re-evaluation of the system is planned for the year 2000. However, delays will result in either more abrupt adjustment for the middle-age generation or heavier burdens on the younger generations. Reforms should also involve making room in the budget to cover the payment of non-contributory benefits – which the Government envisages financing from general resources – and thus facilitate a gradual build up of a reserve fund.

A fundamental reform of the health system will be elaborated following the recent parliamentary commission agreement on an overall framework. To date, piecemeal reform has been introduced in various areas by regional authorities which have accepted responsibility for their public health care systems, notably in the area of hospital management. Many of these experiments have had positive results which point to potential benefits from a wider reform. A systemic reform should improve the gatekeeping role played by primary care doctors, extend successful pilot hospital management reforms throughout Spain and control expenditures on pharmaceuticals, especially by introducing means testing for pensioners, who account for 65 per cent of drug consumption, largely reflecting their free access to pharmaceuticals. Since regional governments are gradually taking over the responsibility for public health care, comprehensive reform is inexorably linked to the issue of regional financing.

Fiscal restraint will also require co-ordination of regional financing

The new financing agreement with the regions for the period 1997-2001 provides them with important new fiscal responsibility. The objective is to increase the share of regional governments' revenue raised from taxes which they control toward the level of expenditures which they have assumed. The agreement also provides the regions with a cushion against revenue shortfalls and additional funds to facilitate a regional convergence of per capita incomes. Although the devolution of more financial autonomy to the regions to match their increased expenditure competencies should enhance efficiency in the long run, during the transition improved co-ordination is needed to avoid the duplication of services at different levels of government and to achieve nationwide consistency of fiscal targets. Risk-sharing mechanisms for revenues and regional equity considerations will also need to be balanced carefully against the objective for overall macroeconomic stability. An internal stability pact is under consideration, but its implementation will require a significant improvement in the monitoring of regional fiscal developments as well as the introduction of a credible enforcement mechanism.

EMU will require more flexible, and better functioning, labour markets

The new convergence programme recognises the need for the Spanish economy to become more flexible, not least because of EMU. Reform of the labour market is indispensable as market rigidities are the root cause of an inordinately high unemployment rate. Dismissal costs, which are among the highest in the OECD, are mostly responsible for the excessively large share of fixed-term contracts and the resulting three-tier segmentation of the labour market between workers with permanent contracts, those with temporary contracts and the unemployed. The middle tier has been the source of a large part of the employment creation during the last decade. However, its existence has strengthened the job security, and thereby the bargaining power, of workers with permanent jobs and led to segmented pay scales. At the same time the overlapping responsibilities of a complex collective bargaining system provide an additional source of wage inflation.

A new labour market reform promotes employment stability but dismissal costs are still too high

In an important first step to reform the labour market, a noteworthy social consensus was reached by employers and unions to promote more stable employment contracts and to clarify the definition of justified dismissals, which carry lower costs. They also suggested a framework for preventing the re-negotiation of contract terms at successive levels of bargaining. The success of the reform will depend critically on the latter two aspects, as the former only partly addresses the underlying motivation for fixed-term contracts. While dismissal costs have been lowered selectively for workers obtaining new permanent contracts, these costs nevertheless remain among the highest in the OECD. Further encouragement to offer permanent contracts comes from temporary financial incentives while the conditions for hiring and extending fixed-term contracts are being tightened; and the Government is considering a one-year rise in unemployment insurance contributions on fixed-term workers by one percentage point. If these reforms either constrain the use of fixed-term contracts or raise non-wage labour costs, they will discourage overall employment even though the share of fixed-term workers in the total comes down.

To create jobs, wages in real terms will need to increase at a less pronounced pace than labour productivity. The current pick up in activity provides the opportunity for this to occur in an environment of real wage gains, and should be conducive to more ambitious efforts at reform. One of the most important steps to be taken is a reduction of the high firing costs for the two-thirds of the workforce with permanent contracts under the pre-reform terms.

The new initiatives to strengthen active labour market policies and support training contracts, if designed properly, should be useful in providing work experience. Similarly, the reduction of fraud under the temporary invalidity scheme – which is reportedly often used as a substitute for

9

unemployment benefits – should encourage job search. Finally, the successful implementation of land reform, especially abolishing licensing as an important source of local authority financing, would serve to reduce the high price of land in a country where land is abundant, and thus improve labour mobility.

Competition should also be enhanced in product markets, where the Government is undertaking an ambitious programme to modernise public enterprises

The Government has focused its efforts to enhance product market competition mainly in the areas dominated by public enterprises, most of which have already been or are in the process of being privatised. Substantial progress has also been achieved under an ambitious programme which aims to restructure public enterprises controlled by the central government and to sell most of them by the turn of the century. Such an accomplishment will eliminate what was a major burden on past budgets and pushed up the general government debt significantly. Eliminating preferential treatment of public enterprises may also lower wage expectations, as generous compensation packages have – at times – tended to provide inappropriate precedents for other enterprises. A successful conclusion of this programme – equity equivalent to 3 per cent of GDP was already sold during 1996-97 – could provide tangible benefits to the economy in addition to the short-term financial gains. However, more substantial benefits can be realised only if the Government succeeds in its policy to promote competition in the sectors previously dominated by public enterprises, especially as these sectors often produce critical inputs for the economy (*e.g.* energy, transportation and telecommunications) and should provide less expensive and/or more efficient services. The OECD Secretariat estimates that the potential output gains from the full realisation of efficiency gains could eventually be of the order of 4 to 5 per cent of GDP, and with more flexible labour markets these gains would create additional employment.

A speedy implementation of reform in various sectors can yield large payoffs

A speedy implementation of regulatory reforms and the privatisation programme would bring forward the gains and provide Spanish enterprises with a head start *vis-à-vis* most of their competitors. This is the case in the telecommunications and electricity sectors following the 1996-97 reforms. A further important step was the recently approved hydrocarbon law for gas and oil. In sectors which are potentially competitive, the Government can move quickly towards privatisation, as it has already done in the case of the aluminium and steel industries. In sectors which the Government considers important for the implementation of public policies, such as railways, the authorities should review whether parts or all of it cannot be operated by the private sector and policy goals achieved in a more efficient way. For example, the use of concession agreements has proved successful in the running of public bus services and could be used for railways, with the social component of the service included in the terms of the concession. Industries in declining sectors such as coal and shipyards will need to improve efficiency, specialise and adjust their capacity. The trade-off between a longer and shorter restructuring period should be re-evaluated, especially for the coal sector which creates significant ripple effects on the efficient operation of the electricity sector and also raises environmental concerns.

Reforms should focus on achieving equitable access to the natural monopoly component...

Industries with network characteristics require difficult decisions regarding the creation of an industry structure which spurs competition. Equitable access to the natural monopoly component of the sector is a necessary condition for the creation of a contestable environment. All the key sectors contain network characteristics (for instance, the electricity or telecommunications grids, and even airport slots). The recent restructuring of the electricity sector, which provides appropriate ring-fencing around the high

11

voltage electricity grid and sets up a price auction, could be used as a model for some of the other sectors, notably oil and natural gas. Technological improvements are reducing the natural monopoly elements in fixed-line telecommunications. However, in the immediate future the level of the interconnection prices will be critical to enhancing competition from the newly created second operator in basic telephony; and at present these prices appear to be very high. In the airline industry consideration should be given to moving further than current EC directives, and slots assigned to the current holders could be auctioned as concessions for fixed periods.

... contestability of markets...

Even if equitable access to the network component of the industry is achieved, the establishment of contestability requires the existence of potential entrants and/or competitors. In the Spanish context, most sectors were formerly dominated by a public enterprise, so that sufficient horizontal competition is often lacking; *e.g.* the basic telephony and gas sectors are *de facto* monopolies, and the oil, electricity and aviation sectors are highly concentrated oligopolies. With competition from abroad constrained by geographic factors in the energy sector, the Government may need to foster domestic competition through new entrants and/or a more drastic restructuring of this sector. The experience of other countries which have preceded Spain in privatisation suggests that delaying restructuring of an industry has been very costly in terms of foregone potential efficiency gains.

... and appropriate regulatory arrangements

The process of introducing competition must by necessity continue to evolve and react to sectoral developments. With competition unlikely to develop quickly in most of these sectors, price cap regulations appear necessary to protect consumers. Their level is difficult to set and therefore periodic reviews should not be too far apart, especially in cases where firms are allowed to pass on large historical sunk costs to consumer prices, as is the case in the Spanish electricity sector. International experience attests to the positive role of well-functioning and independent regulators. To achieve this end, the new regulator for the electricity, gas and fuel sectors should be independent and have broad decision powers. Ownership structure is also important for a firm's economic performance, and extensive cross-shareholder arrangements between critical firms and sectors provide poor incentives for competition and could impede economic growth. The current policy to increase the role of small shareholders' and institutional investors' participation in privatised enterprises should be continued as it could lead to a more independent ownership.

Enhancing entrepreneurial activity should reinforce growth prospects...

Increased product market competition would help entrepreneurial activity, which is an essential feature of a dynamic economy. More risk-taking and an on-going commitment by the business sector to develop new products and processes would strengthen economic performance. Several aspects of the institutional arrangements in Spain are not, however, conducive to entrepreneurship and point to areas where reforms are needed. Barriers to entry are still in force in a number of sectors and, while many measures necessary to stimulate competition are being introduced and further reform has been identified, they have not yet been acted upon. Specifically, opening a new business is a particularly lengthy and complicated process and undermines the development of more innovative and flexible businesses. The Government's expressed intentions to streamline the administrative processes will be a welcome step in the right direction. A shift towards a more business-oriented economy also requires efforts to improve the efficiency of the judicial system to provide more effective enforcement of contracts and more rapid resolution of disputes. Just as importantly more flexible labour markets would make it easier and less costly for firms to take the risks inherent in entering new markets and to respond quickly to changes in market demand. Lower unemployment, especially for the young, could provide the job experience often abetting entrepreneurial activity.

... but requires a broad-based policy approach

For small and medium-sized enterprises in particular, finance has in the past been costly and relatively difficult to obtain. The venture capital market remains relatively undeveloped, which may to some extent reflect the restrictions placed on institutional investors. It may however, also reflect a lack of strong investment proposals. With relatively few researchers who have links to the business sector, the scope for technical innovation in Spain may be more limited than in other countries. But on the other hand, much entrepreneurial activity does not necessarily involve technological innovation. For example, the high degree of fragmentation in certain services, where significant economies of scale and/or scope have been shown to exist in other countries, suggests that there is considerable room for more innovative arrangements. However, their exploitation requires a more conducive environment for entrepreneurship. While it would take time to yield results, a greater emphasis on the development of entrepreneurial skills in the education system would help Spain make the most of the increased opportunities arising from structural reforms.

Summing-up

Conditions are in place for a continuation of very good economic performance. There has been a substantial improvement in macroeconomic policy settings, and the recently approved product and labour market reforms represent important first steps to alleviating supply-side constraints to non-inflationary growth; the successful implementation of the 1998-2000 convergence programme would reinforce this process. The window of opportunity provided by current economic circumstances should be used to make bolder reforms to address several long-standing structural problems, especially in the labour market. Such an approach would give the Spanish economy the best chance to perform successfully within the EMU and be conducive to achieving per capita income convergence with its EU partners.

I. Recent economic trends and prospects

The Spanish economy has experienced remarkable buoyancy during the past two years. Economic activity has been accelerating rapidly following the pause of late 1995, and Spain is expected to be among the fastest-growing countries of the OECD in 1997. The resumption of output growth was initially driven by exports but was subsequently reinforced by a strengthening of total domestic demand in 1997 (Figure 1). With profits booming and financial costs falling sharply, business investment was the engine of domestic demand growth in late 1996 while private consumption has gradually gathered steam as disposable income and consumer confidence recovered. Private sector activity intensified in the face of a tight fiscal policy, which held back demand growth in 1996 and 1997.

The strengthening of the economy has been accompanied by strong employment growth, with a large share of the newly employed under permanent contracts. The unemployment rate has fallen rapidly, though it remains above 20 per cent and has a large structural component. Despite the tightening in the economy, declining financial costs combined with important transitory factors as well as lower imported input costs and diminished inflation expectations, have pushed down the headline inflation rate. Wage demands have been slow to adjust to this new low-inflation environment and have risen considerably in real terms over 1996 and in the first half of 1997. Though the consequent rise in unit labour costs surpassed those of the main trading partner countries by a significant margin, international price competitiveness was not affected in 1996 and improved somewhat in 1997 following the depreciation of the peseta in effective terms due to the appreciation of the US dollar. Combined with buoyant demand from North and Latin America and strong tourist seasons, the current account surplus widened.

Figure 1. CONTRIBUTIONS TO GDP GROWTH
Change over same quarter of previous year

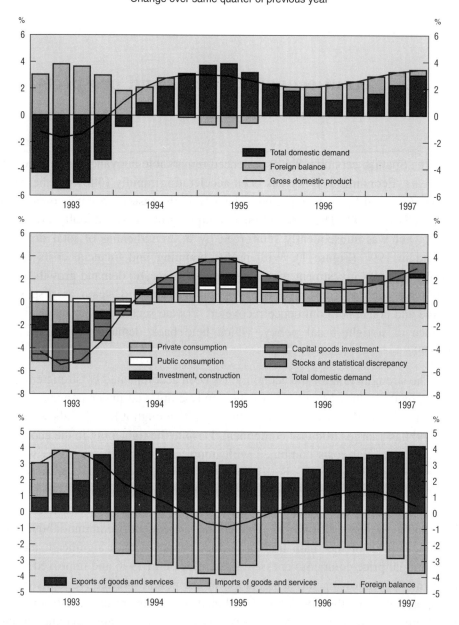

Source: Ministry of Economy and Finance and National Institute of Statistics.

Demand and output

Private consumption gathered steam though the saving rate remained high

Long awaited, the signs of a consumer spending recovery became clear in the second half of 1996 and private consumption has subsequently gathered steam. For 1997 as a whole, private consumption is expected to have risen by over 3 per cent, attaining a growth not experienced since before the 1993 recession and one which contrasts with the sluggish recovery of consumption in most other European countries. The recovery in private consumption was based on rapid employment creation and rising wage gains which boosted households' real earnings despite a public sector wage freeze (Figure 2, upper panel). These developments, as well as a booming stock market and the stabilisation of the share of fixed-term contracts in total employment, appear to have steadily bolstered consumer confidence from late 1996. Further support to consumption has been provided by fiscal incentives for new car purchases (*Prever* plan).[1] Nevertheless, households' saving ratio remained high – near 12½ per cent. The high propensity to save probably reflects the still large share of employment under short-duration fixed-term contracts, their large turnover, and possibly uncertainties surrounding the future of the social security system, especially as regards pensions. The consequences for consumption from the combined impact of income and wealth effects arising from recent asset market developments is ambiguous. On the one hand, prices of housing (households' primary source of wealth) have picked up while mutual fund and equity values have increased by far more (an increasingly larger share of households' financial wealth) (Table 1).[2] On the other hand, interest income is lower as rates on deposits (households' main element of financial wealth) have declined. A reduction in capital gains taxation is inducing a switch out of deposits into mutual funds, diminishing interest income further (but raising household wealth).

Business investment remains strong, reflecting profits and capacity constraints

Total investment was hesitant in 1996 and early 1997. The weakness in total investment masked an acceleration in business investment from the second half of 1996, bolstered by a high and rising capacity utilisation rate which attained its

19

Figure 2. **COMPONENTS OF FINAL DOMESTIC DEMAND**

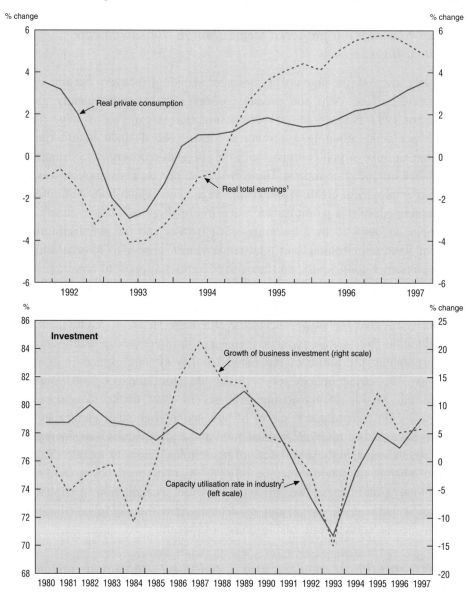

1. Average monthly earnings per employee multiplied by total dependent employment and deflated by the private consumption deflator.
2. 1997 is based on the first 3 quarters.
Source: Ministry of Economy and Finance and National Institute of Statistics.

Table 1. **Outstanding financial assets and liabilities of households**[1]

	1990	1995	1996
Net financial wealth (billion Ptas)	29 001	49 438	57 587
(as a percentage of gross disposable income)	83.2	100.3	110.9
Liabilities (billion Ptas)	29 937	40 904	44 773
Assets (billion Ptas)	58 938	90 342	102 360
of which (as a percentage):			
Deposits	61.2	54.6	48.4
Mutual funds	1.7	11.8	12.5
Other shares and equities	13.1	9.3	15.9

1. Households and private non-profit institutions serving households.
Source: Bank of Spain, *Financial accounts of the Spanish economy, 1987-1996.*

highest level since the late 1980s (Figure 2, lower panel). Declining financial costs and the resulting healthy firm profits have produced high rates of return on capital investment (Table 2). A possible sign of the durability of the recovery is that business fixed capital has sustained a growth path parallel to that of employment during the past years (capital widening) rather than substituting for labour (capital deepening) (Figure 3). Regarding the other components of investment,

Table 2. **Financial performances of non-financial firms**[1]

Percentage change

	1994[2]	1995[2]	1996[2]	1996: Q1-Q3/ 1995: Q1-Q3[3]	1997: Q1-Q3/ 1996: Q1-Q3[3]
Gross value added	8.0	8.1	2.6	2.1	4.7
Labour costs	0.8	3.8	3.7	3.8	2.6
Employment	–2.5	0.9	0.1	–0.3	–0.6
Financial costs	–16.6	–0.8	–13.9	–12.0	–15.8
Memorandum items:					
Net income [4]	5.6	7.4	10.8	16.0	20.8
Debt ratio[4]	48.8	45.6	42.7	40.6	39.7
Leverage ratio[5]	–1.5	–1.0	0.4	1.7	4.2

1. Data coverage is biased towards large, public and industrial enterprises.
2. *Central de balances,* annual sample.
3. *Central de balances,* quarterly sample.
4. As a percentage of the gross value added.
5. Rate of return of assets less financial costs on total liabilities (in percentage points).
Source: Bank of Spain, *Central de balances.*

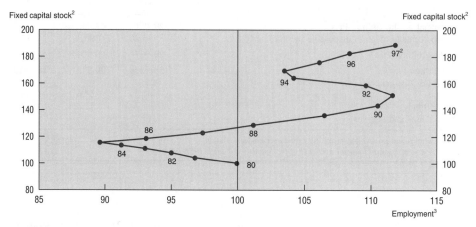

Figure 3. **FIXED CAPITAL STOCK AND EMPLOYMENT**[1]

Business sector, volume indices (1980 = 100)

1. Non-farm employment.
2. OECD estimates.
3. Employment is corrected for the bias introduced by the rebasing of the labour force survey by the gradual introduction of the 1991 census.
Source: OECD Secretariat.

private non-residential building activity remained depressed in 1996 but appears to be recovering in line with the gradual rise in commercial rents. Residential investment, bolstered by the increase in households' disposable income and cheaper mortgage loans, also recovered in 1997. In sharp contrast, public investment was cut by 16 per cent in volume terms in 1996 and stagnated in 1997 as part of fiscal consolidation. Overall, investment continued to increase as a share of GDP, and represented an estimated 22.5 per cent in 1996, which is high compared with most other OECD countries (Figure 4).

With all components of domestic demand strengthening, final domestic demand is expected to have steadily recovered to grow by about 3 per cent in 1997. Total domestic demand growth is expected to have been lower due to a significant reduction in stocks.[3] The sharp contraction in inventories may initially have reflected a correction of involuntary stockbuilding in the industrial sector subsequent to the slowdown in demand in the first half of 1996, but the continuation of the rundown may have been involuntary, induced by an acceleration in

Figure 4. **INVESTMENT IN SELECTED OECD COUNTRIES**[1]

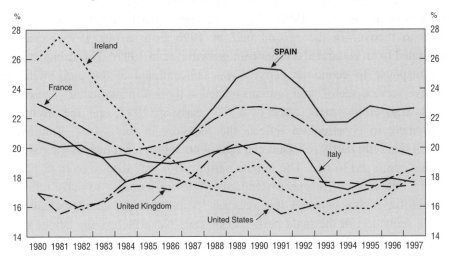

1. Ratio of investment to gross domestic product at constant prices.
Source: OECD Secretariat.

demand in a context of emerging tensions on installed capacities. Finally, the rundown reflects a drop in the large agricultural stocks following a bountiful 1996 season.[4] The external accounts provided an additional boost to output. Net exports' contribution to growth, though envisaged to have slackened somewhat in 1997, remained sizeable, mainly reflecting the strong competitiveness of Spanish exports. Overall, the pace of output growth is estimated to have gradually accelerated to an estimated 3.4 per cent in 1997 from 2.3 per cent in 1996.[5]

The labour market

The employment response to the output recovery was strong

The response of employment to the economic upturn came earlier and was far stronger than in the previous recovery. The approximately ¹/₂ million new jobs created in 1996 and 1997 is estimated to have raised the employment ratio for persons aged 15 to 64 to near 49¹/₂ per cent, a level still far below that of other

European countries but one approaching the recent peak for Spain of about 50 per cent in the early 1990s (Figure 5, upper panel). Employment creation started to recover in the second half of 1996 from a late 1995 pause, and accelerated to an estimated 2.6 per cent growth rate in 1997.[6] The strong employment response to economic activity was concentrated in the buoyant labour-intensive service sector, and tourism-related activities in particular. The decline in industrial employment came to a halt early in 1997, and the strength of employment in construction reflects the recovery in this sector. Employment creation was only partly reflected in a falling unemployment rate, as the participation rate continued to rise. The female participation rate rose to over 47 per cent in 1997, still low by European standards. A lower recourse to early retirement schemes for males between the ages of 55 and 64 has counterbalanced the gradual reduction in the male participation rate. Nevertheless the labour market has tightened as the unemployment rate is estimated to have fallen by one percentage point in 1997 to near 20 per cent by year end.[7]

Despite the employment creation being concentrated in permanent jobs, the share of workers on fixed-term contracts – which tend to have poor career prospects and to be low paying – remained very high (over 33 per cent of total wage earners in 1997 compared with approximately 15 per cent for the European Union as a whole).[8] The turnover rate of fixed-term contracts continued on a rising trend, with their average duration falling to below 6 months (see Figure 5, lower panel). Reinforcing the poor prospects of such contracts, the corresponding average earning is about half that of a worker with a permanent job. An important part of the May 1997 labour market legislation aimed to secure a larger share of indefinite contracts through a variety of financial and contractual incentives (see Chapter III). It is too early to gauge its full impact, especially in view of the concomitant effect of the economic recovery. However, the information on new job contracts revealed that the share of indefinite contracts among all new contracts had doubled, from around 4 per cent in 1996 to around 9 per cent from June to December 1997. Moreover, most of the new indefinite contracts appear to be the result of this agreement.[9] Part-time employment also rose steadily in 1996 and 1997, albeit from a low level compared with other OECD countries (about 8 per cent in 1997, half the EU average).[10]

Figure 5. **EMPLOYMENT**

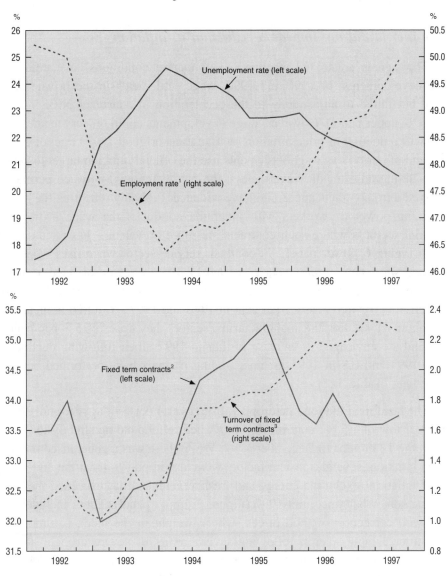

1. Total employment as a percentage of population aged 16-64 years old, data from the Labour Force Survey.
2. Ratio of fixed term salaried employment as a percentage of total salaried employment.
3. Ratio of fixed term new contracts (annualised) to fixed term salaried employment.
Source: National Institute of Statistics, Ministry of Economy and Finance and OECD, *Main Economic Indicators.*

Wages and prices

Wage inertia did not impede a reduction in inflation

The signals are mixed whether labour market conditions have influenced wage developments. In 1996 and 1997, wage settlements in the private sector abated but failed to adjust fully to the deceleration in consumer price inflation (Figure 6, upper panel). However, wage developments could reflect the unexpectedly swift reduction of price inflation relative to its original 1997 target of 2.6 per cent (end of period), as wage settlements use the official inflation target to set the cost of living adjustment. Nevertheless, the pay differential between permanent and fixed-term contracts appears to have widened. Probably reflecting the greater bargaining power of workers with indefinite contracts, the wage drift in the industrial sector – where such contracts are more prevalent – has risen significantly (Figure 6, lower panel). In contrast, service-sector wage rises were very moderate since new employment consisted to a large degree of fixed-term and part-time jobs (*e.g.* in tourism activities). Wage developments combined with low productivity growth – below 1 per cent in 1996 and 1997 – resulted in increasing unit labour costs. For the manufacturing sector, they rose by 5.3 per cent in 1996 and are envisaged to increase further in 1997 albeit following declines of 2.4 in 1994 and 0.8 in 1995; Spain's trading partners have performed better in this respect (Table 3).

The headline inflation rate dropped from over 4 per cent at year-end 1995 to a 30 year low of 1.5 per cent in May 1997, before rebounding slightly to 2.0 per cent in the 12 months to December 1997. While there was a generalised moderation in inflation, several transient factors were also at play, so that the underlying rate of inflation (excluding energy and fresh vegetables) has exceeded the headline rate somewhat since mid-1997 (Figure 7, upper panel). These included: the downward correction of food prices (whose weight in the index is almost one third) after a bumper crop following several years of severe drought and the waning impact of mad-cow disease on meat prices; the reduction of electricity tariffs in 1997, as well as the decline in international petroleum prices. The underlying moderation in inflation was facilitated by the significant drop in financial costs and imported input prices, which alleviated cost-side pressures on price margins and left firms' profitability at very high levels. In addition, inflation developments have probably been dampened by diminished inflationary

Figure 6. **WAGE SETTLEMENTS, TOTAL WAGES
AND THE CONSUMER PRICE INDEX**

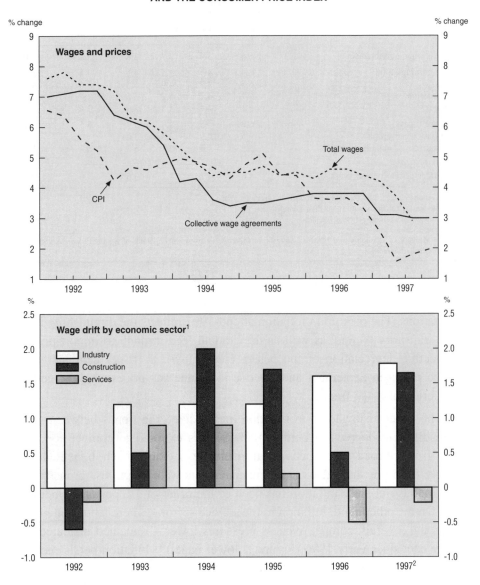

1.   Wage drift is calculated as the average increase in earnings less salary pacts.
2.   Average of the first 9 months.
Source: Ministry of Economy and Finance, Síntesis de indicatores económicos and OECD *Main Economic Indicators.*

Table 3. **Wages and labour costs**

Per cent change, annual rate

	1993	1994	1995	1996	Jan.-Sept. 1996[1]	Jan.-Sept. 1997[1]
Collective wage agreements	5.4	3.4	3.7	3.8	3.8	3.0
Average earnings total[2]	6.4	4.7	4.5	4.5	4.5	3.6
Industry	6.5	4.7	4.9	5.5	5.6	4.7
Construction	6.7	4.7	5.2	4.5	4.4	4.4
Services	6.1	4.1	3.8	3.3	3.4	2.9
Basic hourly pay[3]	6.8	4.5	4.8	5.3	5.5	4.1
Compensation per employee[4]	9.5	2.9	2.3	3.6	..	..
Unit labour costs, manufacturing	5.2	–2.4	–0.8	5.3	6.1	1.2
Memorandum item:						
Consumer prices (period average)	4.6	4.7	4.7	3.6	3.6	2.0

1. Percentage change over the same period of the previous year.
2. Wage survey for firms with more than 5 employees.
3. Ordinary pay excluding annual bonuses.
4. Private sector.
Source: Ministry of Economy and Finance, *Síntesis de Indicadores Económicos*, Bank of Spain, *Boletín Estadístico* and OECD Secretariat.

expectations. The pick up in inflation at end-1997 reflects the diminishing impact of the transitory factors, as well as the gradual feed-through to import prices of an effective depreciation of the peseta (see below), a 10 per cent increase in tobacco prices in September and the rise in butane gas prices after the end of a long period of price freeze.

The general slowdown in inflation masks diverging trends between sectors facing different degrees of competition. Sectors exposed to competition, especially from abroad, and the capital intensive sectors which benefited more strongly from the sharp decline in financial costs were much less prone to raise prices. Industrial price inflation has been of the order of 1½ per cent since early 1997. On the other hand, inflation in the service sector – where labour intensity is higher and, overall, competitiveness pressures lower – remained unabated, near 3½ per cent since early 1996 (Figure 7, lower panel).[11] Inflation persistence may reflect Spain's still low level of openness for a country of its size (Figure 8). Finally, administered prices have been increased at a pace well below that of inflation. In part, this reflects restructuring efforts in certain sectors (electricity) while in other cases (butane gas) price controls reflected explicit efforts to influence inflation expectations.

Figure 7. **CONSUMER PRICES**
Growth rates

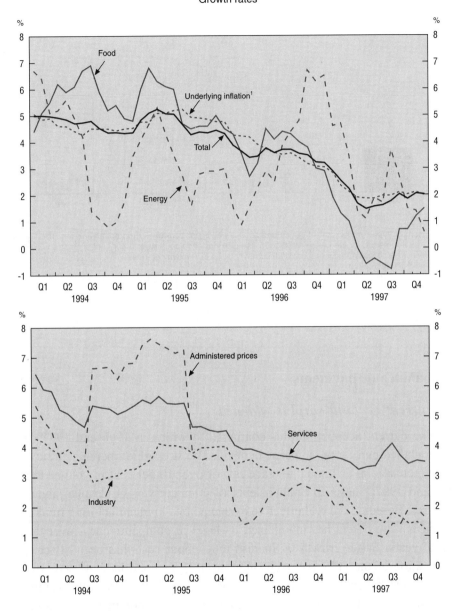

1. Excluding non-processed food and energy.
Source: Ministry of Economy and Finance.

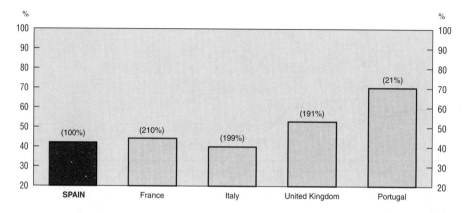

Figure 8. **DEGREE OF OPENNESS OF THE ECONOMY**[1]
1990-1996

1. The sum of import and export of goods and services as a per cent of GDP in nominal terms. The figures in brackets represent, for the period 1990-1995, the GDP for each country as a per cent of Spanish GDP; each country's GDP is converted into a common currency using PPP exchange rates.
Source: OECD Secretariat.

The balance of payments

The current account surplus widened

The current account surplus continued to widen in 1996 and 1997 despite the strengthening of total domestic demand. The strength of merchandise exports, which increased at an annual average rate of over 10 per cent in volume terms in 1996 and 1997, attests to Spain's level of competitiveness, despite labour cost pressures. Based on the real effective exchange rate in manufacturing (unit labour cost basis), the peseta has maintained its level of competitiveness over the past several years. Faster growth in Spanish unit labour costs has been offset by the depreciation of the effective exchange rate in the second half of 1996 and first half of 1997 basically reflecting the appreciation of the US dollar (Figure 9). Moreover, the unit labour cost measure understates the competitive position as it does not take into account the sharp reduction in financial costs. Evidence of the underlying level of competitiveness is confirmed by the estimated 10 per cent

Figure 9. **EXTERNAL COMPETITIVENESS**
1991 = 100

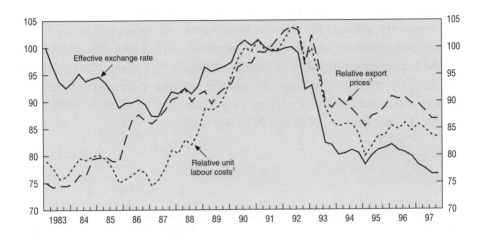

1. Manufacturing.
Source: OECD Secretariat.

gain of merchandise export market share during 1996 and 1997, underpinned by automobile, agriculture and capital good exports and by exports to non-EU markets particularly to Latin America, Asia and North America.[12] External demand for consumer goods remained weaker, reflecting the sluggish recovery in private consumption in most other European countries. Spain's imports responded to the recovery in domestic demand but with a lower income elasticity than in the past. Subdued imports partly reflect good weather conditions (mild weather and above normal rains which prompted a good domestic performance of agricultural output and hydro-energy production). The competitiveness of domestic tradeable sectors and the effective depreciation of the peseta also helped dampen the demand for imports.

A crucial contribution to the improvement of the current account came from a highly competitive tourism sector. Tourism receipts rose to the equivalent of 3.9 per cent of GDP in 1996, and the number of nights spent in hotels by foreigners during the 1997 spring and summer seasons were records, permitting Spain to overtake France and Italy to become the second most important tourist

destination in the world in terms of revenues. During 1996 and 1997, the containment of the trade deficit and the rising non-factor service surplus largely offset
the sharp deterioration of the net factor income deficit (Table 4). Developments in
the latter mainly reflected the increase in payments due to the rise in the external
liabilities of the banking system and the increase in dividend payments stemming
from the improved profitability of Spanish firms. With capital transfers (mainly
from the EU) remaining strong, the current account balance combined with
capital transfers widened to a surplus of 1.4 per cent of GDP in 1996 and an
estimated 1.6 per cent of GDP in 1997 (Box 1).[13]

Table 4. **The current and capital accounts of the balance of payments**

	1993	1994	1995	1996	Jan.-Oct. 1996	Jan.-Oct. 1997
	Pesetas billion					
Trade balance[1]	−1 897	−1 967	−2 194	−1 886	−1 695	−1 633
(per cent of GDP)	(−3.1)	(−3.0)	(−3.1)	(−2.6)	..	..
Exports	7 876	9 889	11 345	12 936	10 552	12 554
Imports	9 773	11 856	13 539	14 822	12 248	14 187
Non-factor services (excluding tourism)	−475	−371	−385	−343	−279	−332
Credits	1 425	1 671	1 818	2 120	1 742	2 074
Debits	1 900	2 042	2 203	2 463	2 020	2 406
Tourism	1 911	2 322	2 610	2 881	2 478	2 828
Net investment income[2]	−448	−1 095	−483	−752	−649	−728
Net current transfers	181	183	593	324	339	427
of which: Net EU transfers	−13	−13	382	126	177	213
Current balance	−728	−928	141	224	194	562
(per cent of GDP)	(−1.2)	(−1.4)	(0.2)	(0.3)	..	..
Capital balance	418	361	780	807	609	532
(per cent of GDP)	(0.7)	(0.6)	(1.1)	(1.1)	..	..
of which: Net EU transfers	401	349	743	776	588	488
	Per cent change, annual rate					
Terms of trade, goods and services[3]	−1.7	−1.1	0.6	−0.3	−1.5	0.0

1. F.o.b.
2. Investment and labour income.
3. National accounts basis, which differ somewhat from customs basis.
Source: Bank of Spain, *Boletín Económico* and *Boletín Estadístico*, Ministry of Economy and Finance, *Síntesis de Indicadores Económicos.*

Box 1. EU transfers to Spain

Net EU transfers to Spain have amounted to around 1 per cent of GDP per year since 1996, with the implementation of the Delors II package as well as the cohesion pro-gramme (applying only to Greece, Ireland, Portugal and Spain) resulting in a doubling of this share from the mid 1990s. This new source of funds is targeted to structural investment and expenditure to promote economic and social cohesion. During the same period, transfers to the agriculture sector remained broadly constant as a share of GDP. As a result, structural and cohesion funds now account for over half of total EU transfers to Spain (on a gross basis). Spanish transfers to the EU have also risen during this period and currently exceed 1 per cent of GDP. The distribution across countries of structural and cohesion funds for the 1994-99 period envisaged in the Delors II package makes Spain the largest recipient in absolute ECU terms – accounting for about one fourth of the total budget of ECU 152 billion – followed by Italy and Germany which will receive about one fifth of these funds. In terms of EU structural and cohesion funds received per capita, Spain ranks third, after Portugal and Greece. This distribution of resources reflects their use being concentrated on geographical areas whose per capita income is below 75 per cent of the EU average.

Table 5. EU transfers to Spain
Billions of pesetas

	1990	1992	1994	1996	1997	1998
EU transfers received by Spain	510	990	1 166	1 664	1 691	1 890
(as a percentage of GDP)	(1.0)	(1.7)	(1.8)	(2.3)	(2.2)	(2.3)
of which:						
Agriculture (FEOGA)	274	463	700	647	760	864
Structural funds	219	505	389	788	783	791
Cohesion funds	0	0	61	210	130	221
Net EU transfers	126	331	352	914	756	938
(as a percentage of GDP)	(0.3)	(0.6)	(0.5)	(1.2)	(1.0)	(1.1)

Source: Ministerio de Economia y Hacienda, *Presentacion del proyecto de presupuestos generales del Estado 1998.*

... net capital inflows continued and foreign exchange reserves rose steeply

Spain was a large net recipient of financial capital in 1996, amounting to $3^1/_2$ per cent of GDP, and this trend persisted in 1997 (albeit at a diminished pace) (Table 6). These flows mainly correspond to a sharp increase in net foreign borrowing by commercial banks, partly related to ''convergence trading'' which

Table 6. **The financial account of the balance of payments**

Transaction basis, pesetas billion

	1993	1994	1995	1996	Jan.-Oct. 1996	Jan.-Oct. 1997
Current and capital balance	−310	−567	921	1 031	803	1 094
Net financial account[1]	−49	728	−1 002	2 492	2 019	1 100
(per cent of GDP)	(−0.1)	(1.1)	(−1.4)	(3.4)	..	..
Investment	6 836	−2 130	2 828	61	563	−1 562
Inflows[2]	8 043	−1 355	3 348	1 125	1 141	1 587
of which: Non-marketable securities[3]	1 027	1 263	765	811	647	705
Marketable securities	7 016	−2 618	2 583	314	494	882
of which: Government paper	6 214	−3 080	2 093	250	381	975
Outflows[4]	1 207	775	520	1 064	578	3 149
of which: Direct and real estate	337	522	448	586	416	1 068
Portfolio	870	253	72	478	167	2 081
Other net capital inflows	−6 885	2 858	−3 830	2 431	1 456	2 662
of which: Non financial private sector	−204	−709	−1 166	−1 110	−1 452	−2 109
Financial sector	−6 622	3 467	−2 855	3 665	3 033	4 784
General government	−58	100	192	−123	−125	−13
Errors and omissions	−216	−169	−764	−451	−289	−590
Change in official reserves	−574	−7	−846	3 072	2 533	1 602
Memorandum items:						
Official reserves (level)	6 130	5 775	4 536	7 930	7 377	10 500
Reserves/months of imports	6.0	4.8	3.3	5.3	5.0	6.1
Factor payments to exports ratio	16.4	15.5	13.3	13.6	..	..
Net external position/GDP	−18.2	−19.1	−17.5	−15.2	..	..

1. Reserves are excluded.
2. Change in liabilities vis-à-vis the external sector.
3. Including real estate and other direct investment.
4. Change in assets *vis-à-vis* the external sector.
Source: Bank of Spain, *Boletín Económico* and *Balanza de Pagos de España.*

anticipated the decline in Spanish long-term interest rates. They also reflected the unwinding of transactions made in 1995 in the wake of the international capital market turbulence. In 1997, capital inflows are estimated to have been partly offset by the continued foreign expansion by Spanish firms, mostly toward Latin America countries. As a result, foreign exchange reserves rose to over US$70 billion in 1997, more than recouping the losses experienced during the 1992 EMS crisis, and reaching a historic high for Spain.

Prospects for 1998-99

Total domestic demand should strengthen further...

The prospects for the continued recovery in output are very promising over the short-term projection period of 1998-99. All domestic components of demand appear set to strengthen. Private consumption should continue to gather steam as wage gains in real terms and employment creation sustain increases in disposable income. Moreover the household saving ratio could decline somewhat from its current high level. Consumer confidence should be boosted by declining unemployment but could also benefit from several other factors: specifically, an improvement in the stability of job tenure through the reduction in the number of fixed-term contracts and/or the lengthening of their duration, as well as the intangible effect of joining EMU with the first group of countries.

Forward looking indicators for investment remain very positive. Order books are booming, both for domestic and external markets, the level of inventories in the industrial sector is declining rapidly, and capacity utilisation continues to rise steeply (Figure 10). Construction should continue to reinforce business investment, as the strong demand for building permits suggests. The lower interest rate environment, including an anticipated further decline in short-term rates, should support all investment sectors. With international economic prospects set to improve – including a gradual recovery in Spain's main European trading partner countries – export markets for goods are expected to remain buoyant and increase by an annual average of 7 per cent in 1998 and 1999. In addition, macroeconomic policies will be less restraining (see below).

... and produce some tensions on productive capacities and, in turn, wages and prices

The acceleration in total domestic demand to $3\frac{1}{2}$ per cent in 1998 and to 4 per cent in 1999 will probably mean that the external sector's contribution to growth will turn slightly negative in 1998 and 1999 (Table 7). Overall, GDP growth may pick up from 3.4 per cent in 1997 to 3.6 per cent in 1998 and 1999, significantly faster than OECD estimates for potential output growth. The strong output growth should continue to create many new jobs and, as a consequence, the unemployment rate is expected to fall rapidly to about 19 per cent. Without further labour market reforms to reduce the very high level of structural

Figure 10. **CONJUNCTURAL INDICATORS**

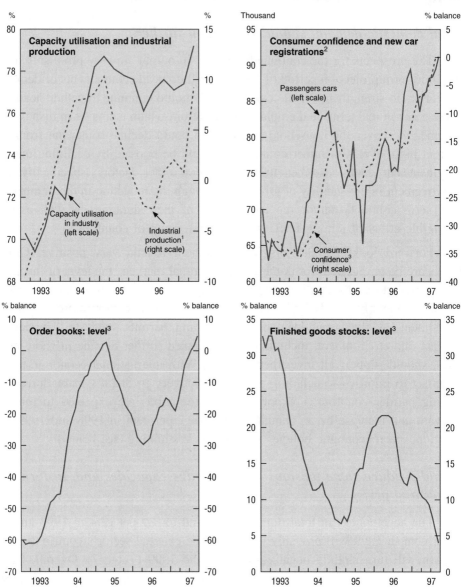

1. Year-on-year growth rate.
2. Three-month moving average.
3. Per cent, balance of replies.
Source: Ministry of Industry, Trade and Tourism and OECD, *Main Economic Indicators.*

Table 7. **Short-term prospects**

	1997	1998	1999
	Per cent change, annual rate		
Private consumption	3.1	3.3	3.5
Government consumption	0.7	2.4	2.4
Gross fixed investment	4.7	5.9	6.4
Total domestic demand	2.7	3.7	4.0
Exports of goods and services	12.9	9.0	8.1
Imports of goods and services	10.1	9.3	9.1
Foreign balance[1]	0.7	–0.2	–0.5
GDP at constant prices	3.4	3.6	3.6
Private consumption deflator	2.0	2.4	2.4
Memorandum items:			
Total economy:			
Unit labour costs	2.5	2.5	2.6
Productivity	0.7	1.2	1.3
Employment	2.6	2.3	2.2
Unemployment rate (per cent)	21.0	20.0	19.0
	Per cent of GDP		
Current external balance[2]	0.8	0.6	0.4
Government net lending[3]	–2.9	–2.4	–2.2
of which: Gross saving	0.3	0.7	1.0
Primary balance	1.5	1.5	1.4

1. Contribution to growth of GDP
2. On a transactions basis.
3. A minus sign indicates a deficit.
Source: OECD Secretariat projections.

unemployment, a tightening labour market is likely to be accompanied by some acceleration in wages in real terms. With unit labour costs projected to increase by 2½ per cent in both 1998 and 1999, and import costs reflecting the feed through of the recent effective depreciation, cost pressures will push up inflation. Moreover, demand side developments will reinforce these cost-push factors. There are signs of capacity tensions, as suggested by developments in stocks and capacity utilisation and, despite buoyant investment, the output gap will fall rapidly and probably be nearly closed by 1999. The confluence of these factors is projected to lead to price inflation of about 2½ per cent in both 1998 and 1999.

The main risk to the projections is that inflationary pressures will be stronger than projected, either due to stronger demand pushing the economy against its potential or to heightened wage pressures. A particular uncertainty surrounds the behaviour of private consumption since the wealth effect stemming from asset market developments, the impact of declining interest rates, and the boost to confidence due to the imminence of Spain joining EMU, are difficult to assess. With faster than projected consumption growth, tensions on production capacities would intensify. Potentially offsetting, the emerging economic crises in Asia could slow output growth significantly in important trading partners, especially if a "reverse tequila effect" dampens Spanish exports to the important Latin America market. On the cost side, wage demands could intensify in a rigid and tightening labour market. Moreover, collective wage negotiations in 1998 may be influenced by the timing of the expected rebound in consumer prices, as the impact of transitory factors fades in the early part of 1998. Again a potentially mitigating factor could come from the envisaged steps towards deregulating product markets. If sustained over the medium-term, price pressures arising either from an economy operating near capacity, or from high wage demands, could ultimately erode the competitiveness of the tradable sectors.

II.   Macroeconomic policies

The centrepiece of macroeconomic policy during the past two years has been a welcome reduction in the general government budget deficit from 6½ per cent of GDP in 1995 to an estimated 3 per cent of GDP in 1997. Fiscal consolidation was achieved without raising taxes significantly; the burden of adjustment was borne by discretionary expenditure, notably public consumption and investment. The overall impact on the economy has been positive. The prospect of joining monetary union from the outset as well as an improvement in the policy mix have spurred a sharp reduction in interest rates and provided a remarkable boost to business and consumer confidence. At a time of an improving economic conjuncture internationally, this confluence of events has spurred private sector investment, and economic growth more generally, as well as strong employment creation. These developments have created a virtuous circle whereby fiscal consolidation is furthered by lower interest payments and cyclical factors. Moreover, fiscal policy tightening facilitated the task of the monetary authorities.

Inflation has been consistently below the inflation target set by the Bank of Spain during 1996 and 1997, an accomplishment which greatly enhanced the central bank's anti-inflationary credentials. A monetary policy that was severely tightened in mid-1995, in combination with moderating wage and import costs, have guided Spanish inflation below the Maastricht ceiling. With disinflation progressing as planned, the Bank of Spain has gradually relaxed monetary policy. Looking forward, however, the prospective convergence of Spanish interest rates to the level appropriate for the EMU as a whole suggests a further loosening of monetary conditions in the period to end-1998; and one that perhaps would not have been warranted by developments in the Spanish economy. With a loss of autonomy over monetary policy, in the future macroeconomic adjustment for Spain itself would need to rely on fiscal and structural policies.

The objective of the 1998-2000 convergence programme is to prepare the Spanish economy for the challenges of the third stage of EMU, including the loss of autonomy regarding monetary policy. It outlines the steps the Government plans to take to prepare for the fiscal discipline embodied in the Stability and Growth Pact, and to improve the flexibility of the economy. The Government expects these measures to improve the capacity to generate output growth and jobs, as well as to absorb asymmetric shocks. The programme balances macro-economic and structural policies, and essentially strengthens the policy pursued during the past two years. It sets forth an agenda for further reductions in the general government deficit to 1.6 per cent of GDP by 2000 and a series of structural reforms which will liberalise product and factor markets.

The 1998 Budget and the accompanying legislation are the first step in this process, and the general government budget deficit is targeted to fall to 2.4 per cent of GDP. The Government strategy for consolidation will continue to be based on a more efficient use of resources, especially as regards government consumption and public enterprises, and on curbing the abuse of social spending programs. However, most of the fiscal adjustment is set to come from the fall in interest payments and improvements in the cyclical components of the deficit. Following two years of fiscal restraint, the Budget takes advantage of the growth in revenues coming from the positive economic conjuncture to raise spending on health, education and active labour market policies. The deficit could be lower in the event the economic recovery is stronger than expected, since the Government has committed itself to use any excess revenues to reduce the deficit. However the current pace of economic growth in combination with the prospects for a further relaxation of monetary policy suggests that fiscal policy may need to be tighter.

Looking forward to future budgets, preventing a breach of the limits under the Stability and Growth Pact in the event of a cyclical downturn will require consolidation over and above that contained in the convergence programme. In view of a limit to the savings that can be squeezed out of discretionary spending and the Government's commitment to reduce the tax burden, allowing an uncon-strained functioning of the automatic fiscal stabilisers will require structural reform of the large entitlement programmes, namely the public health system, the public pension system and labour market policies, as well as improved co-ordination of spending between the various layers of government. Fiscal adjustment will also be necessary to reduce the public debt burden which stands near 70 per cent of GDP.

Monetary policy

Developments to mid-1997

Following central bank independence in June 1994 and the Bank of Spain's subsequent adoption of inflation targeting from 1995, the conduct of monetary policy has been highly successful in combating inflation. Inflation measured by the CPI has been below the target set by the Bank of Spain by increasingly wide margins, most recently with the target of 2.5 per cent for end-1997 (Figure 11, top panel). These results should permit Spain to observe with relative ease the inflation and interest rate criteria contained in the Maastricht Treaty.[14] Regarding the exchange rate, the Peseta remained close to the central parity during 1996 and 1997. The interest rate differential combined with a stable exchange rate and the expectation of a reduction in domestic interest rates have been partly responsible for capital inflows and a build up of reserves by the Bank of Spain.

Inflation reduction has been supported by a monetary policy stance that was initially quite tight and has been subsequently relaxed as the inflation objectives have been met. Since mid-1995, the Bank of Spain has reduced its intervention rate cautiously. From a peak of 9.25 per cent, it has been gradually decreased to 7.25 per cent in mid-1996, and 5.25 per cent in mid-1997 (Figure 11, middle panel). Adjusted for inflation, the decline in short-term rates was very gradual; from over 4 per cent in mid-1995 to 3.7 per cent in mid-1996 and to 3.3 per cent in mid-1997. The yield curve fell more or less uniformly during this period, and the yield gap between short and long-term interest rates was relatively narrow, staying near 1 percentage point during most of this period.

Reflecting the nominal convergence with the other EU partner countries and the overall performance of the Spanish economy, interest rate differentials with comparable German financial instruments have declined rapidly, especially at the long end of the yield curve (Figure 11, bottom panel). The short-term differential has fallen from a peak of over 500 basis points at end-1995 to about 200 basis points at mid-1997. Over the same period, the long term differential has fallen by

Figure 11.
INFLATION TARGETS AND INTEREST RATES

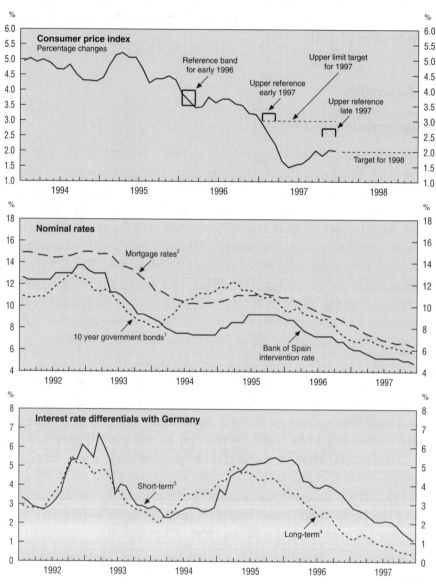

1. Yield from secondary market.
2. Credit and savings institutions.
3. 3-month interbank rate.
4. 10 year government bonds.
Source: Ministry of Economy and Finance and OECD, *Main Economic Indicators.*

almost 450 basis points from a peak in mid-1995 to stand at near 50 basis points – at the time a historic low for Spain. The impressive developments at the long end of the yield curve reflect both "convergence trading" by financial markets as they anticipated Spain's entry as an initial member of EMU and the credibility gains stemming from an improved policy mix.[15] Despite the resulting capital inflows, adding to inflows from a current account surplus, the Peseta has remained remarkably stable against the Deutschemark, near the mid-point of the ERM band (Figure 12, top panel).

Financial conditions, taking into account developments of both the exchange rate and interest rates, reveal a sharper tightening in the latter half of 1995 than if only the development of short-term interest rates are considered, but a more rapid loosening thereafter.[16] In addition to the sharp interest rate hikes in the second half of 1995, the real effective exchange rate appreciated. Subsequently, financial conditions have moderated, as inflation fell and fiscal policy was tightened, and thus supported the recovery in output. First long-term and then short-term interest rates declined in real terms, and this monetary loosening was reinforced by the appreciation of the US dollar as well as the currencies of some European countries (Figure 12, middle and bottom panels).

Reflecting the reduction in interest rates and the strengthening of economic activity, monetary and credit aggregates have been accelerating strongly. The narrow monetary aggregate (M2), which is more closely linked to transactions demand, experienced a 9 per cent increase in real terms in the 12 months to November 1997 (Figure 13). The growth of the broader monetary aggregate, ALP, which used to be the main reference aggregate, has however been more restrained.[17] This development reflects asset switching from time deposits to assets outside the aggregate, especially mutual funds. Specifically, time deposits declined by 12 per cent in nominal terms from the beginning of 1996 to November 1997, while mutual funds (net asset values) have increased by about 90 per cent over this period. A new aggregate which attempts to adjust for this distortion by including fixed income mutual funds (ALPF) has grown at a pace more in line with the strength of aggregate expenditure ($6\frac{1}{2}$ per cent through November 1997 in real terms). Domestic credit expansion to the private sector has been the main source of liquidity during 1996 and so far in 1997.[18] Credit to households and firms has increased steadily over this period, to reach an 11 per cent pace in real terms at end-November 1997. The strong household demand for

Figure 12. **EXCHANGE RATE,
FINANCIAL CONDITIONS AND ECONOMIC PERFORMANCE**

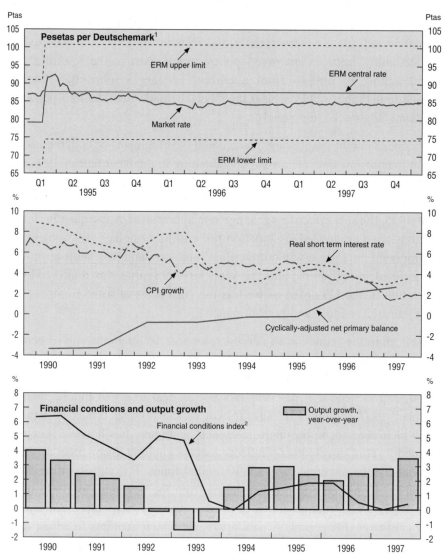

1. The central rate of the peseta was devaluated by 7 per cent in March 1995.
2. The financial conditions indicator contains the weighted average of the short term and long term interest rates in real terms and the real effective exchange rate (based on unit labour costs in manufacturing). The interest rate variable has a unitary coefficient while the coefficient of the exchange rate variable is the ratio of exports to GDP.
Source: OECD Secretariat.

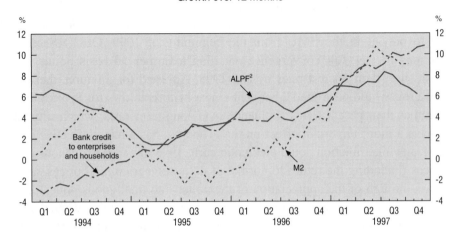

Figure 13. **REAL MONEY AND CREDIT**[1]

Growth over 12 months

1, Deflated by the consumer price index.
2. Liquid assets in the hands of the non-bank public plus holdings in fixed-income mutual funds.
Source: Bank of Spain.

credit is largely associated with mortgage lending and to a lesser extent consumer credit, while credit to firms has been concentrated on the service sector. Overall credit growth has been dampened by the lower financing needs of the public sector. Nevertheless, total credit increased by 7 per cent in real terms in the 12 months to November 1997.[19]

The end to monetary policy independence

From the middle of 1997, the Bank of Spain has refrained from relaxing monetary policy much further, with a view to attaining its 1998 target for the inflation rate: staying close to 2 per cent during the year. The only action since May 1997 was a 25 basis points drop to 5 per cent in the intervention rate after the presentation of the 1998 Budget to Parliament and two reductions of similar magnitude in mid-December 1997 and mid-February 1998 following announcements of moderate monthly inflation figures. In combination with a tightening of policy in Germany, these moves brought the short-term interest rate differential to 100 basis points. The September 1997 Inflation Report of the Bank of Spain foresaw some difficulties in attaining further gains in lowering inflation in the short term, albeit from the best performance of the past 30 years. While certain factors would be putting upward pressure on prices, the central bank's room to implement an independent monetary policy was being constrained by the prospective convergence of short-term interest rates towards the lower levels that are likely to prevail in the EMU from the beginning of 1999. OECD Secretariat projections foresee full convergence entailing a further 50 basis points fall in Spanish short-term interest rates by end-1998. Adjusted for inflation, these rates in real terms would be around 2 per cent – near historical lows for Spain, albeit in euro rather than peseta terms. Influence over long-term rates, which ultimately may have a more important effect on the economy, has already effectively been lost. Meanwhile, inflation could pick up in early 1998 due to *i)* exogenous effects on prices (including the return to normal of domestic agricultural prices, and the full pass-through of the appreciation of the dollar into final goods prices), *ii)* the tightening capacity constraints in the economy, and *iii)* aggressive wage demands in a tightening and rigid labour market. At a time when a central bank would in normal circumstances consider tightening monetary policy so as to satisfy its 1998 target of inflation near 2 per cent during 1998, Spain could face the opposite prospect due to EMU. With the prospective loss of a central bank able to tailor policy towards the requirements of the Spanish economy, the onus of macro-economic policy adjustment falls on fiscal policy in the short term and structural policies over the longer run.

Fiscal policy

Fiscal retrenchment is estimated to have led to a fall in the general government deficit equivalent to 3½ per cent of GDP during the period 1996-97. Faced with a short period in which to achieve substantial adjustment, Spain – as other countries – focused fiscal consolidation on discretionary spending (Table 8). Of the total fiscal consolidation, almost half was the result of cuts in discretionary spending, essentially government consumption and capital outlays (1½ per cent of GDP) but also transfers to public enterprises (½ per cent of GDP). Lower interest rates and cyclical factors accounted for the bulk of the remaining consolidation (each contributing approximately ¾ per cent of GDP). With the objective to attain a general government deficit equivalent to 3 per cent of GDP in 1997 estimated to have been achieved, attention necessarily turns to the future and Spain's commitments under the Stability and Growth Pact, as well as the challenges coming from the structural problems of the budget and a large debt stock.

Table 8.   **General government adjustment efforts: an international comparison**

As a per cent of GDP

	Change between 1995 and 1997						Estimation in 1997	
	Government deficit	Interest payments	Primary current expenditure	Consumption	Net capital outlays[1]	Current revenue	Primary balance	Debt[2]
Canada	4.5	−0.9	−2.8	−1.7	−0.3	0.5	5.4	96.7
United States	1.9	−0.2	−0.7	−0.6	−0.0	1.0	1.9	61.5
Austria	2.1	−0.4	−0.9	−0.4	−0.2	0.6	0.6	65.5
Belgium	1.5	−1.1	−0.5	−0.2	−0.2	−0.3	5.1	124.5
Denmark	2.2	−1.0	−2.1	−0.0	0.4	−0.3	2.7	63.1
Finland	3.9	0.4	−3.0	−0.4	0.1	1.3	0.6	59.4
France	1.9	−0.1	0.5	0.1	−0.8	1.6	−0.0	57.0
Germany	0.3	−0.1	−0.8	−0.3	−0.7	−1.3	0.0	60.7
Greece	4.8	−3.0	−0.3	0.1	−1.0	0.5	5.0	107.3
Ireland	1.7	−0.2	−0.6	−0.8	0.4	1.3	3.7	67.5
Italy	4.0	−1.5	0.7	0.2	−0.4	2.8	5.2	122.3
Norway	4.0	−0.6	−3.9	−1.6	−0.2	−0.7	7.4	40.9
Portugal	2.9	−2.1	1.3	0.8	0.1	2.2	1.7	66.5
Spain	**3.6**	**−0.7**	**−0.5**	**−0.6**	**−1.2**	**1.1**	**1.5**	**69.8**
Sweden	5.5	−0.1	−2.2	−0.1	−0.6	2.6	1.9	76.6
United Kingdom	3.3	−0.4	−1.8	−0.9	−0.8	0.2	0.4	53.8

1.   Gross investment minus net capital transfers received.
2.   End of period. Maastricht definition for EU countries.
Source: OECD Secretariat.

1996: the first step towards the Maastricht target

A reduction in the general government deficit from 6.5 per cent in 1995 to the 1994-97 convergence programme target of 4.4 per cent in 1996 was achieved through a primary balance adjustment equivalent to 2 per cent of GDP (Table 9).[20] Fiscal consolidation in 1996 was achieved mostly through the compression of discretionary expenditure, though revenues were surprisingly buoyant in view of the slowdown in output growth. On the expenditure side, capital outlays and the consumption of goods and services were squeezed (by 0.9 per cent of GDP and 0.2 per cent of GDP, respectively).[21] The improved revenue performance was concentrated in indirect taxes (as excise taxes on tobacco and alcohol were raised in August 1996 to cover the servicing of uncovered expenditure liabilities amounting to 0.8 per cent of GDP), non-tax revenues, and social

47

Table 9. **General government accounts**

National accounts definition, per cent of GDP

	1993	1994	1995	1996	1997¹
Current revenue	**40.9**	**39.5**	**38.3**	**39.1**	**39.5**
Direct taxes	11.9	11.4	11.5	11.6	11.9
Households	9.4	9.3	9.2	9.2	9.1
Business	2.5	2.1	2.3	2.4	2.8
Indirect taxes	9.6	10.1	10.0	10.2	10.5
Social security contributions	14.9	14.6	13.6	13.9	14.0
Other	4.4	3.4	3.1	3.3	3.1
Current expenditure	**43.6**	**42.5**	**41.5**	**41.2**	**40.3**
Public consumption	17.6	16.9	16.7	16.5	16.1
of which: Wages and salaries	12.3	11.8	11.7	11.7	11.4
Social security benefits	16.9	16.5	15.7	15.7	15.7
Interest payments	5.2	5.1	5.3	5.3	4.7
Current transfers and other	3.9	4.0	3.7	3.7	3.7
Net saving	–2.7	–2.9	–3.2	–2.1	–0.8
Gross saving	–1.6	–1.7	–2.0	–1.0	0.3
Fixed investment	4.3	4.1	3.8	3.2	3.0
Net capital transfer payments	–0.9	–0.5	–0.6	–0.3	–0.2
Net lending (+) or net borrowing (–)	**–6.8**	**–6.3**	**–6.5**	**–4.5**	**–2.9**
Borrowing requirement²	12.5	6.0	7.1	6.4	2.6
Memorandum items:					
Net lending					
State	–6.0	–5.1	–5.5	–3.4	–2.4
Social security	0.5	–0.2	–0.3	–0.4	–0.2
Territorial governments	–1.2	–1.0	–0.7	–0.6	–0.3

1. OECD projections.
2. Net lending plus assumption of net liabilities by the government.
Source: Data submitted by national authorities, OECD, *National Accounts* and OECD Secretariat.

security contributions.[22] An improving interest rate environment permitted the government's financing needs to be met mostly from the domestic bond markets. In fact, the Treasury over-financed the deficit by almost Ptas 1 trillion (1.3 per cent of GDP). Partly as a result, the gross debt of general government (Maastricht basis) increased by Ptas 6 trillion (8 per cent of GDP), to Ptas 52 trillion at end-1996 (equivalent to 70 per cent of GDP).[23]

1997 budget: the final step to Maastricht

The Government viewed 1997 as a historic opportunity for Spanish economic policy. Integration into EMU from its creation was at hand, and the benefit of a favourable economic conjuncture could be used to establish a stable macro-economic basis necessary for sustainable economic growth and job creation. The 1997 Budget also reflected a new orientation of economic policy which the Government considered essential to the modernisation of the Spanish economy. Budget consolidation would focus on expenditures and not raise the fiscal burden. Though the structure of revenues would be re-balanced toward indirect taxes, including a more extensive application of user fees, the longer term objective was to reduce taxes. Expenditure reduction would be achieved by reviewing the effectiveness of budget resources in three essential areas: public consumption (personnel and goods and services), transfers to public enterprises, and public investment. Savings would also be achieved by improving the efficiency of operations, especially in the social security system through measures to reduce social benefit fraud and contribution payment arrears.[24]

The target of fiscal policy was a general government deficit of 3 per cent of GDP. Its attainment would require renewed consolidation equivalent to 1.4 per cent of GDP, of which the bulk would be primary balance adjustment, including 0.3 per cent at the level of territorial governments (regional and local). Despite declining interest rates, the large increase in the debt stock in 1996 was expected to keep interest payments (national accounts basis) broadly unchanged as a share of GDP. The economic environment was expected to be favourable, with output growth envisaged to grow by 3 per cent and consumer prices by an average of 2.8 per cent. The improved economic conjuncture was expected to contribute the equivalent of about 0.4 per cent of GDP to the adjustment, mainly through lower social expenditures. Discretionary expenditure would bear the bulk of the remaining adjustment.

The largest savings would come from compressing personnel expenditure through both a wage freeze and the implementation of a policy to replace only one in four retiring employees at all levels of government.[25] Government consumption of goods and services would also be curtailed through the application of new control procedures.[26] Expenditures were also decreased by pushing certain items off budget. First, current and capital transfers to public enterprises and entities would be cut by about a quarter in nominal terms, with their financing needs met from resources outside the budget, essentially from the resources of the profitable public enterprises and privatisation receipts (see Chapter IV for a more detailed description). Second, investment expenditure would decline in volume terms, but the fall would be compensated through the use of alternative financing procedures for investment, including a greater participation of the private sector and the use of turnkey payment procedures (Box 2). Though difficult to estimate the counterfactual, these two policies may have reduced the 1997 budget deficit by about ³/₄ per cent of GDP.

On the revenue side, the collection effort was centred on indirect taxes, which would increase due to the full year effect of the increase in excise taxes in August 1996, the increase in user fees by 8 per cent and the introduction of new charges (*e.g.*, 4 per cent on non-life insurance). A further boost to revenues would come from corporate income taxes, which were increased temporarily by moving forward withholdings and the introduction of the option for firms to re-value their capital stock and imposing a 3 per cent charge on the resulting capital gains.[27] Personal income taxes were affected by the introduction of a simplified flat capital gains tax at a rate of 20 per cent.[28]

Box 2. **New techniques to finance infrastructure investment**

The 1997 budget introduced several new financing techniques. Private sector participation in the construction of motorways, rail tracks, and hydraulic works was encouraged through long-term concession contracts (build-operate-transfer agreements). To promote road construction, the concession agreements were lengthened from 50 to 75 years and the VAT reduced from 16 per cent to 7 per cent.

Two newly created public entities, the *Ente Gestor de Infraestructuras Ferroviarias* (GIF) and the *Aguas de la Cuenca del Ebro* (ACESA), were created and given responsibility for several new railway and water works. Part of their financing will come from the Government, with initial capital injections of Ptas 60 billion and Ptas 40 billion, respectively.

The turnkey method of payment (*metodo del abono total del precio*) has the Government making full payment upon the project's completion, and thus pushing the burden on to future budgets. Projects valued at approximately Ptas 160 billion (0.2 per cent of GDP) were signed in 1997 under this format, not including large military contracts with the publicly owned shipyards and defence firms (Bazan and CASA) for the construction of navy frigates and Eurofighter planes (for an estimated total cost of Ptas 1 500 billion by 2010). In May 1997, turnkey contracts were restricted to 30 per cent of total investments, while individual investments cannot exceed certain limits. It is envisaged that 1998 will be the final year that such contracts will be permitted.

Regarding the outcome for 1997, the OECD Secretariat's assessment based on state government data suggests that the general government budget deficit should attain the Maastricht target of 3 per cent of GDP – and could over-perform slightly. The uncertainties lie with gauging developments at the level of territorial governments where data is received with a lag. The territorial governments are a critical component of the fiscal adjustment as they control about 40 per cent of discretionary spending. In the event, the attainment of the fiscal objective has been facilitated by revenue over-shooting and the savings from the sharper-than-expected fall in interest rates. Of the total adjustment, OECD Secretariat projections suggest that interest payments account for 0.7 per cent of GDP, discretionary measures for 0.6 per cent of GDP and cyclical factors for the remainder.

On the revenue side, the tax elasticity with respect to GDP has been higher than budgeted, partly offsetting a lower-than-projected nominal GDP growth. This development is probably linked to the better-than-expected composition of growth, with higher consumption and an improved profitability of firms. Specifically, corporate income taxes are growing at a very fast pace, though this also reflects large windfall capital gains tax receipts earned by the state from the sale of the final tranche of the national telephone company share (Telefonica) in a booming stock market. In contrast, the lower interest rates and individuals' switch from deposits into mutual funds (in part enticed by the lower capital gains tax) have made personal income taxes lag budget projections significantly.

Primary expenditures at the level of the central government are more or less as budgeted, with the possible exception of the consumption of goods and services.[29] Personnel expenditure appears to be contained by the wage freeze which has been applied consistently at the level of central government. Similarly, unemployment benefits and temporary disability benefits – which have often been used as a substitute for unemployment benefits – have fallen far more dramatically than budgeted. Partial evidence of fiscal developments at the level of territorial government can be provided by movements in their level of debt. Though other factors could account for this development, this increased by about $1/2$ per cent of GDP during the first half of 1997.

The attainment of the deficit target has led to a turnaround of debt dynamics in 1997. The debt to GDP ratio of 70 per cent (Maastricht basis) is projected to fall for the first time since the early 1980s. This result is partly due to the fact that the general government borrowing requirements are envisaged to be smaller than the deficit as the Government planned to run down Ptas 1 trillion of reserves at the Bank of Spain, built up in 1996.[30] In view of the low long-term interest rates, the government's borrowing strategy continued to focus on the longer maturities, thereby extending the average (remaining) maturity of government debt to $3^{1}/_{2}$ years in 1997 from 2 years in 1992.[31] In the lower interest environment, the average yield of new issues has fallen to $5^{1}/_{2}$ per cent in 1997 from over 10 per cent in 1995, and prompted the Government to refinance Ptas 1 trillion of outstanding debt in 1997.[32]

Looking forward: The 1998-2000 convergence programme

To prepare for the third stage of EMU and to meet the conditions under the Stability and Growth Pact which will begin to apply from 1999, the Spanish Parliament passed a new convergence programme in April 1997 covering the period 1998-2000. The programme projects a continuation of the positive trends observed in the Spanish economy over the past two years. The programme contains a relatively detailed set of supporting medium-term term policy objectives.[33] With these measures, the Government seeks to correct what it believes to be the major failure of the Spanish economy – the inability to create sufficient jobs to bring the unemployment rate down to an acceptable level. The blame is placed on macroeconomic imbalances having cut short periods of economic growth and the rigidity in a large number of product and factor markets which has hampered competitiveness. As a result Spain has not realised its economic potential and raised its per capita income to the levels of other EU countries. The structural rigidities are identified to be:

- excessive intervention and regulation by the State in key markets;
- obstacles to competition in strategic sectors;
- the presence of over-sized and inefficient public enterprises, many of which survive only with financial support from the Budget;
- the provision of grants and subsidies to the private sector which distort incentives; and,
- a tax system which deters saving.

The Government believes that the full implementation of the measures taken during 1996 and 1997 should improve the flexibility of the economy (see Chapters III and IV) and reduce the structural deficit of the budget, but it intends to continue its efforts to carry out structural reform. Policies will focus on the following areas:

- reducing public consumption through a rationalisation of the civil service and health expenditure (improving hospital management and limiting the growth of expenditure on drugs);
- containing social benefits through measures to control fraud and the implementation of the ''Toledo Pact'' on pension reform;
- downsizing public enterprises, as envisaged in the Modernisation programme;
- reducing the tax burden by extending the base and matching the structure and rates to the trends in the EU, reallocating the tax burden from labour, savings, and small and medium size enterprises, and emphasising user specific charges. Tax reform would also entail combating tax evasion and improving tax administration procedures;
- finalising and implementing the internal stability pact with regional governments.

The introduction of these measures is projected to produce a primary balance adjustment of 0.7 per cent of GDP over the three year period and reduce the general government budget deficit to 1.6 per cent of GDP in 2000. Fiscal consolidation is based on primary (mostly discretionary) expenditure and interest payment reductions, as the projections entail a reduction in revenues and an increase in public investment expenditures as a per cent of GDP (Table 10). These policies and a favourable international conjuncture are envisaged to lead to an annual average GDP growth rate of 3.3 per cent and average employment growth of 2.2 per cent, entailing a reduction in the unemployment rate of about 4 percentage points. A linchpin assumption of the projections is the subdued behaviour of wages in real terms, which are expected to grow at a rate below productivity and keep unit labour costs in line with those of trading partners.

The 1998 budget: preparation for EMU

The objective of the 1998 Budget is to consolidate the achievements of 1996 and 1997. The fiscal target is a general government budget deficit of 2.4 per cent of GDP. The Government's strategy is to reorient resources to the more dynamic and productive elements of the economy and introduce tax incentives to support savings and entrepreneurial activities. To this end, the Budget increases

Table 10.   **Convergence programme 1998-2000**

	1997	1998	1999	2000
		Per cent change, annual rate		
Output and demand				
Real GDP growth	3.0	3.2	3.4	3.2
Private consumption	2.7	2.7	2.8	3.0
Government consumption	–0.3	1.0	1.0	1.0
Gross fixed capital formation	4.0	7.1	7.8	5.6
External sector[1]	0.4	–0.2	–0.3	–0.2
Prices				
Private consumption deflator	2.5	2.3	2.2	2.2
Labour market				
Employment	2.0	2.2	2.3	2.1
		As a per cent of GDP		
Fiscal account				
General government deficit	–3.0	–2.5	–2.0	–1.6
Primary balance	1.9	2.1	2.3	2.6
Total revenue	40.7	40.7	40.5	40.3
Total expenditures	43.7	43.2	42.5	41.9
Current expenditures	39.4	38.8	38.0	37.4
of which: interest payments	4.9	4.6	4.3	4.2
Capital expenditures	4.3	4.4	4.5	4.5
State	–2.5	–2.1	–1.7	–1.4
Social security	–0.2	–0.2	–0.1	0.0
Territorial governments	–0.3	–0.2	–0.2	–0.2
Gross debt	68.2	67.7	66.7	65.3

1.   Contribution to growth of GDP.
Source: Ministry of Economy and Finance and Bank of Spain.

funding for active labour market policies, research and development, raises spending on education and maintains public investment as a share of GDP. New tax deductions will be provided for contributions to private pensions, and the taxation of SME's is lowered further. Furthermore, advantage will be taken of the higher revenue during this economic upswing to improve the level of protection provided by the social security system. Specifically, social protection will benefit from increased resources for health care and pensions will not be adjusted for the better inflation outcomes relative to the official target in 1997.

The resources for this orientation reflect the improved economic conjuncture framing the budget. The assumptions for the economy are economic growth of 3.4 per cent and average consumer inflation of 2.2 per cent. Despite what might seem to be an improved composition of output for tax purposes, the tax elasticity is expected to fall below one, and overall revenues are expected to decline by 0.3 per cent of GDP. Corporate income taxes will reflect the unwinding of the one-off measures introduced in the 1997 budget (moving forward of tax payments and the revaluation of assets) and personal income taxes will suffer from a lower interest income, as well as a smaller extent of tax bracket creep.[34] Indirect taxes will reflect the strength of the recovery in consumption and the large rise in the price of tobacco in September 1997.[35] Non-tax revenues are expected to decline as a percentage of GDP, reflecting lost dividends as a result of the new public enterprise policy (see Chapter IV). In the event of larger-than-anticipated revenues, the Budget law requires their application towards deficit reduction, excluding their use for financing new expenditure.

On the expenditure side, official projections indicate a reduction in primary current expenditures of the order of 0.6 per cent of GDP. Savings are expected to arise from the maintenance of the strict rule of replacing only one in four retiring civil servants at all levels of government, and limiting cost of living increases to the official projection for CPI inflation (2.1 per cent on an end of period basis). Despite the improvements in social protection and education, spending on goods and services and social benefits are projected to decline by 0.3 per cent of GDP, in part due to lower unemployment and the expected reduction in fraud.[36] Health expenditure will rise $1\frac{1}{2}$ times as fast as nominal GDP as a result of the new multi-year agreement between the central and regional governments covering the period 1998-2001.[37] Finally, interest payments are projected to decline by 0.2 per cent of GDP (Figure 14).

The OECD Secretariat projects a similar outcome for the 1998 deficit (*i.e.* a general government deficit of 2.4 per cent of GDP). However, the Secretariat's revenue projections are somewhat more buoyant, partly reflecting the higher expectations for nominal output. Moreover, the projected decline in interest payments as a per cent of GDP is larger (0.6 per cent). The differences are offset by the Secretariat's somewhat higher projections for social benefits and the consumption of goods and services, reflecting the government's social policy agenda. The cyclically adjusted primary surplus could be reduced by $\frac{1}{2}$ per cent of GDP compared with 1997, and $\frac{1}{4}$ per cent of GDP compared to 1996.

Figure 14. **GENERAL GOVERNMENT BUDGET**
Per cent of GDP

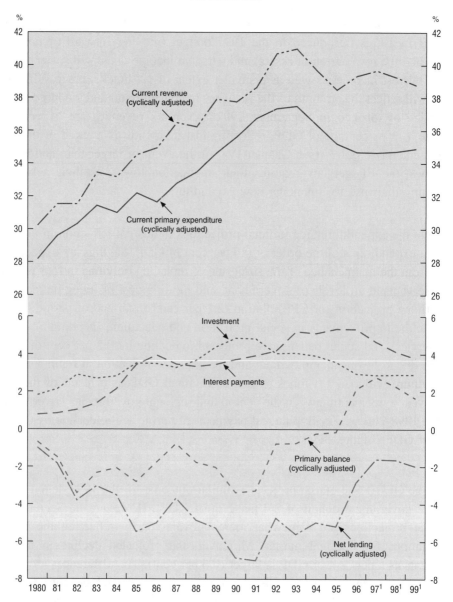

1. OECD projections.
Source: OECD, *National accounts* and Secretariat estimates.

Medium term fiscal adjustment

The recent fiscal consolidation, in combination with the positive economic conjuncture and the convergence of interest rates to those of the prospective EMU, have significantly improved the government accounts during 1996 and 1997. Moreover, the prospects for the next couple of years remain favourable. The OECD Secretariat projections through 1999, which include the impact of the measures of the 1998 Budget (but unchanged policies for 1999) point to a general government deficit equivalent to 2.2 per cent of GDP in 1999. The resulting primary surplus – equivalent to nearly 1 1/2 per cent of GDP – in conjunction with significantly lower interest rates on Government debt and annual output growth in excess of 3 per cent should slowly turn around the debt dynamics. Under these conditions, the ratio of the gross debt to GDP is projected to decline gradually by about 1 percentage point of GDP (similar to the projections in the convergence programme). The evolution of this ratio will obviously be influenced by the extent to which privatisation receipts are used to reduce the debt and conversely asset acquisitions add to the debt.

This seemingly comfortable position for the immediate future is deceptive. There is no room for complacency on fiscal policy as the fiscal balance is quite sensitive to the economic cycle. The primary balance, adjusted for the effects of the business cycle, is estimated by the OECD Secretariat to be equivalent to about 1 1/2 per cent of GDP by 1999.[38] Interest payments would be of the order of 3 1/2-4 per cent of GDP following the full pass-through of the lower interest rates. Thus, the corresponding cyclically adjusted component of the general government budget deficit would be about 2-2 1/2 per cent of GDP. This position does not, however, provide sufficient cushion to prevent Spain from breaching the 3 per cent limit set by the Stability and Growth Pact in the event output growth slows significantly.[39] Based on OECD Secretariat calculations, a one percentage point widening of the output gap would result in a 0.6 per cent of GDP deterioration in the fiscal balances. On this basis, if output growth were to fall by a cumulative two percentage points relative to the current projections, the fiscal deficit would be pushed above the 3 per cent limit.[40] Such an outcome would not be unusual as the output gap has increased in previous economic cycles, on average, by 3 percentage points of potential GDP and by approximately 7 percentage points of GDP during the last downturn. In an average downturn, therefore, the target for the cyclically adjusted deficit would have to be near 1 per cent of GDP in order to stay within the 3 per cent limit. To avoid any possibility of incurring fines associated with a breach of the limit, the fiscal balances would need to be tighter still, and be broadly in balance.[41] Acknowledging the uncertainty surrounding this sort of calculation, these scenarios suggest the need for additional fiscal adjustment to the structural component of the deficit equivalent to at least 1 per cent of GDP compared to the OECD projections, and to provide a safety margin, an adjustment closer to 2 per cent of GDP would be appropriate. With the difference between the OECD's fiscal scenario and the authorities' convergence programme amounting to no more than some $1/4$ per cent of GDP in 1999, the latter – which relies partly on favourable cyclical factors to achieve fiscal adjustment – would need to be more ambitious to meet Spain's commitments under the Stability and Growth Pact.

The task is made more difficult since additional fiscal adjustment will be needed just to keep the structural component of the deficit from increasing in the future. Ageing, as in most other OECD countries, will put pressure on health and pension expenditures.[42] Additional budgetary pressure could arise from several policy commitments. First, the Government is committed to reducing taxes, though success in the fight against tax evasion may attenuate the impact on revenues. Second, the devolution of expenditure authority to regional governments, such as for education and health, may continue to increase overall expenditure, as the increase in regional administrations is not fully offset by reductions at the level of central government. The introduction of an internal stability pact could serve to co-ordinate and control overall expenditure. However, its feasibility will require enhanced monitoring in order to obtain information on a timely basis and also a strengthened co-ordination of policies among the regions and between levels of government. The recent agreement with the regional governments on a new financing arrangement could also lead to additional expenditures for the central government as it entails guarantees for minimum resources to regions (Chapter III). Third, the Government is committed to certain once-off payments. The 1997 judicial decision has required the Government to compensate the victims of the toxic colza oil,[43] and legislation is in place which gradually transforms a conscripted into a professional military force. Finally, while shifting expenditures off budget during 1996 and 1997 could yield potential improvements in efficiency, in certain cases however, expenditures have been postponed to future budgets (the use of turnkey payment contracts for investments, guaranteeing debts of loss making public entities and taking equity participations in new entities, which will need to be profitable to repay the investment). An offset to these one off costs could come from the successful conclusion of the public enterprise privatisation programme.

The insufficient strength of the structural balances will require a more ambitious fiscal effort to be sustained over a longer period – a situation not dissimilar to that applying to many of Spain's EU partners. The recent efforts regarding the restructuring and privatisation of public enterprises are positive steps as they address a major burden on the budget. Similarly, efforts to improve the productivity of civil servants by managing with fewer could continue to provide savings, though the number of civil servants (as a percentage of the labour force) is below the average of most other OECD countries. However, a fiscal adjustment policy focusing primarily on discretionary expenditures will be difficult to sustain – especially as a significant part of the fiscal improvement over the past two years has been based on the compression of civil service wages and the consumption of goods and services. Further cuts in these areas could be difficult. The 1997 wage freeze has been the third during the past five years and has resulted in a cumulative decline in civil service wages of over 3 per cent in real terms between 1993 and 1997, at a time when private sector wages have increased by about 5 per cent in real terms. A widening wedge between public and private pay could result in a resurgence in public wage demands. Furthermore, the consumption of goods and services has been reduced to low levels, as a percentage of GDP, relative to outcomes in recent years and is now substantially lower than the EU average, suggesting that not much more savings can be expected in this area (Figure 15).

Structural reform of the budget will need to tackle entitlement programmes, especially as the government's objective is to contain or reduce the tax burden and increase investment. The main entitlement programme is the social security system, encompassing the public health system and the pension system. The potential savings are large as together these two programmes account for 15 per cent of GDP and about 40 per cent of current primary expenditures. However, in view of the inherent upward pressure on these expenditures, the recent piecemeal reforms will succeed only in slowing the rate at which they increase in the short run. More radical reforms will be necessary to contain pension and health expenditures (Chapter III). Regarding pensions, incentives will need to be

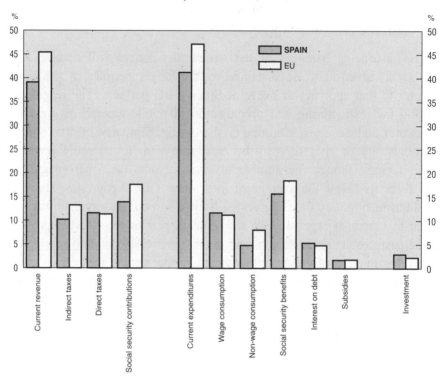

Figure 15. **THE STRUCTURE OF THE GENERAL GOVERNMENT ACCOUNT:
A COMPARISON WITH THE EU**

As a per cent of GDP, 1996

Source: OECD Secretariat.

introduced to delay retirement, especially in the specific regimes, to combat
fraud, and to reduce further the generosity of pension payments relative to
contributions. Health system reform will need to introduce incentives for savings,
especially through an enhanced role for primary care physicians, a more efficient
use of hospital resources, and an improved pharmaceutical policy, including
more competition among pharmacies and the introduction of some form of
means-tested co-payment for pensioners. Similarly, a labour market reform which
succeeds in reducing the high structural unemployment rate would also have a
positive impact on social expenditure. It would reduce benefits accruing to the

unemployed (unemployment as well as various programmes which may substitute for unemployment benefits) but also raise revenues as productive employment is created.

A reform of the taxation system could also alleviate budgetary pressures. Obviously, a successful fight against tax evasion would produce revenues, especially in the social security system where high contribution rates yield receipts significantly below the OECD average. The harmonisation of the VAT system within the EU countries to the levels prevailing on average could raise rates in Spain, which are among the lowest in the EU and subject to a large number of exemptions. Finally, personal income tax rates are high but their effectiveness in raising revenues is also diminished by the existence of a large number of tax expenditures. Most tax expenditures are usually distortionary and a reform of the system of direct taxation should balance a reduction of marginal tax rates with a simplification and reduction of the system of tax expenditures. A reduction of distortions arising from the tax system would help raise the economy's growth potential.

III.   Surveillance of structural policies

The Government has undertaken structural reform in several critical areas during 1996-97, and significant steps were made in liberalising the Spanish economy. The achievements made during this period reflect the strategy put forward in the context of the 1998-2000 convergence programme, which aims to free product and factor markets so as to reduce structural rigidities and support economic development. To this end, the government's reform efforts focused on two areas in particular. First, they aimed for a speedy start to the public enterprise Modernisation Programme, which aims to restructure and sell most of the enterprises under central government control, and as support to this programme, the liberalisation of critical network industries such as telecommunications, electricity and natural gas. Second, the Government introduced two reforms resulting from social dialogue: a pension reform comprising the elements agreed in the "Toledo Pact" and a labour market reform. In addition, a significant step was also made towards the devolution of revenue raising power to regional governments in an effort to catch up with the more advanced process of devolving expenditure decisions. Reforms in other important sectors such as land and water use, which have been key bottlenecks for the economy, and the public health services are under discussion. The reform of the public enterprise sector, and the concurrent reform of the regulatory structures, is described in a special chapter (Chapter IV). This chapter describes the progress with respect to the other structural reforms introduced by the Government.

Labour market reform

In a notable display of unity, trade unions and employers' representatives agreed on a labour market reform in April 1997. The main aim of the agreement, which was quickly passed into law (May 1997 labour legislation), was to foster stable employment and to improve the collective bargaining processes. Regarding the first objective, the new legislation attempts to reduce the large number of workers under fixed-term contracts. The costs associated with these contracts were acknowledged by both the employers and the trade unions: the resulting uncertainty was undesirable in itself, and by weakening longer-term links between employers and workers with fixed-term contracts, human capital formation within firms was impaired. An important contribution of the reform is that it recognises that the segmentation created by the generous job protection for those with permanent contracts (*i.e.* the high firing costs) crowds new entrants out of the labour market and fosters the rotation of fixed-term jobs with no dismissal costs. The reform of the multi-tiered collective bargaining system may prove to be even more important. The aim is to introduce more flexibility into the process by focusing the "most appropriate" level of negotiations on specific contract issues. In this fashion, the measures embodied in the Labour Act attempt to address a few of the key recommendations presented by the follow-up on *Implementing the OECD Jobs Strategy* contained in the previous *OECD Economic Survey of Spain* (Table 11).

The most noted aspect of the reform was the introduction of a new permanent contract, with reduced severance payments. This contract was targeted to two groups: the population most exposed to unemployment (*i.e.* youth, the long-term unemployed, women and men above age 45), and workers on a temporary contract who converted to an indefinite one during the one-year period following the implementation of the May labour market legislation (*i.e.* up to May 1998). The new contract reduces severance payments in the event of an unjustified dismissal – from 45 days' pay per year of service, up to a 42 month maximum, to 33 days per year up to a 24 month maximum – which nevertheless remain above the EU average. Also critical to the reduction of dismissal costs is the reform's attempt to clarify when employers are justified in laying off workers on permanent contracts (and can thus pay lower severance payments of 20 days per year up to a 12 month maximum). Under the new legislation, a dismissal is considered to be fair when it allows the enterprise to reorganise its workforce in order to surmount difficulties related to its competitive performances or demand weakness. This aspect of the reform takes another step in the direction embarked on by the 1994 labour market reform, which had tried to make the definition of a justified dismissal less restrictive by adding to the range of criteria ones related to

Table 11. **Implementing the OECD Jobs Strategy – an overview**

Proposal	Action	OECD assessment/recommendation
I. Reform employment security provision:		
a) Reduce the legal minimum severance payments for justified dismissals.	a) Creation of a new indefinite contract for targeted groups with reduced severance payments for unjustified dismissals while restricting the use of fixed-term contracts.	a) Severance payments remain among the highest in the OECD and should be reduced significantly.
b) Ensure that the decisions of the labour courts, as concerns severance payments, conform to the spirit of existing legislation.	b) Some clarification in the conditions for fair dismissals.	b) Ensure that the decisions of the labour courts, as concerns severance payments, conform to the spirit of existing legislation.
		c) Elimination of the administrative approval for collective dismissals.
II. Reform unemployment and related benefit systems:		
a) Review the eligibility conditions for unemployment assistance benefits.	a) Reduce fraudulent use of temporary invalidity benefits.	a) Incentives to job search need to be further enhanced.
b) Maintain work incentives.		
c) Review the replacement rates and the maximum duration of unemployment benefits.		
III. Increase wage and labour cost flexibility:		
a) Increase the flexibility of working conditions and wages (by reducing the range of provisions included in the clausulas normativas and Ordenanzas laborales).	a) All Ordenanzas laborales have been suppressed and are now negotiated within the collective bargaining process.	a) Collective bargaining needs to take advantage of the potential new flexibility in negotiations and permit new wages to reflect the economic circumstances.
b) Take more into account the entreprises' specific situation in collective agreements.	b) New voluntary framework for collective bargaining which proposes decentralisation of wage bargaining to the firm or regional level.	
c) Abandon automatic indexation.		

Table 11. **Implementing the OECD Jobs Strategy – an overview** (*cont.*)

Proposal	Action	OECD assessment/recommendation
IV. Expand and enhance active labour market policies:		
	a) Consider active placement and job search assistance programmes as well as work-fare or employment subsidies for targeted groups.	*a)* Employment subsidies should be linked to training and/or work-fare.
	a) Social contribution rates on the new indefinite contract were temporarily reduced for targeted groups.	
V. Improve labour force skills and competence:		
	a) Enhance the educational attainment of youth cohorts.	
	b) Ensure that vocational education is given appropriate emphasis.	*a)* Training programmes should maximise work experience.
	b) Creation of a new contract with training certificate.	
VI. Enhance product market competition:		
	a) Restructure and privatise government owned enterprises.	*a)* Rapid implementation can provide large opportunities for job creation.
	a) Implementation of the June 1996 modernisation programme of public enterprises.	
	b) Relieve regions' restrictions on shop-opening hours.	*b)* Restrictive land-use regulations which reduce worker mobility should be relaxed.
	b) Two packages of measures liberalising, *inter alia*, telecommunications, electricity, professional services.	
	c) Reduce the prerogatives of the "colegios profesionales".	

the economic situation of the firm (*i.e.* organisational and production-related reasons).[44] Despite the attempt in 1994 to broaden the justifications, the labour courts have nevertheless continued to rule overwhelmingly in favour of workers, and in practice, many companies opt simply to pay more than the full rate foreseen for unfair dismissals to avoid the costs and delays involved with the courts.[45]

To give an additional incentive to the use of new indefinite contracts, in May 1997 the government lowered the employers' share of the social contribution rate for workers under such contracts. In most cases, the reduction only applies to the first two years of the contract and varies between 40 and 60 per cent of the standard share paid by employers (23.6 per cent).[46] The only population group that cannot benefit from a contract with these two enticements (lower firing costs and lower social security contribution) are prime age males (age 30-45) excepting the long-term unemployed. The reform appears to be succeeding in increasing the number of indefinite contracts. Over the period from May to December 1997 their number increased two times more than in 1996, and almost 70 per cent of the new contracts benefited from reduced social contribution payments. The success of this reform in achieving a lasting increase in more stable contracts will depend critically on firms' reactions at the end of the two year subsidy period.

The attempt to reduce recourse to fixed-term contracts also involved penalising their usage. Conditions required for using fixed term contracts were tightened considerably, and their maximum length shortened.[47] In addition, certain types of fixed-term contracts were suppressed, such as the one for so-called new activities, and all existing financial incentives were withdrawn from hiring under fixed-term contracts (except for the handicapped). Furthermore, fixed-term contracts may incur a one percentage point higher contribution rate for unemployment coverage: the 1998 budget law gives the Government the authority to take this decision if the above-described incentives do not succeed in raising the share of indefinite contracts.

The 1997 agreement between social partners also aimed to simplify and improve the collective bargaining process. The agreement between the social partners recognised that collective bargaining in Spain is extremely complex since it involves negotiations at various levels and lacks a clear definition of the responsibilities at each level, resulting often in cascading negotiations and possible inconsistencies. Specifically, the system has a strong inflationary bias since wage increases agreed at a higher level of collective bargaining have often been taken as a floor in subsequent bargaining at lower levels. The agreement between social partners provides some general guidelines on an optimal division of responsibilities between the (national) sectoral level collective bargaining and bargaining at a regional or firm level. In particular, wage bargaining should preferably be undertaken at the regional or firm level, since this would permit wage settlements to better reflect the specific labour market situation – either a region's own unemployment rate or an enterprise's specific financial situation. Further functional flexibility on the labour market could be facilitated by the additional recommendation contained in the Labour Act to broaden the definition of professions and job status. This aspect of the agreement takes a further step in the direction initiated by the 1994 labour market reform to introduce more flexibility into the collective bargaining process.[48] Specifically, the 1994 reform provided the potential to include a broader variety of work-related terms in the bargaining process and has resulted in the introduction of many clauses which have improved functional and geographical mobility. However, little use has been made of the option created in 1994 to insert a clause permitting an opt-out of higher level wage negotiations in the event of an individual firm's financial distress.[49]

Though it is still far too early to fully assess the achievements of the 1997 labour market reform, it serves to point the way for future efforts to create a more flexible labour market. The social partners have taken an important step in agreeing that high dismissal costs are partly responsible for a segmented labour market. In this situation, workers with more secure permanent contracts (''insiders'') are able to bid up their wages as their bargaining power is increased by the existence of a large share of fixed-term contracts (''outsiders''), for which there are few redundancy costs. Though partly compensated by the lower wages of workers under fixed-term contracts, overall wage costs are bid up and employment flexibility constrained, with both factors restricting employment creation. Acknowledging that the new permanent contracts carry lower unjustified dismissal costs, these nevertheless continue to be higher than in most other EU countries, and such contracts will only apply to certain categories of workers, effectively segmenting the labour market even further (Figure 16).

Figure 16. **LABOUR MARKET CHARACTERISTICS IN SELECTED EU COUNTRIES**

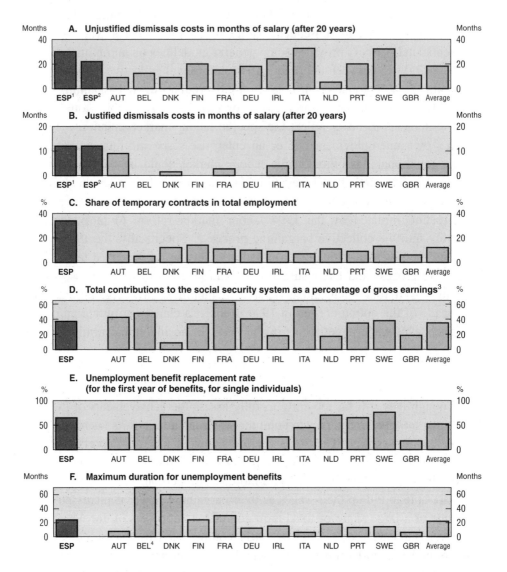

1. Existing indefinite contracts.
2. New indefinite contracts for targeted groups.
3. Effective employee's and employer's contributions for a married individual with 2 children earning a salary equivalent to the average production worker.
4. Indefinite duration for single person and one-earner couple.
Source: OECD (1997) *The tax/benefit position of employees, Implementing the OECD Jobs Strategy* and *Employment Outlook.*

To reduce this stimulus to market segmentation, effective dismissal costs will need to be reduced substantially. Such costs are high because the existing regulations defining a justified dismissal, or equivalently their interpretation by the labour courts, are deficient. The large majority of the labour courts' decisions rule in the favour of the employees, leading firms to avoid their use. The move to clarify the economic basis for a justified dismissal is a step in the right direction, but the non-effectiveness of a similar 1994 reform is telling, and suggests a more ambitious reform of dismissal regulations may be required. Additional reform should not be delayed in order to gauge the effectiveness of the current reform. It should focus on reducing decisively the high effective dismissal costs *i)* by taking the necessary measures to ensure that the decisions of the labour courts conform to the spirit of the regulations pertaining to justified dismissals, *ii)* abolishing administrative approval for collective dismissals or, *iii)* more directly, by reducing statutory dismissal costs. Further reform in this direction is important since a large majority of employees continue to be under the pre-reform permanent contracts. Steps in this direction will facilitate the intended shift in the wage bargaining process to lower levels of collective negotiations with such relative wage flexibility supporting employment creation.

Spain's pluri-annual employment programme (1997-2000) presented in September 1997 states that the Government would foster employment by providing appropriate macroeconomic and institutional frameworks. Similar to the main lines of the Luxembourg Accord, the employment programme stresses the need to enhance "employability" (*i.e.* ensuring that people have the right incentive and skills to exploit work opportunities) through better education and training opportunities throughout the life cycle. To this end, the programme envisages devoting approximately Ptas 2 500 billion (more than 3 per cent of the 1997 GDP) over this 4 year period to promote active labour market policies and training. For the most part, the programme does not involve expending significant additional revenues, as many of the individual programmes under the overall umbrella already exist under the control of different ministries. A notable change in active labour market policy concerns the emphasis on part-time workers. In an effort to raise the low share of part-time work in Spain, the Government is raising unemployment contributions on overtime work (to the level applying to normal hours) and lowering them on part-time work. Regarding passive benefits, reform of temporary disability benefits is envisaged. But broader reform of the system of unemployment and related benefits - characterised by high replacement rates and long duration for those eligible for unemployment insurance, both of which discourage job search – will have to be considered.[50]

Pension reform: the implementation of the Toledo Pact

In July 1997, Parliament approved legislation introducing several notable reforms to the pension system. The new law on the Consolidation and Rationalisation of the Social Security System implements the agreement between social partners of October 1996, which in turn was based on the recommendations of the Toledo Pact.[51] The reform contains measures which aim to improve the financial situation of the system and make the system more equitable. The most important measure generating saving is the gradual widening of the pension base from the last 8 years of contributions to the last 15 years. The result will be an approximately 5 per cent reduction in the average pension (compared with what would have been the case without the introduction of this measure) after the year 2000 when the full impact of the measure would be in force.[52] Another measure which aims to improve the system's financing will gradually unify the different contribution ceilings at the level of the highest one.[53] Finally, a reduction of the front-loaded accumulation of pension rights, which provides incentives to retire early by having an accumulation rate which diminishes in relation to the years of contributions. Further savings could arise from the efforts to clarify eligibility to the different degrees of permanent invalidity as well as its transformation to an old-age pension at age 65. Measures to improve the equity of the system ease the eligibility conditions for receiving an old-age pension as well as retiring early.[54] They also raise the minimum pension received by younger widows and broaden the age conditions for the receipt of an orphan's pension.

In total, the net savings produced from the full impact of these measures do not appear to be very significant compared with the magnitude of the future problem, especially as the equity-enhancing measures partly compensate the gains stemming from the other measures. The other important change introduced by the new legislation is its stipulation that the financing of non-contributory pensions would no longer be made from contributions, but would have to be undertaken by general sources of taxation by the year 2000.[55] Any resulting surplus in the social security system would be used to build up a reserve fund.[56] Finally, the legislation incorporates into law the recent practice of indexing pensions to inflation.[57]

This reform implicitly recognises the concern over the long-run viability of the pension system and plans a re-valuation of the system in the year 2000. Similar to the situation in most continental European countries, Spain faces population ageing which will place a heavy strain on the financing of the pay-as-you-go pension system if pension regulations are not tightened.[58] The old-age dependency ratio is projected to rise from its current 25 per cent to about 67 per cent in 2055. Spain's predicament is magnified by the existence of a rather generous, yet still not mature, system.[59] The benefit formula is one of the most generous in the OECD and will remain so even after the above-described widening of the pension base (the replacement rate for 35 years of contributions will be about 85 per cent of the final wage and even higher for wage paths with flat profiles). In most other countries – where the viability of the system is also an issue – the average annual accumulation rate for 35 years' contributions is significantly lower than the $2^{1}/_{2}$ per cent implied by the Spanish system, and ranges from $^{1}/_{2}$ to $1^{1}/_{2}$ per cent.

Another significant source of pressure on the system is early retirements which hinder the build up of a reserve fund during the current maturation stage of the system. In 1996, the average age of new old-age pensioners was 62 in the largest regime (the general regime), with 70 per cent of new pensioners below the statutory pension age of 65, out of which 45 per cent are at age 60. The incentives for early retirement may be due to the existence of a front-loaded accumulation rate. Despite the improvement introduced by the new reform, 50 per cent of the old-age pension is still accumulated after 15 years of contributions and 80 per cent after 25 years of contributions, implying that the formula continues to be front loaded. Nevertheless, the fact that approximately 60 per cent of pensioners have contributed for 35 years and retire early with a reduced pension suggests that the generous level of the pension (compared with the corresponding level of contributions) is providing the main incentive to individuals to retire early.[60] The average age of pensioners as a whole is reduced by the large share of invalidity pensions – approximately 23 per cent of total pensions. The rate of increase of invalidity pensioners was quite high during the past 15 years, with their number increasing at twice the pace of old-age pensions.

However, it has slowed considerably and is now growing at 1 per cent annually compared with 2½ per cent for old-age pensions. The fact that many invalidity pensions are received near retirement, in conjunction with the generosity of such benefits, has been interpreted as a sign that recourse to an invalidity pension has been a way of obtaining early retirement.[61] The recent reform in this area could reduce some of these incentives to early retirement. However, the recent erosion of the restriction requiring all post-1967 members of the work-force to retire only after reaching age 65, weakens a significant stabilising element contained in the legislation.

There is a general consensus that the need to reduce the high unemployment rate rules out increasing social security contribution rates (they are above the OECD average and represent nearly 60 per cent of the average wage). In any event, raising contributions – as through the unification of the ceiling for all contributors – will provide for some additional financing in the short term, but could also eventually entail larger pay outs of pensions.[62] Although contribution rates may not be raised, the authorities' increased efforts to reduce payment fraud could improve contribution collection. Specifically, efforts to contain the fraudulent access to the minimum pension supplement may reduce incentives to evade contributions as well as reduce pension expenditure. These incentives to evade would originate from the guarantee of a minimum pension level – irrespective of contribution years – which therefore reduces the need to accumulate pension rights.[63] This phenomenon could be more prevalent in the special regimes (for the self-employed, including farmers) where the average number of contribution years by pensioners is significantly below 35 years and the share of pensioners receiving the minimum pension supplement is the highest.[64]

Reforms to the pension system need to be introduced early, as changes to current entitlements can be introduced only gradually, while delays will magnify the burden that future generations will bear. The recent reforms may provide a small reprieve but certainly do not provide sufficient relief for the system.[65] As a simple illustration of the pressures exerted on the system, equilibrium at any one point in time requires the ratio of the effective contribution rate to the effective replacement rate to equal the ratio of pensioners to contributors (see Annex I).[66] Currently, the latter ratio is about 55 per cent (more than twice the old-age dependency ratio due to early retirements) while the effective contribution rate is 25 per cent and the effective replacement ratio 35 per cent. The fact that the system is in surplus is indicated by the fact that the former ratio is larger than the latter (25/35 > 0.55). However, if the ratio of pensioners to contributors follows even partially the projected path of the old age dependency ratio mentioned above (an increase of about 150 per cent) then the replacement rate must fall drastically to keep the system in balance. Maintaining equilibrium will be made more difficult if the effective replacement ratio increases towards its much higher statutory level as the system matures. In contrast, the effective contribution rate appears closer to its statutory level. Though a very rough indication of the magnitude of the problem, this simple example reveals that future reforms should raise the effective pension age, as well as reduce replacement rates. Timely action will permit the build up of a reserve fund, which will attenuate the severity of reforms which will have to occur at a later date.

The new financing system for the regions

In September 1996, the Spanish authorities approved a new system to finance the regions (*Comunidades Autonomas*) for the period 1997-2001, which gives the regions an important new dimension of fiscal autonomy.[67] Since the establishment of the regional governments by the 1978 constitution, the process of decentralisation had been rapid but asymmetric in the devolution of spending and revenue raising powers. The expenditures ceded to the regions have comprised the two large spending items of education and health care, while the central government retained most of the taxing powers and transferred resources to the regions to cover ceded expenditures (Table 12).[68] Until 1997, fiscal devolution was confined to the collection of the so-called ceded taxes (*tributos cedidos*), mainly on property, whose rates and conditions were nevertheless set by the central government. These ceded taxes only covered about one-quarter of regional expenditure.

The 1997-2001 regional financing plan granted the regional governments important new responsibilities to raise tax revenues. The main innovation is that the regional governments are able to set a component of the personal income rates applying to their own region. Specifically, marginal rates are divided into a State and a regional component. The regional component can vary within a 20 per cent band around their 15 per cent share of the marginal rate, *i.e.* the marginal tax brackets for individuals could vary by as much as plus or minus

Table 12. **Regional governments' expenditure and revenue**

As a percentage of respective general government budgetary component

	1985	1990	1996
Total consumption	14.6	18.1	20.9
Wage consumption	17.6	21.0	24.3
(Employment)	24.0[1]	25.5	29.5
Non wage consumption	7.0	10.8	12.7
Investment	31.4	31.3	35.1
Debt	1.5	3.7	7.9
Total taxes	6.5	7.1	6.8
Indirect taxes	10.9	13.0	12.1
Direct taxes	1.5	2.3	2.3
Memorandum item:			
Current transfers received by regional governments			
as a percentage of their current receipts	62.5	65.9	73.0

1. 1987.
Source: Bank of Spain.

3 per cent.[69] The introduction of a lower limit reflects a perceived risk of excessive tax competition. The regional percentage will pass to 30 per cent when all regions have the responsibility for compulsory education transferred to them, envisaged to occur in 1998. Regions were also granted the possibility to vary income tax exemption thresholds, and gained more powers to modify taxes already transferred to them (taxes on wealth, inheritances, donations, property transactions, legal acts and on gambling). As a result, it is estimated that over the period 1997-2001, taxes over which regional governments will have at least some capacity to change the base or the rate will increase from about one-quarter to over one-half of current revenues; of course, total current revenue may need to be increased as regional governments are devolved additional expenditure responsibilities (*e.g.* for health care in many regions).[70]

The new financing system includes some guarantees aiming to protect the regions against possible temporary revenue shortfalls and thus ensure a sufficient level of resources for the provision of regional public services. This decision partly reflects that a large part of the regions' financial resources will henceforth depend on personal income taxes, which will likely make regional revenue more volatile. Personal income tax revenue has historically varied more than GDP and more importantly some regions have a concentrated production and tax base (Figure 17). The guarantees consist of the State's commitment to partly compensate a region with transfers in the event its personal income tax collection or total revenues grow more slowly than the respective national averages.[71] The risk-sharing mechanism could conceivably put pressure on the central government budget as it is asymmetric. It requires the central government to guarantee transfers to regions in the event of bad states of nature but does not receive any resources in the event of good states. While previously the centralised taxation system pooled risk related to regional tax variations and acted as an insurance system, the new system provides insurance against shortfalls without having a source to finance these risks. Additionally, there exist mechanisms which promote real convergence among the regions. First, there is an additional guarantee when the level of financing per capita falls below the national average. Second, there is the existing Compensation fund (*Fondo de Compensacion Interterritorial*), which aims to correct economic imbalances between regions through investment expenditure.[72]

Figure 17. **VARIABILITY OF GENERAL GOVERNMENT REVENUE**
Annual growth rate

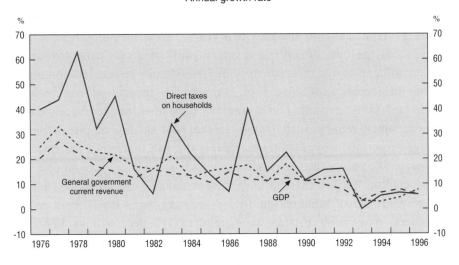

Source: OECD Secretariat.

Though the new system increases the fiscal responsibility of regional governments, it has not introduced new instruments to secure fiscal discipline. With Spain committed to fiscal consolidation at the general government level, further decentralisation requires enhanced co-ordination and monitoring so as to ensure that the regions do not put Spain's convergence process at risk. In the past, limits were set for the regions' debts and deficits, in accordance with Spain's convergence programme. However regional governments have turned to the financial markets to fund any additional expenditure and have often exceeded these limits, since there were no penalties imposed for non compliance. Additional constraints imposed on the regions' recourse to borrowing have also not been effective.[73] The problem for setting national policy is made more difficult by the unavailability of data to assess the regions' fiscal performance, with the exception of the regions' indebtedness. The regions' debt to GDP ratio rose from 5.7 per cent in 1995 to 6.3 per cent in 1996, and increased by the equivalent of 1 per cent of the 1996 GDP in the one-year period to September 1997, compared with a convergence programme deficit target for territorial governments of 0.6 per cent of GDP in 1996 and 0.3 per cent of GDP in 1997.

Reforming the health care system

Health care reform has been sporadic at the level of both central and regional governments over the past two years.[74] New measures have aimed to improve both the cost effectiveness and quality of health care provision, as quality is still considered unsatisfactory in Spain despite an acceleration in health spending in recent years. Areas of concern are specialised care, which is characterised by long waiting lists, and the high level of pharmaceutical consumption, which reflects such factors as the poor quality of preventive care, excessive prescription by doctors, as well as the fact that drugs are free for all pensioners.[75] To reduce drug expenditure (which accounts for around one fifth of total expenditure on health), the Government reduced the sizeable administratively set pharmacists' retail margin by 2 percentage points (to 27.9 per cent) and wholesalers' margin by 1 percentage point (to 11 per cent) in 1997.[76] The Government is also promoting the use of generics, whose penetration in Spain is still very low compared with most other EU countries. As part of the agreement with the regions for the period 1998-2001, the Government has decided to reduce the number of pharmaceuticals on the social security system's eligibility list. A similar measure was implemented in 1993, however it led to large substitution towards other, often more expensive, listed pharmaceuticals. The agreement also entails an accord between the Government and the pharmaceutical industry to pay Ptas 29 billion from the latters' profits and to reduce drug prices. The combined savings from these three measures is estimated to reduce public health expenditure by Ptas 75 billion.

At the regional level, several promising pilot programmes have been implemented. However, to take advantage of the experience obtained from these decentralised programmes in formulating national health policy will necessitate improved information flows between the central government and the regions. At the regional level, steps have been taken to improve incentives to reduce costs by introducing private management practices in several health care centres and public hospitals. In addition, some possibilities for choice among providers have been offered to patients. While the norm is for hospital staff to be paid exclusively on a salary basis and effectively have the status of civil servants, several health care centres (particularly in Cataluña) and public hospitals have linked some components of staff remuneration to productivity. To further increase efficiency, more flexibility in hiring practices, job contracts and working hours has also been introduced. In Andalucía, patients were offered a choice among public hospitals in 1997, which should help introduce more competition into the system, and thus reduce waiting lists. In public hospitals in Madrid and Aragon, the waiting lists for surgery were reduced by providing financial incentives to use equipment more intensively, which is envisaged to increase the number of surgeries per day.[77] Regarding pharmaceuticals, the Basque region health administration has introduced a reference price system for pharmaceuticals: doctors prescribe the active ingredient and the patient is reimbursed on the basis of the corresponding reference price.

The demand for health care will continue to grow, *inter alia*, as the population ages and Spain's per capita income catches up to the level of its EU partners. Maintaining control over public health care expenditure and safeguarding the objective of the new agreement between the central and the regional governments will likely require reform efforts on several fronts. The commitment to maintain the growth of health care financing through the budget of the national institute of health (INSALUD) equal to that of nominal GDP during 1999-2001 would otherwise be jeopardised.[78] Looking at the health care system from the financing side, the fact that regions (the seven out of 17 that have had health care devolved to them) are not responsible for raising the financing for their respective public health care system, in combination with the transfer from the central government being effectively based on historical costs, provides no incentives to cost savings. Until the requisite transfer of sufficient revenue-raising capabilities to the regional governments to cover their health expenditures, efficiency gains could arise if all regional expenditure financed by the central government is provided through a general transfer, thus providing the incentive to regional governments to achieve savings which can be applied elsewhere.

Nevertheless, expenditure control will require improvements in the incentives of providers and users of health care services. In many other countries, there is movement towards the creation of an internal market for health care. In this manner, though public health care could still be provided without charge, the system's efficiency is enhanced by the introduction of competition among health care providers as "the money follows the patient". Such a system should lead to more efficient use and allocation of increasingly scarce resources and improve the quality of service. Looking at the main components of the health care system, well-functioning primary care is a necessity in any system, as preventive care can produce much savings down the road, and primary care physicians can play a useful gatekeeper role in curtailing access to more expensive and scarcer hospital care. In this regard, the role of the health care centres could be improved if their responsibility for patients were enhanced. This would help reduce the long waiting lists that exist for hospital care. Other reforms to improve the efficiency of hospital care could involve the use of case-mix funding in lieu of historical cost budgeting, recourse to contracting out services (with penalties for non-performance), as well as more flexible hours, the more extensive use of day surgery, and the replacement of civil service status for hospital staff with productivity-based labour contracts. Health care reform will necessarily need to focus on pharmaceutical consumption which absorbs a larger-than-average share of total health care expenditure (20 per cent). A main factor is the free access to pharmaceuticals for pensioners, which partly accounts for their large share of drug expenditure (65 per cent). The introduction of means-tested co-payment for this segment of the population could help reduce over-consumption of drugs. Other reforms to contain health care reform would be to further encourage the use of generics and prescriptions based on active ingredients and daily dosages as well as more competition among pharmacies. The parliamentary committee agreement in December 1997 provides a general framework for a systemic reform which could include several of the above-described recommendations.

Other product and factor deregulation measures

In June 1996 and February 1997, the Government announced two large packages of measures whose eventual implementation will "liberalise and re-activate the economy" and thus facilitate employment generation. Most of the measures focus on enhancing product market competition in the critical economic sectors where public enterprises had a dominant position (telecommunications and energy sectors, and infrastructure development). These reforms are described in Chapter IV. However, the proposals covered other important areas such as land and water use, as well as the liberalisation of professional associations (e.g. lawyers and architects). A reform of professional services has already occurred, while important reform of regulations for land and water use are currently under discussion in Parliament.[79]

Despite the abundance of land in Spain, the supply of urban land is artificially constrained and as a result urban land prices are high – a fact which also deters the geographical mobility of workers.[80] Supply is constrained by complex procedures for transforming non-urban land to urban land and subsequently obtaining a building licence. It reportedly takes five years for the transformation of land which can not be urbanised to urban land and then receiving a license.[81] In a first step at reform, April 1997 legislation simplified some aspects of these complex procedures. However, the low supply of urban land also reflects the dependency of local authorities on revenue sources which are based on land values (approximately 30 per cent of their total revenues and over 50 per cent of the revenues they raise), and thus provides them with the incentive to keep land prices high. The draft law on land reform currently in Parliament takes a step towards reducing land prices. It would lower the direct licensing cost to the urban land developer by reducing the amount of land that has to be ceded to local authorities in order to obtain a building licence. From 15 per cent of the development project, the ceded share would drop to a maximum of 10 per cent, with the share within this range left to be set by the local authorities. The reform also aims to reduce the arbitrariness of local government licensing and urban planning decisions by setting basic rules for promoting urban land. An apparent obstacle to its passage is the loss in revenue for local authorities, suggesting that the main challenge to land reform is finding a substitute source of revenue for local authorities.

Water use is also marked by an allocation system which is distortionary. Part of the misallocation problem arises from low water prices, which are among the lowest in the OECD for households while the price for agriculture use is based on land size rather than actual volume of water used. Allocation is made inflexible as concession rights are usually granted for up to the maximum of 75 years according to a pre-determined order of preference.[82] Moreover, the concession rights can only be nullified if the concession has not been used for 5 years. Reflecting, *inter alia*, the albeit declining importance of agriculture in Spain, the rigid allocation mechanism, and the use of water supply policy as an instrument of income distribution to farmers and sustaining a rural population, over 80 per cent of water consumption in Spain is accounted for by agriculture. The allocation of water is also complicated by the need to cover the water deficit in southern Spain through a very large array of infrastructure projects. These are mostly covered by resources from the central government with user fees covering up to 4 per cent of the value of the investment used by the respective consumer.

The draft law on water use aims to improve the management and allocation of water use, *inter alia*, by increasing the role for water fees, and introducing a market for water and new financing techniques for infrastructure investment. Greater recourse will be made of user fees, including the increase in discharge fees so as to encourage the cleaning and re-use of water (polluter pays principle), and the placement of levies on the users of water concession rights (user pays principle). The market for water rights – as currently envisaged – would permit the transfer of a concession. But with few exceptions, transfers would be only permitted between the same type of users – effectively segmenting the market between the large but potentially declining agricultural component and the more dynamic components such as hydro-electric use. The final major initiative pertains to the opening of opportunities to larger private participation in the financing and construction of hydraulic works. Other aspects of the reform entail the requirement of metering for all consumers and the liberalisation of salt water desalination. Though the law entails a major step forward, reforms to ensure a more efficient use of water would need to entail a fully integrated market for water rights, and a more thorough implementation of the principle of the user pays, especially as pertains to the large agriculture sector. Income and regional policies if desired, would be better implemented through a targeted subsidy policy.

Overall, many important steps have been taken during the past two years – or are about to be taken – which would serve to reduce the structural rigidities constraining the output growth potential of the Spanish economy. Nevertheless, many restrictions remain as a result of Spain's corporatist legacy. The 1998-2000 convergence plan has rightly placed an important emphasis on the need for pushing further ahead with reform of product and factor markets, especially as flexibility will become more important for the economy in light of the approach of EMU, and the potential of asymmetric shocks. The first order of importance should be further labour market reform, while the enhancement of competition in product markets, especially those producing key inputs for other markets, will also be of critical importance. Finally, macroeconomic stability will require significant reforms of incentives in the health and pension systems, which would induce savings in these expenditures. Though the list of reforms may be long, the interlinkages of sectors suggests that the effect of concurrent reform efforts will be reinforcing.

IV. Reforming the public enterprise sector

The Spanish Government has accelerated the process of restructuring and privatising public enterprises. A modernisation programme – announced in 1996 – aims at improving the financial performance of enterprises, and to sell all but a select few over the next 4 to 5 years. This strategy reflects the viewpoint that public control of the enterprises has resulted in efficiency losses for the economy as well as huge budgetary costs. Contemporaneously with this modernisation programme, the Government is introducing new legislation to promote competition in the sectors previously dominated by public enterprises. The most significant innovations pertain to the changing structure of the telecommunications and electricity sectors. Moreover, further reforms will be implemented in the gas and oil sectors in line with the recent approved hydrocarbon law. Though progress has often been spurred by EC directives, the Spanish liberalisation effort has achieved rapid progress and in certain areas has surpassed that of many of its European partners. The completion of this modernisation programme will nevertheless leave enterprises which implement public interest policies under state control (trains, postal services and public television) as well as the perennial loss-making coal mines, which will however undergo a further restructuring effort.

The objective of this chapter is to analyse the main problems with the public enterprise sector and assess the current policy framework as well as planned changes to it. First, the key features of the public enterprise sector are outlined including their impact on public finances and the labour market. Second, the recent changes in government policy towards public enterprises are reviewed. Third, the economic conditions – mainly the competitive structure and pricing policy in the main sectors – are examined. Fourth, an attempt is made to quantify the potential gain in output and employment from introducing competition and an appropriate regulatory framework. The chapter concludes with a set of recommendations.

Key features of the public enterprise sector

Spanish public enterprises are controlled by various bodies.[83] Until September 1997, the loss-making industrial enterprises were grouped under the *Agencia Industrial del Estado* (AIE) while the profitable ones were under the SEPI holding (*Sociedad Estatal de Participaciones Industriales*). The remaining important public enterprises are controlled by the Ministry of Finance – *Direccion General del Patrimonio del Estado (DGPE)* and its agent responsible for privatisations, *Sociedad Estatal de Participaciones Patrimoniales (SEPPA)* – or are public entities with agency status (Table 13). Public enterprises with a public policy role are under the supervision of the respective ministry (*e.g.* the railway company *RENFE* is under the auspices of the Ministry of Fomento). Finally, territorial governments (regional and local) also have formed public enterprises which are under their direct control.

This universe of Spanish public enterprises comprises a diverse set of firms, representing many different sectors and having divergent financial situations – circumstances similar to most other countries. As a result, few conclusions can be drawn from aggregate public enterprise data, and a deeper analysis will require sectoral reviews. Nevertheless, before taking that route, some indications of the main issues can be found from reviewing the aggregate data for 1995 (Table 14).[84] Reflecting the high capital intensity of many public enterprises, aggregate labour productivity was unsurprisingly higher in public enterprises compared with the combination of public and private ones (and therefore by inference the private sector), as was the aggregate rate of return on assets and aggregate compensation as a share of value added.[85] However, public enterprises received significantly larger support in the form of current and capital transfers than the private sector, and despite this assistance, were relatively more indebted. A breakdown by the respective controlling body (*e.g.* SEPPA and Ministry of Fomento, SEPI, AIE), reveals a high productivity for the firms in SEPI, reflecting the large representation of the energy sector, yet even this set of firms received large state assistance while its rate of return on assets was lower than in the private sector. The composition of the firms in the AIE (*e.g.* loss-making coal mining and shipyards) results in relatively poor productivity. The performance of firms under SEPPA and the Ministry of Fomento are more difficult to interpret, most likely because they included telecommunications but also rail and television services (according to the Bank of Spain classification). Enterprises under the

Table 13. **Institutional groupings of public enterprises at end-1996**

Holding Sociedad estatal de participaciones patrimoniales (SEPPa-DGPE)

	Sector	State participation %
Aldeasa	Duty free shop	80.0
Minas de Almadén	Mining	100.0
Paradores de Turismo	Hotel	100.0
Tabacalera	Tobacco	52.4
Transmediterránea	Sea transport	95.2
Argentaria	Banking	25.1
Telefonica	Telecommunications	21.0
Enausa	Motorways	100.0
Alimentos y Aceites S.A.	Edible oils	100.0
Cesce	Insurance	50.2

Holding Agencia industrial del Estado (AIE)

	Sector	State participation %
Astilleros Españoles, (AESA)	Shipbuilding	100.0
Astilleros y Talleres del Noroeste, ASTANO	Shipbuilding	100.0
Sta. Bárbara (ENSB)	Defence	100.0
E. Nacional Bazán Constr. (BAZÁN)	Defence	100.0
Hulleras del Norte, S.A. (HUNOSA)	Mining	100.0
Minas de Figaredo, S.A. (FIGAREDO)	Mining	100.0
Productos Tubulares, S.A.	Iron and steel	100.0
CSI Corporación Siderúrgica, S.A.	Iron and steel	100.0
AHV-Ensidesa Capital, S.A.	Iron and steel	100.0
Altos Hornos del Mediterráneo, S.A. (AHM)	Iron and steel	99.5
Prerreducidos Integ. Sureste España, S.A. (PRESUR)	Iron and steel	100.0

Holding Sociedad estatal de participaciones industriales (SEPI)

	Sector	State participation %
Enagas	Gas	9.0
Astilleros del Atlántico	Shipbuilding	45.0
Auxini	Engineering and construction	60.0
Aviaco	Air transport	67.0
Babcock Wilcox	Equipment goods	100.0
CASA	Defence	99.3
ENCE	Chemicals and paper	51.0
ENDESA	Electricity	66.9
Iberia	Air transport	99.9
Inespal	Aluminium	99.7
Potasas del Llobregat	Mining	58.2

Others public entities

	Sector	State participation %
Hispasat	Satellite	100.0
RTVE	Radio and television	100.0
AENA	Airport	100.0
Puertos del Estado	Harbour	100.0
Enatcar	Bus transport	100.0
Retevisión	Radio and television	100.0
FEVE	Train transport	100.0
Renfe-Feve	Train transport	100.0

Source: A. Cuervo Garciá, "Las privatizaciones en España"; *Cuadernos de Información Económica*, Núm. 119, Febrero 1997 and OECD Secretariat.

Table 14. A comparison of public and private enterprise performance in 1995[1]

	Number of enterprises in the sample[2]	Number of employees (Thousands)	Share under fixed term contracts (Per cent)	Average annual compensation per employee (Thousand Ptas)	Productivity (Million Ptas per employee)	Total compensation	Operating surplus	Corporate taxes	Dividends	Current and capital transfers	Net lending	Gross liabilities	Return on assets[3]
						As a per cent of respective value added at factor cost							
Public enterprises	128 (10.6%)	300	5	5 862	12.1	48.4	49.9	3.1	8.2	27.5	17.1	256.9	12.8
SEPPA[4]	18 (5.5%)	157	8.5	5 562	12.0	46.3	51.6	5.7	2.5	27.4	7.8	231.6	21.0
SEPI and AIE	101 (4.7%)	121	6.4	6 056	13.2	48.6	50.0	12.0	4.2	24.5	28.6	296.7	9.2
SEPI	80 (3.9%)	80	6	6 835	16.8	40.5	58.0	14.3	4.4	21.4	39.0	271.6	11.4
AIE	21 (0.8%)	42	0.3	5 548	6.1	90.3	8.5	..	3.1	40.7	-25.2	427.5	-3.2
Under the control of Territorial Governments	7 (0.5%)	21	0.4	5 081	7.3	71.9	27.7	..	..	60.1	12.4	154.9	15.2
Non-financial enterprises (private and public)	5 445 (29.9%)	1 096	15	4 969	9.4	53.0	45.4	3.6	6.4	12.2	9.7	221.5	12.1

1. Sample of largest firms issued by Bank of Spain *Central de Balances*.
2. The figures in parentheses represent the share of value added at factor cost of the enterprises in the sample as a percentage of the total value added of the non financial enterprise sector.
3. Gross saving divided by non-financial assets.
4. Includes the national rail company RENFE, the national television company RTVE and the DGPE group entreprises not included in SEPPA.
Source: Bank of Spain.

control of territorial governments also had low productivity and poor financial positions (though the survey may not be representative as the few firms contained in the sample are mostly in television and urban underground transport).

The public enterprise sector is not large and is shrinking

An international comparison concerning the relative size or performance of public enterprises is made difficult by the above-described composition effect. Nevertheless, if employment is used as a proxy for the size, the Spanish public enterprise sector, though comprising a not insignificant share of employment, is not very large by international standards. At all levels of government, it employed 3½ per cent of the wage earners in 1996, compared with over 10 per cent in France, and only 1½ per cent in the United Kingdom.[86] Moreover, its direct weight in the Spanish economy has been reduced rapidly, primarily through the restructuring of loss-making industries that has taken place since the mid 1980s. As a result, there was significant labour shedding in the coal mining industry, the shipyards, and in the rail and air transport companies. Overall, employment was cut by nearly 50 per cent in the group of loss-making industrial enterprises between 1985 and 1995.[87]

More recently the size of the public enterprise sector has been diminished through a privatisation effort that has gathered steam, particularly during the last two years, and has now moved faster than in many other European countries. In 1996 and 1997, the State sold its remaining shares in the telephone company (Telefonica) and its international call subsidiary (TISA), the oil company (Repsol), the gas company (Gas Natural), the Steel Company (CSI), the aluminium company (Inespal) and tranches of shares in the electricity company (Endesa) and the second telephone operator (Retevision). As a result public sector participation has been broadly eliminated in the petroleum, natural gas, and steel sectors, adding these sectors to the low public presence in banking and insurance. This situation contrasts with many other continental European countries. These sales raised over Ptas 2 trillion (equivalent to 3 per cent of 1997 GDP), adding to the Ptas 1½ – 2 trillion raised during the previous 10 years (Table 15). However, while public enterprises controlled by the central government have been gradually downsized and privatised, those controlled by territorial governments appear to be increasing rapidly in number. Though information on activities of these public enterprises is scarce and incomplete, available evidence suggests that their employment – albeit from a low base – rose by almost 30 per cent over the

Table 15. **Main privatisations in Spain, 1986-1997**

Society	Date	% of capital sold	Receipts (Billions Ptas)
Seat	1986	75.0	19
Telefonica	1987	..	82
Endesa	1988	20.0	74
Repsol	1989	26.4	135
Repsol	1989	4.2	21
Repsol	1990	2.9	19
Seat	1990	24.0	20
Repsol	1992	9.9	64
Repsol	1993	14.0	106
Argentaria	1993	24.9	69
Argentaria	1993	25.0	99
Endesa	1994	8.7	138
Repsol	1995	19.0	130
Telefonica	1995	12.0	165
Repsol	1996	11.0	140
Argentaria	1996	25.0	155
Gas Natural	1996	3.8	36
Telefonica	1997	20.9	630
Repsol	1997	10.0	169
Auxini	1997	60.0	6
Endesa	1997	25.0	660
Telefonica International (TISA)	1997	23.8	131
CSI (Aceralia)[1]	1997	60.0	222
Elcano	1997	100.0	6
Inespal	1997	100.0	62
Retevision	1997	70.0	181
Aldeasa[2]	1997	100.0	56

1. Comprises four separate transactions: a sale of 35 per cent to the Luxembourg-based Arbed, and subsequently three sales to domestic firms.
2. Comprises two separate transactions: a sale of 30 per cent to the publicly controlled Tabacalera, and an IPO for 70 per cent.
Source: OECD Secretariat.

period 1986-95.[88] Another indication of the expansion of public enterprises at the regional level of government is the rapid increase in their number, which rose by 45 per cent during the period 1990 to 1996 (Table 16).

... but remains dominant in some industries providing critical inputs and public services

As in many other OECD countries, public enterprises have dominated, at least until very recently, sectors which provide critical inputs to the rest of the

Table 16. **The growth of regional public enterprises,**
1990-1996

Region	Number of enterprises[1]	Share created since 1990
Andalucia	39	48.7
Aragon	9	88.9
Asturias	16	25.0
Baleares	16	37.5
Canarias	25	52.0
Cantabria	10	70.0
Castilla-Leon	17	41.2
Castilla la Mancha	0	n.a.
Cataluna	44	56.8
Extremadura	17	70.6
Galicia	22	68.2
Madrid	25	28.0
Murcia	12	66.7
Navarra	27	18.5
Pais Vasco	74	36.5
La Rioja	3	33.3
C. Valenciana	18	27.8
Total	374	45.2

1. Controlled by regional governments as of end-1996.
Source: Ministry of Economy and Finance, *Sector Publico Autonomico.*

economy. These sectors have included the telecommunication services, electricity, gas and petrol, air and rail transport, mining and steel (Figure 18), most of which operate in a quasi-monopolistic or tightly regulated environment where network externalities may be present. Entry restrictions have been seen as instrumental in guaranteeing a rate of return on basic investment, and allowing these enterprises to expand coverage and to adopt newer technology. Nevertheless, this policy has often been extended from the truly network-based activity of a certain enterprise to its other vertically integrated but essentially competitive activities. Enjoying a dominant position, some of the firms operating in these sectors have set prices much above the OECD average, and earned high profits (electricity, oil, natural gas and telecommunications). In many cases, these profits have been used in a substantial international expansion, in particular to Latin America, where Spanish public enterprises have become leaders, or key players, in their respective sectors over the past five years.

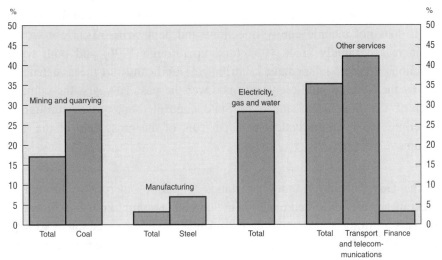

Figure 18. **SHARE OF PUBLIC EMPLOYEES IN KEY SECTORS**
As a percentage of total employment in the first quarter of 1996

Source: INE, Encuesta de Poblacion Activa.

Nevertheless, some public enterprises have a less satisfactory financial situation. In activities more open to competition, the financial performance has for the most part been weaker (*e.g.* the transportation sector). Poor financial performances also arises in sectors where Government policy intentionally price discriminates or places firms under public-service obligations – *e.g.* rail, postal system and television. Finally, there are loss-making public enterprises in declining, but inherently competitive, industries which receive large amounts of financial assistance (coal mines and shipyards). These firms face severe restructuring, with difficulties in adjusting promptly compounded by political constraints; many are located in the north of Spain (Asturias, Galicia and the País Vasco) and in Andalucia, where the unemployment rates are high.

Assistance to public enterprises has burdened the budget significantly

It is these two latter groups of enterprises, for the most part, that have been a large burden on the State budget. State operating subsidies and capital transfers to public enterprises have averaged approximately 1¹/₂ per cent of GDP per year between 1987 and 1996 (Table 17). Cumulated over this period, these amount to the equivalent of about 20 per cent of the gross debt of the general government at end-1996. Such a figure vastly understates total support to public enterprises since it does not include equity injections and debt write-offs. Debt write-offs have increased rapidly since 1993 (and up through 1996) and both types of transactions taken together have contributed significantly to the assistance provided by the State to public enterprises. Over the past 10 years, the cumulative impact of the State's assistance to State controlled-enterprises through such transactions has been equivalent to 5 per cent of the gross debt of the general government.[89]

The Government provides assistance to public enterprises through more indirect means as well. Such methods include the assumption of liabilities arising from early retirement and separation packages, and State-guarantees to support enterprises' borrowing, especially that of the loss-making enterprises or entities. Though the value of many of these items could be sizeable, precise estimates are difficult to make. Nevertheless, the implicit pension liabilities stemming from restructuring agreements in loss-making industrial firms controlled by the State (those previously under the AIE umbrella) are estimated to be approximately Ptas 1.2 trillion in 1997 (nearly 2 per cent of the gross debt of general government), while the total guaranteed debt of loss-making public entities and enterprises amounts to approximately another 3 to 4 per cent of the gross debt of general government.[90] Support was also provided through public enterprises' prices (such as the carbon levy in electricity prices), the incidence falling finally on consumers.

Local and regional authorities are another source of assistance to public enterprises. Though of a smaller amount, transfers by local and regional authorities to their own public enterprises, have been rising steadily to approximately ¼ per cent of GDP. These enterprises are nevertheless representing a mounting economic cost since they receive about twenty per cent of total operating subsidies and capital transfers paid to public enterprises (*i.e.* from both the central and regional governments) and contribute about 4 per cent to total value added by public enterprises (Table 18). Despite these transfers, their debt has tripled since 1990 to about 1 per cent of GDP.

Table 17. **Central government assistance to public enterprises, 1987-1998**

	1987	1988	1989	1990	1991	1992	1993	1994	1995	1996	1997[1]	1998[1]
						Billion pesetas						
State budget transfers to public enterprises[2]	703	651	807	706	642	611	797	744	1 146[3]	935[3]	525	517[4]
(as a percentage of GDP)	(1.9)	(1.6)	(1.8)	(1.4)	(1.2)	(1.0)	(1.3)	(1.2)	(1.6)	(1.3)	(0.7)[5]	(0.6)[5]
Current transfers	292	375	367	417	385	308	416	447	429[3]	391[3]	326	318[4]
Capital transfers	410	276	440	289	257	302	381	297	717[3]	544[3]	199	199
State assistance to State controlled public enterprises[2]	379	418	574	572	572	560	578	772	946	919	725[6]	n.a.
(as a percentage of GDP)	(1.0)	(1.0)	(1.3)	(1.1)	(1.0)	(0.9)	(0.9)	(1.2)	(1.4)	(1.2)	(0.9)[5]	n.a.
Current and capital transfers	266	302	442	400	413	400	351	424	492	404	333	n.a.
Financial transactions (including equity purchases)	13	16	22	46	61	50	65	106	66	66	392[6]	n.a.
Debt assumption	100	100	110	126	98	110	162	243	388	449	0	0
of which (as a percentage of the State transfers to state-controlled enterprises):												
Railways (RENFE + FEVE + GIF)	49.0	49.5	46.5	48.3	51.7	50.0	42.1	36.3	34.1	29.0	45.1	n.a.
National Industrial Institute (INI)[7]	26.4	23.9	26.1	22.0	17.1	19.6	28.0	27.5	23.0	0.0	0.0	n.a.
Coal mines (Hunosa + minas de Figaredo)	6.7	6.1	7.8	8.6	8.3	8.5	9.0	6.8	5.6	8.7	14.6	n.a.
Postal services	6.3	5.5	6.6	8.2	6.6	4.6	7.1	9.3	7.5	5.3	0.0	n.a.
National radio and television (RTVE)	0.1	0.0	0.0	0.0	0.0	0.0	0.0	7.4	12.4	14.4	1.5	n.a.
Financial institutions	4.0	3.8	1.7	1.0	0.3	2.3	5.7	2.7	0.7	0.5	0.0	n.a.

Table 17. **Central government assistance to public enterprises, 1987-1998** *(cont.)*

	1987	1988	1989	1990	1991	1992	1993	1994	1995	1996	1997[1]	1998[1]
						Billion pesetas						
Memorandum items:												
Regional government operating subsidies to public enterprises	54	69	86	128	134	158	176	174	160	178	n.a.	n.a.
Debt of public enterprises and entities controlled by territorial authorities (regional and local)	162	176	231	279	386	471	573	613	631	749	846[10]	n.a.
Debt of the State[8]	..	15 023	16 595	19 402	21 089	23 798	31 154	34 217	38 493	43 702	44 471	n.a.
Debt of public enterprises[9]	..	..	..	6 451	8 687	8 653	9 291	9 319	8 753	..	..	n.a.

1. Budget data.
2. Data submitted by IGAE for the State budget transfers and by the Ministry of Finance for the State assistance.
3. Estimation from Banco de Espana, *Cuentas Financieras*, State operating subsidies to private schools have been excluded.
4. Transfers to the newly created Institute for the restructuring of the coal mine industry, amounting to Ptas 106 billion in the 1998 State budget project, are not included.
5. The GDP is an OECD estimate.
6. Include a Ptas 275 billion loan with a state guarantee to the AIE holding (redistributed to its subsidiary companies).
7. The INI holding has not existed since August 1995. INI's liabilities amounting to Ptas 578 billion were transferred to the SEPI in 1995.
8. Maastricht definition.
9. Based on a sample of largest firms issued by Bank of Spain *Central de Balances*.
10. Data for the third quarter of 1997.

Source: IGAE, Banco de Espana, *Cuentas financieras, 1987-96* and *boletin estadístico* and other data submitted by the National authorities.

Table 18.   **Total transfers received by non-financial public enterprises**[1]

	Value added	Operating subsidies	Capital transfers[2]	Total direct transfers	Net lending (+) Net borrowing (–)
Total as a percentage of GDP	5.1	1.1	0.8	1.8	0.2
of which (as a percentage of total):					
Non-financial enterprises controlled by the State	95.8	71.7	80.6	75.5	175.6
Non-financial enterprises controlled by regional governments	1.9	22.2	16.2	19.7	–70.5
Non-financial enterprises controlled by local governments	2.4	6.1	3.1	4.8	–5.1

1.   In 1994.
2.   Does not include debt take-overs by the general government.
Source: IGAE, *Cuentas de las empresas publicas,* 1993-1994.

These high transfers partly reflect high labour costs

The monopolistic or oligopolistic environment in which some public enterprises operate and/or the continued receipt of transfers from the budget have not provided appropriate incentives to control labour costs. On a national level, a comparison of the level of aggregate wages in the private and the public sector is biased by the different productivity mix and age structure. Nevertheless, wages appear to be too high in the public enterprise sector. International comparisons indicate that Spanish wage levels exceed their counterparts in many sectors (such as air transport, rail and telecommunications), while the wages provided by the loss-making firms under the AIE umbrella, which are broadly equal to the national average, are certainly excessive. Similar inferences can be drawn from wage rate developments. Up to the early 1990s, wage increases in public enterprises consistently exceeded those for the private sector by a large margin, notwithstanding the high proportion of loss-making firms within the public enterprise group, while in sectors with both private and public enterprise participation, sectoral collective agreements distort wage bargaining in the private sector. The Government's reaction to these developments was to introduce an Interministerial Commission in 1993 which would approve collective agreements covering public state-owned enterprises and oversee their implementation.[91] This policy appears to have been successful, so far, as wages in State-owned public enterprises have subsequently increased broadly in line with those in the private sector. However, the sustainability of such administrative controls could be restricted by the

Figure 19. **WAGES AND EMPLOYMENT: A COMPARISON WITH THE PRIVATE SECTOR**

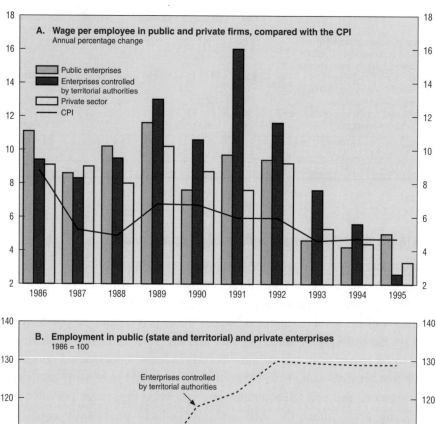

A. **Wage per employee in public and private firms, compared with the CPI**
Annual percentage change

Public enterprises
Enterprises controlled by territorial authorities
Private sector
CPI

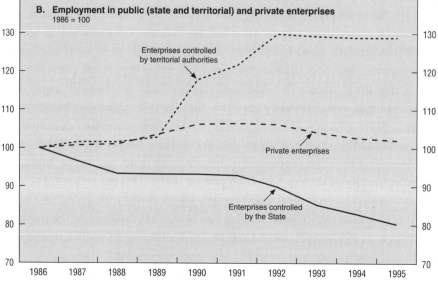

B. **Employment in public (state and territorial) and private enterprises**
1986 = 100

Enterprises controlled by territorial authorities

Private enterprises

Enterprises controlled by the State

Source: Bank of Spain, *Central de balances,* 1995 and Negociacion colectiva, various issues.

inadvertent introduction of relative wage distortions. In public enterprises controlled at a lower level of government, which were not covered by this commission, wage increases have in general continued to far exceed those for the private sector (Figure 19).

Obtaining wages that reflect firms' economic situation will require addressing the more rigid labour market conditions prevalent in the public enterprise sector. For example, firms face less flexible employment contracts, as a higher proportion of workers is on indefinite contract. This situation results in a much lower job turnover rate (less than half turnover of the private sector level in 1995) and higher dismissal costs. Public enterprises' internal labour organisation is also characterised by a lower functional and geographic mobility of the workforce. For example, clauses providing for functional flexibility appear ten times less frequently in their collective agreements than in the private sector (Table 19,

Table 19. **Main features of labour in public enterprises**

A. Labour force characteristics

	Public enterprises	Private enterprises
Share of permanent contracts[1]	84.6	60.7
Turnover rate[2]	15.5	33.9
Firing costs[3]	188.7	162.9
Share of wage-earners above age 40[4]	62.1	38.9
Functional mobility[5]	0.21	2.33
Geographical mobility[5]	0.32	0.58

B. Trade unions' concentration, conflicts and hours worked (1995)

Type of enterprise	Unions' concentration[6]	Negotiation length (in days)	Conflicts[7]	Worked hours per year[8]
Private, Spanish	46.3	157	0.9	1 677
Private, Foreign	73.2	101	0.5	1 683
Public, State	69.2	294	5.4	1 594
Public, local	52.0	245	0.4	1 621

1. Wage-earners with a permanent contract as a percentage of total wage-earners. Data for year 1997.
2. Sum of new and leaving employees as a percentage of total employment. Data for year 1994.
3. As a percentage of the wage bill per employee. Data for year 1995.
4. Data for year 1997.
5. As a percentage of the firms' labour force. Data for year 1995.
6. Share of the two dominant trade unions (UGT and CCOO) to the negotiation assembly.
7. Lost hours per worker.
8. Including extra-hours.
Source: Encuesta de Población Activa and *La negociación colectiva en las grandes empresas en 1995.*

part A). Another factor which could explain the wage pressures and more rigid work conditions in public enterprises may be the strength of trade unions (Table 19, part B). Overall, the stylised fact suggests that until recently there was an incentive to seek employment in a public enterprise due to higher wages, shorter hours worked, more secure employment, better training opportunities and other fringe benefits (*e.g.* family and maternity).

A major change in policy towards public enterprises

The overall policy framework

In June 1996, the Government announced an ambitious programme to modernise the State-owned enterprise sector so as to ensure its future viability and, consequently to maintain employment in this sector. The Modernisation Programme is based on the following principles: *i)* separate the management and the ownership of public enterprises so as to improve efficiency during the restructuring and privatisation process; *ii)* conduct the modernisation process with transparency – part of this commitment entailed the creation of an institution to report on the fairness and transparency of the privatisation process (*Consejo Consultivo de Privatizaciones*) and *iii)* among financially acceptable bids, to favour those which entail investment and maintain employment. The programme plans to shift public enterprises to private hands as soon as possible. Under the current timetable, public enterprises are to be privatised by the year 2000 or 2001. The programme does not include the coal sector, or enterprises which are seen as different in that they also implement public policies, such as railway, television and the postal services. The strategy recognises the very different financial situations and competitive environments of the various public enterprises. Accordingly, it groups them into four categories and offers a different timeframe and strategy for each group, based on their financial prospects and their competitive environment (Table 20).

Reducing public enterprises' direct burden on the budget

The modernisation programme was accompanied by a sharp reduction of on-budget resources to public enterprises in nominal terms in the 1997 and 1998 budgets.[92] Moreover, the Government ruled out further debt write-offs in

Table 20. **The modernisation programme's privatisation strategy**

		Current financial position of firms	
		Profitable	*Non profitable*
Competitive environment of firms	*Competitive*	Privatise immediately	Restructure then privatise
	Non-competitive	Deregulate the sector then privatise	Improve management and "restructure" so as to eliminate need for public transfers

1997 and 1998. To compensate for the rapid reduction in assistance, the Government permitted the AIE holding and loss-making firms outside the AIE to turn to the loan market, with an explicit State guarantee.[93] However, much of the resulting increased indebtedness is by public enterprises and entities which have little likelihood to service their debt, and may eventually need to be taken over by the State or other public entities. For example, the financial position of public television company (RTVE) has been greatly affected by this policy. Budgetary assistance has been drastically reduced, despite mounting operating losses resulting from a failure to adjust to a declining market share caused by the opening of the market to private operators in the late 1980s. As a result, its indebtedness has more than doubled in the past two years to Ptas 600 billion (equivalent to $3/4$ per cent of GDP), mostly with government guarantee. Public television companies run by regional governments reportedly face a similarly grim financial situation with debts reportedly amounting to some Ptas 100 billion.

With a view to facilitating the financing of loss-making enterprises from sources other than the State budget, the institutional groupings of State-controlled industrial enterprises were reshuffled in September 1997. Assets and liabilities of loss-making State-controlled industrial enterprises, formerly grouped within AIE, were transferred to SEPI. Starting from 1998, neither the new SEPI nor its subsidiaries will be able to obtain support from the state budget, with the exception of the coal mines. Thus, financial and implicit liabilities of the loss-makers will have to be financed by SEPI through privatisation proceeds, its own resources (profits) as well as loans.[94] In a related move, the Government intends to recognise the implicit pension liabilities arising from past restructurings of public enterprises. A special fund will be created – fully capitalised (in present value terms) using privatisation receipts – and subsequently auctioned to the private sector to manage. The authorities do not expect significant further losses to arise from firms under the AIE umbrella (excluding coal), though if they do occur, they – as well as any future restructuring costs – will not be covered by budget resources but most likely by SEPI resources. Subsequent to this change in the institutional setting, direct financial support from the State budget remains highly concentrated on a small number of large chronic loss-makers; the national railway company – *RENFE* – which received around 50 per cent of the State transfers; the public coal mines, *HUNOSA* and *FIGAREDO*; the national radio and television company, *RTVE*; and postal services, *Correos*.

In addition, the government designed new schemes to foster the co-financing of public enterprise investments by the private sector.[95] These have been used mainly to finance infrastructure developments in water supply, railroads and the highways. New public entities were created, through which private co-financing as well as loans from capital markets could supplement the equity injections from the State Budget. The most visible example was the creation of the *Ente Gestor de Infraestructuras Ferroviarias* (GIF) to build new railroads. The high-velocity track Madrid-Barcelona link should be one of the first new projects to be built under the supervision of the GIF (see below). Similarly, private co-financing for water infrastructure and highways relies mainly on the granting of longer concession periods to private companies.

Controlling wages and prices

Cuts in transfers to public enterprises were accompanied by new measures to contain labour costs. In the context of the wage freeze for civil servants in 1997, the government tightened wage norms for State-controlled enterprises and, for the first time, linked wage increases to productivity gains. Specifically, in profitable enterprises, nominal wage increases were made conditional on productivity gains, though the overall upper limit for the wage bill was set at the official projected inflation rate for the year (2.6 per cent). For loss-making enterprises, the total wage bill was frozen in nominal terms in 1997. For 1998, the wage norms are less restrictive: no wage increases in real terms but some nominal increases depending on productivity gains.[96] Wage moderation will facilitate the implementation of a price cap – the so-called CPI-X formula – on administered prices of several public enterprises; a measure which accompanied the June 1996 modernisation programme. Although the adjustments have not yet been announced for the "CPI-X" formulae except in the electricity sector, legislation indicates that their determination should take into account management improvements, productivity gains and technological innovation.

Competition surveillance

To support the change in strategy towards public enterprises, the Government is currently contemplating further reforms of competition policy. These would improve the efficiency and the independence of the existing institutions in charge of competition surveillance. The framework consists of a two-tier system: the *Servicio de Defensa de la Competencia* which forms part of the Economic Ministry, and the independent *Tribunal de Defensa de la Competencia*. The *Servicio,* acting on its own initiative or, increasingly, private complaint, decides which cases to investigate and bring them before the *Tribunal* for consideration and decision (appealable to the courts). In addition to their case work, both the *Servicio* and the *Tribunal* have issued reports concerning competitive conditions in many sectors and recommendations for reform. Overall, the system appears to function well. The *Tribunal,* is widely respected for its independence, which is well evidenced by its cases against two large state-owned monopolies, Tabacalera and Iberia. The former was accused of discriminating against other producers by abusing its dominant position as *de facto* monopoly distributor of tobacco products (as well as being a major producer). The latter was accused of colluding with private carriers in setting prices. However, there are complaints that the *Servicio* takes too long to prepare its cases. To improve the situation, the authorities are considering a unification of the two arms under the authority of a new organisation, the *Instituto de Defensa de la Competencia* which will be functionally independent from the Government and will be in charge of implementing competion policy. The unification of the institutions will provide independence to the *Servicio* and should shorten case duration due to the envisaged unification of case procedure, with the *Servicio* in charge of investigations and the *Tribunal* responsible for making the case decisions. Competition issues go beyond the concerns usually addressed by competition authorities in the network industries where the existence of regulation is required: the issue of ensuring market contestability in these situations is addressed below sector by sector.

Ownership structure

The ownership structure of the recently privatised public enterprises reflects the Government's effort to foster the role of the small shareholders. Recent privatisations have targeted about one-half the share offerings to small domestic shareholders and included price discounts for small domestic buyers relative to other potential buyers. Further diversification of the ownership structure has arisen from the significant percentage of the shares recently offered to international institutional investors. Nevertheless, the large banks have also obtained critical shares of the recently privatised or partly privatised enterprises, while these enterprises also have developed significant cross-share holdings, with strong relations in vertically-related sectors. As a result, the ownership structure still revolves around two bank pairings – Banco Bilbao Vizcaya (BBV)/La Caixa and Banco Central Hispano (BCH)/Banco Santander - with each pair controlling a large player in oil refining/gas, the electricity sector, and telecommunications (see Figure 20).[97] These relationships reflect banks' traditionally close ties with industrial groups, purportedly as a means of securing customers. But the narrowing of lending margins during the past 5 to 10 years has provided a further impetus. When large monopolistic industrial sectors began to be sold, they provided attractive alternative investment opportunities for banks. *Cajas* (regional savings banks) have recently followed the banks and also obtained large equity shares in these same enterprises.[98] These moves have been reinforced by legislation which provides financial incentives to purchase large blocks of equity.[99]

Despite efforts to diversify ownership, links between banks and industry remain strong. This ownership structure resembles the one existing in several continental European countries. The purported strength of such a corporate governance arrangement is that the long-term relations create a stable environment for managers to make investment decisions with a long payback period. In this relationship, banks' monitoring functions are associated with their double capacities as lender and significant shareholders. Its purported weakness, on the other hand, is that it impairs incentives for competition between firms with intertwined interests but in overlapping markets.[100] Cross-share holdings may also create systemic problems such as a less liquid stock market, and diminish attractiveness to foreign investors. Nevertheless, the continued encouragement of small shareholders and openness to foreign institutional investors could serve to achieve the

Figure 20. **KEY ELEMENTS OF OWNERSHIP STRUCTURE FOR THE MAIN SPANISH ENTERPRISES**[1]

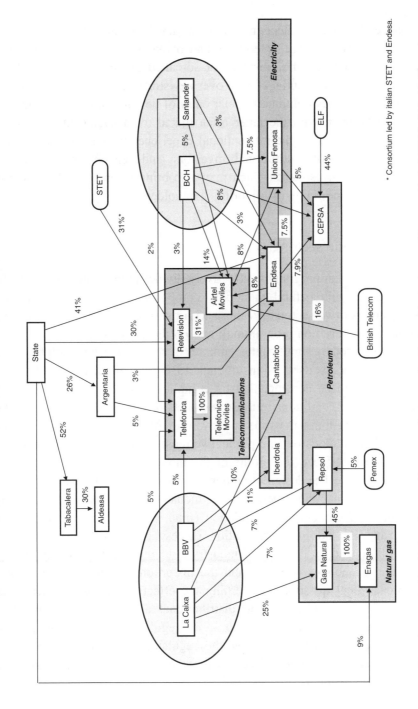

1. The information in this table intends to provide an approximate snapshot of ownership structure as of the second half of 1997. Individual holdings change over time.
    Source: OECD Secretariat.

* Consortium led by Italian STET and Endesa.

right balance. This trend reflects international developments where cross-owner-ship relations between large enterprises and banks are being weakened. In the case of Spain, however, the existence of so-called golden shares whereby the Government retains substantial control over key strategic decisions, such as large share transactions, may continue to deter entry of new investors and mitigate the threat of a take-over, with the latter often linked to management efficiency.[101] This practice goes against the international experience which has been to foster the ownership role of institutional investors (independent from banks), to encourage foreign investment (which may also bring technological know-how), and to strengthen the rights of minority shareholders.

Reform in specific sectors

The privatisation programme effectively divides public enterprises into four groups: *i)* those with natural monopoly components; *ii)* those which are in potentially competitive sectors; *iii)* those with overriding social concerns (which are not in the privatisation programme); and *iv)* those which are down-sizing. In sectors characterised by significant economies of scale associated with large fixed costs, privatisation by itself is insufficient to ensure efficiency gains for the economy. It has to be accompanied by complicated policies which foster and protect competitive conditions in those segments of the respective sectors where this is feasible. At the same time, policy must often face potentially difficult trade-offs between allocative and productive (cost) efficiency, and address sensi-tive distributional effects (the profits of the monopoly enterprise and universal service obligations). The design of an appropriate regulatory framework involves three critical elements: the structure of the industry (horizontal, vertical, regional separation), the form of price regulation (final price and access price to the network), and the non-price regulation (access rights and service quality). Choices will depend, in the case of industry structure, on the trade-off between any potential economies of scope and the distortions arising from integration, taking into account questions concerning the effectiveness of conduct regula-tions. Price setting centres around distributional issues and the provision of incentives to reduce costs. Finally, non-price regulations relate to the informa-tional asymmetries existing between the regulators and the enterprises. The sectoral analysis that follows discusses these issues for the individual sectors with network components.

In potentially competitive sectors the objective is to sell the enterprises as quickly as possible after appropriate restructuring – acknowledging the potential difficulties such operations entail in practice. The candidates for this group of enterprises may be expanding as technological progress is rapidly blurring the differences between network and competitive industries, for instance, telecommunications and airlines. In sectors where the Government decides to maintain public policy objectives, the goal is to achieve social objectives in the most cost efficient manner. This policy path offers the choice of several new techniques, including contracting out the service (including the social component) to the private sector, or targeting subsidies directly, without distorting enterprise behaviour. Finally, the restructuring of firms in sectors with declining technologies will be more difficult and will require finding a niche market or else reducing their production significantly. Restructuring will need to be accompanied by supporting adjustment policies, such as re-training.

Network industries

Electricity sector

The essential economic characteristics of an electricity sector are the non-storability of supply, high demand variation, and the capital intensity of production, which entails large sunk costs. The industry can be divided into generation, the transportation activities of transmission (high voltage) and distribution (low voltage), and retail supply. The non-storability of electricity and the fact that the laws of physics prevent electricity from following contractual paths requires a high degree of co-ordination between the various stages. However, any losses in economies of scope arising through separating generation from the natural monopoly transmission and distribution functions are more than offset by competition-induced efficiency.

In the case of Spain, the industry structure is highly concentrated, and firms are burdened by past large investment programs and a requirement to support the coal sector. Generation and distribution currently are vertically integrated oligopolies with two firms together controlling over 80 per cent of generation and distribution (the publicly controlled Endesa group and privately owned Iberdrola), while the high-voltage transmission grid is owned by state-owned Red Electrica.[102] There is excess capacity in generation, arising from past government-encouraged large investment programmes; available generating capacity accounts for 120 per cent of peak load demand.[103] However, a large share of the existing generating technology (especially for coal) is quickly becoming outdated, and generation using the more efficient combined cycle gas turbine technology is being introduced only gradually.[104] Imports account for about 3 per cent of potential capacity. These are restrained by the small capacity of interconnections with France, due partly to geographic and environmental factors.

Electricity prices are high in Spain compared with those in other OECD countries; they exceed the respective averages for OECD Europe by 20 per cent for industry and 54 per cent for households (Figure 21).[105] Several factors account for the higher prices. First, the electricity tariff contains several charges, which amount to about 5 per cent of the average tariff for households and industry. They are used to finance, *inter alia*, the cost of the nuclear moratorium and nuclear waste management.[106] Second, subsidies to the domestic coal sector amount to another 5 per cent of the average electricity tariff. Assistance to the coal sector also comprises a priority to buy domestic coal – approximately 95 per cent of domestic coal is used in electricity generation and currently about 25 per cent of electricity production is generated by coal.[107] Third, the electric utilities' heavy investment programme during the 1970s and 1980s has left them with heavy debts. Fourth, overmanning exists in state-controlled Endesa (and it plans to implement a 20 per cent reduction in personnel). Despite the fact that under current legislation the range of electricity tariffs is set by the Ministry of Industry based on standard costs for the overall system,[108] electricity firms have earned high profits, which have been used to diversify into foreign, especially Latin American, markets.

Parliament passed a new electricity law in November 1997 which introduces a major restructuring of the sector and should provide, along with the envisaged full privatisation of Endesa, a significant boost to competition in the sector. The reform is quite radical compared with the situation in many other European countries and is more ambitious than commitments under EC directives issued in late 1996.[109] The main components of the new legislation are the following:

- First, competition and efficiency in generation will be enhanced by a new wholesale spot market where orders will be accepted according to the attractiveness of price bids, and the marginal price of the pool will determine the price for electricity generation. Stranded costs (the unamortisized costs of prior investments) and coal subsidies (including the

Figure 21. **ENERGY PRICES IN AN INTERNATIONAL PERSPECTIVE**

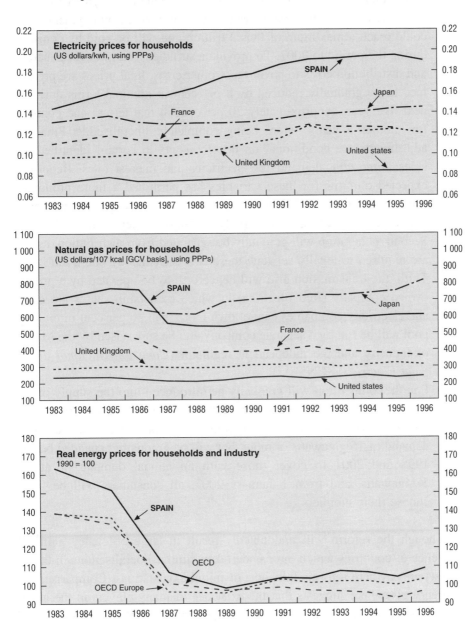

Source: International Energy Agency.

105

requirement that at least 15 per cent of total generation must be based on domestic coal for the next 10 years) will be covered by payments which could reach a maximum of Ptas 2 trillion and will be paid by consumers during the period to 2007. To provide a sufficient margin over generating and distribution costs to cover these other costs, final prices are programmed to be gradually reduced by 8 per cent in nominal terms during the next five years (approximately 20 per cent in real terms) and controlled for another 5 years before being completely liberalised.[110] Final-price adjustments are conditional on developments in certain identified variables, *inter alia*, demand for electricity and interest rates. Better-than-expected outturns for these variables has permitted a more pronounced price reduction in 1998; average electricity prices were reduced by 3.6 per cent rather than the initially envisaged 2 per cent.

– Second, generation will gradually be separated from distribution, as firms are required to legally separate these two activities by end-2000.

– Third, the transmission grid will henceforth to be operated by a privately owned company (Red Electrica) in which ownership shares are capped and electricity companies cannot own more than 40 per cent in total. The pool will be run by a separate company and be supervised by the Ministry of Industry and the independent regulator (*Comisión Nacional del Sistema Electrico* – CNSE).[111]

– Fourth, competition will gradually be introduced into the supply of electricity, as large consumers are gradually allowed to choose their suppliers; initially choice will only be permitted for consumers with an annual demand of 15 gigawatts or more, but will be gradually expanded between 1998 and 2001 to cover those with an annual demand of at least 5 gigawatts, and from 1 January 2007, all consumers will be free to choose their suppliers.

Though the reform will undoubtedly result in large efficiency gains, the experience of countries which have undertaken similar liberalisations in the past suggests areas where reforms fall short of initial expectations. Comparison with experience elsewhere suggests that the existence of many players in the generation of electricity is as important for competition as vertical separation. The Spanish generation market has two dominant players (plus two smaller ones) and has little competition from imports. Despite eventual legal separation, the close links that will remain between generation and distribution, and the incomplete liberalisation of the distribution market (some 30 per cent of supply will eventually be liberalised by 2001, but most of it will be the low margin segment), could form obstacles to the development of competition.

Allocative and distributional issues arise from the delayed liberalisation of operational control, the pre-commitment to meet stranded costs, and the rate of price reductions. Regarding the control over operational decisions, the experience of the United Kingdom was that the moment that the so-called vested contracts between electric utilities and coal mines expired, there was a "dash for gas" used in the more efficient combined cycle gas turbines. This incident suggests that the operational control constrained firms' choice of technology and reduced the efficiency of operations. Regarding the recovery of stranded costs through the electricity tariff, the strategy in the United States is for the compensation not to be predetermined, and compensation calculations to be constantly revisited. These considerations may permit a far more rapid reduction of prices in the event the initial estimate of the stranded costs were overestimated.[112] Finally, most countries have found the role of an independent regulator critical in the efficient functioning of the sector. The powers of the CNSE are more limited than those in other countries. The CNSE has wide scope for collecting and verifying information but it does not have the authority to approve tariffs or, develop best practices and has only limited authority to impose decisions. Restrictive practices are reported by CNSE to the *Servicio de Defensa de la Competencia*.

Natural gas

The economic characteristics of the natural gas sector are similar to those of the electricity sector, and the large fixed costs of transmission bestow natural monopoly characteristics to this segment of the sector. A big difference between the two sectors is that gas is storable and thus less co-ordination is required between upstream and downstream sectors of the industry. Many countries are promoting the gas sector due to its environmental-friendly properties and the availability of new technologies, especially in electricity generation. The demand for gas is rapidly rising because of its low price relative to alternative energy supplies reflecting large world-wide reserves. The gas sector in Spain, however, is less developed than in other EU countries: it meets only 7 per cent of energy needs versus 22 per cent for the EU as a whole, despite the provision of several financial and tax incentives. In an effort to promote the gas sector within the EU, a new directive which would liberalise the internal market for large consumers (those with annual consumption larger than 25 million cubic meters) has recently been approved by the Council of EC Ministers. The directive may also provide regulations regarding compensation in the event of disruption to long-term take-or-pay contracts arising from consumers' switching to alternative suppliers.

Liberalisation is necessary to promote competition in the Spanish gas sector, as it is currently dominated by a *de facto* integrated monopoly. Recently privatised Gas Natural accounts for 90 per cent of distribution and owns ENAGAS which is the sole importer of natural gas and operates most of the high pressure transmission system.[113] Third party access to the transportation system has been restrictive despite the September 1996 reform which permitted access to very large consumers (consumption exceeding 350 million cubic meters annually, which effectively excludes all but a handful of firms in the fertiliser and electricity sector). The extent of the reform is also limited by the fact that use is constrained to own-consumption, access is not guaranteed under certain circumstances, and the terms of access are negotiated directly with ENAGAS. Thus, competition in the core market of households (where margins are higher) remains extremely limited. The creation of a second operator, with links to France, is being contemplated by Endesa, a private oil company, Cepsa, and Banco Central Hispano so as to attain bargaining power in its negotiation with Gas Natural. Draft legislation introduced in December 1997 should improve third party access and facilitate the entry of new operators.

The price of gas is much higher than in most other OECD countries. According to the International Energy Agency, natural gas prices (adjusted for purchasing power) for households are about double those in Europe generally, slightly below those in Japan, and three times above prices in the United States.[114] Natural gas prices for electricity generation are about 20 per cent above the European average and about double the comparable price in both the United States and Japan. The high prices, though still lower than for substitute products, are probably related to the government policy aiming to encourage the development of this sector and to permit Gas Natural to recover its large investments. The maximum price is regulated, and the price formula based on the cost of alternative fuels, permits full pass through of international price changes, and provides cross subsidies to industry through higher prices to households.[115]

The Government understands that the impending EU directive, and the restructuring of the electricity sector to which natural gas will be a critical future input, provides an opportunity to introduce a significant reform of the natural gas sector. In this light, a new hydrocarbon law was presented to Parliament in late 1997. The main innovations of the draft legislations are the following. First, prices will be gradually liberalised over a 15 year period, starting first with large consumers (initially those with demand exceeding 25 million cubic meters annually, but extending in 5 year intervals, respectively, to those with annual demand of at least 15 million cubic meters, 10 million cubic meters, 5 million cubic meters and finally to all consumers). Second, when firms are involved in more than one activity, it requires separate accounts for transport, storage, and wholesale and retail distribution. Moreover, firms involved in these activities are prohibited from also being involved in commercialisation. Finally, a uniform government-approved fee will be introduced for accessing the network and conditions for third party access will be improved (though access can still be limited in several cases such as supply constraints, and obligations of the operator arising from supply contracts).

The United Kingdom experience in liberalising its gas sector – one of the first natural monopoly sectors to be liberalised in that country's extensive privatisation cum liberalisation programme – provides useful insights.[116] Specifically, it suggests potential shortcomings in a strategy of privatising the industry as a fully integrated monopolist without clear rules concerning third-party access to the distribution system. The United Kingdom authorities were subsequently forced to restructure the privatised industry (restricting British Gas's market share and forcing British Gas to divest from supply activities) and provide appropriate ring-fencing around the natural monopoly component.

Oil-refining and distribution

The general economic characteristics of the oil distribution sector resemble those of the gas and electricity sector, though the small scale economies in transportation and storage reduce the natural monopoly characteristics of this critical segment of the industry. In Spain, the up-stream refining stage is an oligopoly dominated by three firms; recently privatised Repsol, and the private companies Cepsa and BP. Refinery capacity utilisation is near 90 per cent but is concentrated in less-efficient technology using heavier fuels. Transportation and storage are *de facto* controlled by the three main players in the refining market through their joint ownership of *Compania Logistica de Hidrocarburos* (CLH) which owns 95 per cent of storage capacity and the only pipeline, and transports about 95 per cent of fuels. Access by other (non-owner) companies has depended on availability, and they have complained of their exclusion by CLH from the inter-enterprise market in oil. Specifically, the companies that own CLH could input oil into the CLH distribution system at any point and out-take at any other, thus reducing their transportation costs. The wholesale market is again dominated by the three main players, with regulation stipulating large storage limits and thus restricting entry (currently 90 days demand, reduced from 120 days in 1994). The draft hydrocarbon law contains reforms which should make access to the distri- bution and transportations system more equitable. Most importantly, access can only be limited when there exist supply constraints or firms are not current in their payments to the network operator. In addition access prices must be made public and must be non-discriminatory. Furthermore, a procedure for conflict resolution will be established.

Vertical constraints and other restrictions permeate the retail sector and stifle competition. Approximately 90 per cent of the petrol stations operate on conces- sion agreements with the wholesale/refining companies. These contracts have fixed margins and are of long duration (with 10 years being the standard length). Recent reforms which eliminated minimum distances between petrol stations could become effective in promoting competition only following the expiration of the existing concession contracts.[117] Retail competition could also be impeded by abstruse licensing regulations, with local government responsible for issuing licenses to most petrol stations. Partly reflecting these constraints, Spain has about double the ratio of inhabitants and vehicles per service station and the largest distance between petrol stations compared with the respective European average. Recent legislation has also aimed to open up access to distribution by permitting companies with large annual demand (exceeding 50 million tonnes) direct access to CLH installations, but the conditions are restrictive.[118] Neverthe- less, the component of the draft hydrocarbon legislation which permits service stations to renegotiate their concession agreements, to shift to supplier agree- ments whereby they have control over the final price, could be an important step in introducing competition in the downstream part of this sector.

Some fuel prices are unconstrained (high octane gasoline and, from June 1996, diesel), while for low octane and unleaded gasoline there exist maximum prices set by the government which apply uniformly to the whole country, effectively cross subsidising more remote regions. The price formula is based on the international price (thus allowing full raw material cost pass through), and provides a mark-up derived from the average of several European countries, plus a margin of Ptas 2 per litre, and adds indirect taxes. The fact that the market has rarely taken advantage of the Ptas 2 per litre margin has been viewed as an indicator of the lack of competition in this sector. In the event, industry profitability is high, permitting Repsol to invest heavily in foreign acquisitions (*e.g.* Argentine Astra and Pluspetrol).

Telecommunications

Spain had initially negotiated a five-year grace period with respect to the EC directive on liberalising basic telephony by 1 January 1998. The need for advances in infrastructure development in order to better prepare the ground for a competitive environment was an argument by the Spanish authorities for delaying the deregulation of the sector and maintaining a state-sanctioned monopoly. Despite much progress, especially in the quality of service, the coverage of the population and the pace of introduction of new technologies lag behind those of other OECD countries. Specifically, the average waiting time for line installation was reduced to about 3 days in 1996, from 8 in 1993 and other quality indicators such as call failure rates, fault incidence and repair time have also improved.[119] However, the number of mainlines per capita is still much below the OECD average, and in 1995 only 56 per cent of the fixed network was digital compared with an average of 82 per cent for the OECD average.

Though it is not clear whether the monopolistic situation attained its intended objectives, it could be partly responsible for the high and distorted pricing schemes. Telefonica's prices for long distance calls, both domestic and international, are among the highest within the OECD area, while the price of local calls and the monthly service fee are in the low range (see Figure 22, panel A). As a result Telefonica has been very profitable and, following the pattern established by other Spanish monopoly utilities, has invested heavily in Latin America, despite the obvious requirement for domestic infrastructure investment. Profitability does not appear to have been affected by excessive labour costs, in contrast to other enterprises that formed part of the public sector. Labour productivity, when measured by the number of mainlines per employee, is high compared with the OECD average for telephone operators and largely

Figure 22. **LABOUR COSTS, PRODUCTIVITY AND PRICES
IN THE TELECOMMUNICATION SECTOR**

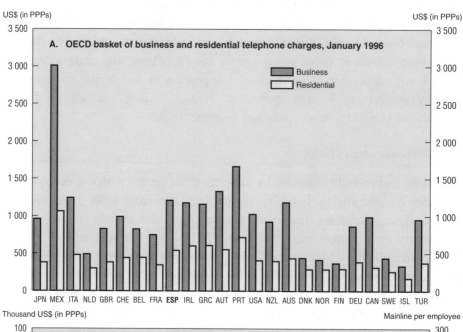

US$ (in PPPs)

A. OECD basket of business and residential telephone charges, January 1996

Business
Residential

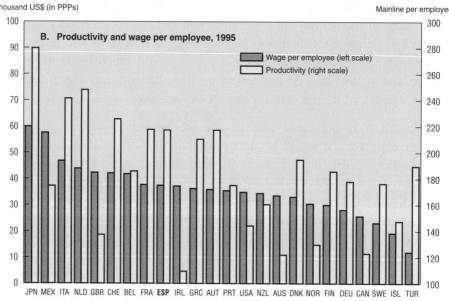

Thousand US$ (in PPPs)

Mainline per employee

B. Productivity and wage per employee, 1995

Wage per employee (left scale)
Productivity (right scale)

Source: OECD.

compensates for the high personnel costs per employee (see Figure 22, panel B).[120] Nevertheless, further improvements in labour productivity are expected (after an average rise of more than 5 per cent per year between 1985 and 1995) and should stem from a new reduction in Telefonica's workforce.[121]

In the second half of 1996, Spain and the European Commission reached an agreement to liberalise fully the provision of all telecommunication services by December 1998, waiving all but 11 months of the five-year grace period. To set up the conditions for a more competitive environment, the Government passed new telecommunication legislation in June 1996 that created, *inter alia*, a second operator in basic telephony (using the TV signals transmitter, Retevision), which started to compete with Telefonica in January 1998 (Box 3).[122] The State also sold its final holdings in Telefonica in early 1997 (and thus became the 'second country in the EU after the United Kingdom to fully privatise its telecommunications monopoly).[123] Thus, the monopolistic market structure was converted into a private duopoly for fixed telephony for the brief transition period to December 1998. It follows the successful creation of a duopoly in mobile telephony in 1995. Airtel, a private consortium, received a 25-year licence which broke Telefonica's monopoly in mobile telephone services. Intense competition ensued, producing sharp reductions in the price of connections and equipment.

The June 1996 legislation also created an independent regulatory body, the *Comisión del Mercado de las Telecomunicaciones* (CMT), defined the responsibilities and the financing of universal service provision and dealt with the issue of numbering (ensuring an equal access to numbers for operators and number portability for users). However, the Government will continue to set interconnection prices until December 1998, after which this responsibility is envisaged to be passed to the CMT. Moreover, the responsibility for final prices for the dominant operator Telefonica will remain within the Government's domain subsequent to this date, with a view to gradually correcting the distorted price structure.[124] As a first step, in March 1997 the Government allowed Telefonica to further rebalance its tariffs, by reducing the cross-subsidisation from long distance to local calls.[125] Retevision is free to set prices lower than those stipulated for Telefonica.

Despite the regulatory reform, certain obstacles to the generation of effective competition could remain. Following the strategy of most other OECD countries, Spain chose to privatise Telefonica as one integrated company. The exception is the United States where the dominant telecommunication company

---

Box 3. Recent regulatory changes in telecommunication services

In June 1996, Spain began to introduce important regulatory changes in order to commence the transition to a competitive market for telephone services. These included:

  i) A second basic telephony licence was granted to a public entity (Retevision) which started operating in January 1998. A third licence for basic telephony is to be granted in January 1999.

  ii) A new regulatory body was created in April 1997. The Telecommunications Market Commission (*Comisión del Mercado de Telecomunicaciones, CMT*) has the authority to:

  – arbitrate disputes between network operators and service providers;
  – advise the Government with respect to tariffs and regulatory proposals;
  – assign numbering to telephone operators; and
  – take the necessary measures to promote competition, with particular attention to access conditions to the networks, operators' prices, and sale practices.

  iii) The requirements and responsibilities for the provision of universal service, as well as its financing, were defined.

  iv) Interconnection conditions and prices for fixed telephone operators were set in March 1997.

  v) A new numbering framework was approved in November 1997 so as to ensure that Telefonica and new entrants will have access to numbers on an equal footing. A plan for number portability was also approved which will allow customers who want to shift to another operator to keep their existing number. The numbering framework will be in place from April 1998 and the portability scheme will be available by end-1998.

The Government keeps various powers. Specifically, the Government has set prices for the dominant operator (Telefonica), the initial interconnection prices, and access conditions for both fixed and mobile telephone operators.

---

was split into a number of vertically separated companies as a result of a court decision. The rationale for maintaining an integrated firm is partly based on the rapid technological advancements of this sector since the United States decision, which have prompted competition from various other sources. In these circumstances, critical to the development of effective competition will be the independence and rapid response of the regulator (CMT). Retevision, the second operator, will need full support if it is to succeed in becoming a full fledged competitor and not follow the unsuccessful path travelled by UK's second operator,

Mercury. The latter has become a true competitor to British Telecom only in small niche markets, such as the large-firms segment. The CMT's recent quick decision to arrest Telefonica's discount offers to large consumers, on the basis that it was potential predatory pricing, has provided a positive signal to the market in this regard.

Several factors could restrain Retevision's ability to compete more effectively with Telefonica. First, the interconnection prices are high by international standards, especially for long-distance calls, though this could partly reflect the recent surge in investment spending (*e.g.* the expanded use of digital lines) (see Table 21). Nevertheless, the European Commission has recommended that Spain lowers substantially interconnection prices. Based on the average of the three least expensive interconnection prices in the EU, it recommends a reduction of 30 to 60 per cent depending on the type of call. It argues that interconnection prices should be based on forward-looking (incremental) long-term marginal costs. Factors which support setting lower interconnection costs, which would not cover Telefonica's past investments, could be: *i)* Telefonica has accumulated significant assets due to its past profitability; *ii)* the desire to provide an explicit initial advantage to the new entrant, and *iii)* rapidly changing technology that has resulted in a rapid depreciation of existing fixed assets.

Telefonica's strong incumbent position could also restrain competition. The population without digit lines cannot select Retevision as a long-distance operator and around 30 per cent of the population continues to be without digital lines

Table 21. **Interconnection prices for basic telephone companies to the dominant operators**

Operator	Interconnection price (Ptas per minute)[1]
Telefonica (Spain)	5.10
British Telecom (United Kingdom)	1.66
Bell Atlantic (United States)	2.74
Cincinnati Bell (United States)	2.80
Ameritech (United States)	2.82
Telia (Sweden)	3.07
NTT (Japan)	5.30
TNZ (New Zealand)	7.24

1.   Average prices. Using PPP exchange rates.
Source: Cinco días, 27 March, 1997 and *El País,* 30 March, 1997.

as of June 1997 – though Telefonica is committed to providing digital lines country-wide by June 1998. Retevision could circumvent this obstacle to expanding its customer base by using new wireless technology for concentrated areas (such as wireless in the local loop). Similarly, under the current set-up, Retevision customers will not be able to connect with mobile telephone users, which will likely be a substantial disincentive to switch operators. Differences in the range of services offered by telecommunications operators may also reinforce the incumbent position. If Telefonica's competitors offer only a small range of telecommunication services, customers are less likely to switch to another operator, *e.g.* for long distance calls, if they still depend on the dominant operator for several other service applications. This facet of competition is presumed to have been a major factor in the poor development of Mercury as a second operator. Finally, Retevision's potential advertising strategy based on charging calls by the second – a system which has long been supported by consumer associations – will be made difficult by interconnection charges by the minute. In mobile telephony, competition is stronger. Nevertheless the low number of firms raises the possibilities of collusion – for example, the simultaneous rise in handset prices by Telefonica and Airtel in 1997 could be seen as a case in point. Entry is restricted, but the authorities envisage granting a license to a third mobile telephone company and thus complying with EC directives.

Potentially competitive sectors

Air transport

Since the early 1990s Spain has deregulated many aspects of the air transport sector, with some moves ahead of schedule with respect to successive EC directives. The domestic air transport market was liberalised in 1994, and since then two private carriers have been competing with the state-owned Iberia Group. On domestic flights where there is effective competition, Iberia Group's market share dropped from 100 per cent in 1992 to 70 per cent in 1996. The increased competition on the domestic market has led to a sharp drop in prices and on competitive routes full-fare domestic flights are now among the cheapest in Europe in terms of cost per mile (estimates are around 30 per cent less expensive). The price decline was accompanied by an increase in the variety of fares, and in the quality of services (*e.g.* the number of flights and the quality of facilities). In handling operations, Iberia's monopoly position was lost when the sector was liberalised in 1996. There are now three handling operators in Spain, with two in almost every large airport.[126] Introducing competition has led to a close to 50 per cent fall in handling prices.

The publicly-owned Iberia group incurred losses for six consecutive years before returning to profits in 1996, helped by three years of strong international demand for air transport. The major reason for the financial troubles of Iberia was that it was late to adjust to fiercer domestic competition. In early 1996, a three-year viability plan was agreed with the European Commission aiming to cut costs and raise productivity in preparation for privatisation. The agreement also allowed the Spanish Government to inject Ptas 87 billion in 1996 after a first package of Ptas 120 billion in May 1992.[127] The 1996 capital transfer aimed to recapitalise the company and reduce its debt and finance staff reductions. Employment was cut by almost 15 per cent (3 500 out of a workforce of 23 500, mainly through early retirement and voluntary redundancies) and wages were frozen. However, recent surveys concur in showing that Iberia still is an expensive European carrier in terms of cost per passenger-kilometre, mainly reflecting the fact that it is overstaffed and wages remain high for certain categories of personnel (pilots and crew).[128] In addition, some critical negotiations are still pending for Iberia. In particular it needs to reach understandings with pilots and other unions over the wage scale to follow the unification of Iberia Group airlines. It also needs to renew its ageing fleet. However, recent agreements on an international strategic alliance with British Airways and American Airlines and restructuring within the Iberia group should help to consolidate its position and facilitate its partial privatisation (the government plans a 50 per cent share offer in 1998 or 1999).[129]

Despite significant improvements in a more competitive environment, Iberia still enjoys some *de facto* advantages. The market share of the second largest air carrier remains lower than in most other European countries, and foreign companies have difficulties in entering the domestic market. This may reflect partly some remaining institutional features hindering competition. Among them, congested airports and slots allocation which – partly through complying with the European ''Code of conduct'' under which historical rights cannot be denied – favours the established airline. The lack of slots suitable for flights aimed at business travellers (early in the morning or late at night) in key airports (Madrid and Barcelona) inhibited private carriers from competing with the established carrier but also prevented European companies taking advantage of the opening of Spanish domestic routes after the liberalisation of cabotage in 1993 and the full liberalisation of the European market in April 1997.[130] Other factors which provide Iberia with incumbent advantages are the following: first, in Spain, unlike in some other EU airports, congestion costs are not included in the calculation of airport tariffs;[131] and second, terminal charges include a volume discount. In addition, Iberia was recently promised its own terminal building in Madrid.

Enterprises the Government is using to implement public policies

Rail transport

As in many OECD countries, rail transport in Spain has lost market shares to road and air transport over the past two decades. It also has been able to cover only about one-half of its operating costs and thus absorbs a sizeable amount of State transfers – it is among the largest recipients of State transfers as a percentage of operating revenue among all OECD rail companies. Over the past decade, budgetary transfers to RENFE represented almost 0.5 per cent of GDP annually and accounted for around one third of State transfers to non-financial enterprises in the form of operating subsidies and capital transfers.[132] A substantial cut in employment over the same period has helped to improve dramatically labour productivity, which now compares well with most European railways. However, this has not led to an improvement in the financial performance of RENFE, and labour costs as a proportion of total costs, as well as per employee, remain high by international standards (see Figure 23, panel A). RENFE's difficulties are mostly due to low passenger and freight rates. In the early 1990s, these rates were among the lowest in Europe reflecting an approximately 50 per cent reduction in real terms since 1978 (see Figure 23, panel B). At the same time, expenditure on infrastructure improvement has been delayed, thus making train services less attractive. Indeed, rail route kilometres per capita and average speed of train services are low compared to the European average.[133] As a consequence, train traffic has experienced declining demand during the past decade, except for the recently operating high speed passenger services and suburban and combined transport.

Improving infrastructure and service quality, and utilising transfers more effectively could be facilitated by the recent decision to separate the accounts of RENFE's business units.[134] This institutional feature could permit an increase in

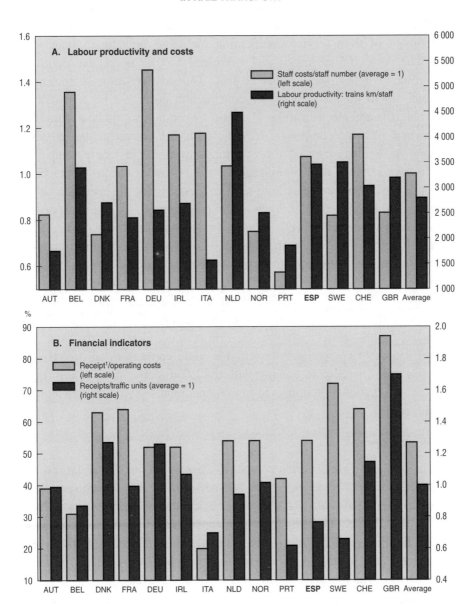

Figure 23. **LABOUR COSTS, PRODUCTIVITY AND PRICES
IN RAIL TRANSPORT**

A. Labour productivity and costs

Staff costs/staff number (average = 1) (left scale)
Labour productivity: trains km/staff (right scale)

AUT BEL DNK FRA DEU IRL ITA NLD NOR PRT **ESP** SWE CHE GBR Average

B. Financial indicators

Receipt[1]/operating costs (left scale)
Receipts/traffic units (average = 1) (right scale)

AUT BEL DNK FRA DEU IRL ITA NLD NOR PRT **ESP** SWE CHE GBR Average

1. Rail business only.
Source: Preston J. and C. Nash, 1994: "European Railway comparisons and the future of RENFE".

119

accounting transparency, and thus permit a social costs-benefit analysis in setting prices and subsidies for each train service. Just as importantly, better accounting data should result in more transparent access charges, thereby facilitating the development of train service competition including through co-financed new entry. The new co-financing model envisaged for the Barcelona-Madrid high speed route is a first step in this respect. The private sector is envisaged to contribute up to 40 per cent of the construction costs and be responsible for railway signals and electrification. The train's operation would be handled by the state-owned railway company, *RENFE*, with the infrastructure consortium receiving an agreed share of the operating revenues. Private participation to provide train services is also envisaged if the private sector proves to be cost-competitive. The auctioning of long-term concessions for the operations of some sections could be envisaged, following the Spanish model for bus transport which seems to work reasonably well. A more fundamental reform would follow the recent UK experience where the responsibility for railroad infrastructure and track signalling was separated from rail operations, and the latter was split into approximately 25 different franchises, each including contracts with service standards.[135] An independent regulator was made responsible for ensuring equitable access to the network and monitoring the fairness of track charges. Competition in UK freight services is tighter, as firms can compete over the same routes. Another source of competition for RENFE could come from abroad. However, Spain has thus far failed to comply with the EC directive on granting rights of access for international groupings to run international services, though legislation is forthcoming.

Postal service

The national postal service company, *Correos*, is one of the largest public enterprises in term of employment (65 000 persons in 1996). Postal services have consistently incurred losses and absorbed a significant share of State transfers over the past decade. Operating losses amounted to Ptas 37 billion in 1996, down from 45 billion in 1992, while current and capital transfers in 1997 were projected to be Ptas 40 billion. The main factor behind these losses is the mail service tariffs, which are among the lowest in the OECD.

In December 1997, a draft law project to reform postal services was presented to Parliament. It aims to reduce the losses of *Correos* and to open segments of the domestic market to competition before the liberalisation of the sector in 2003 in accordance with the EU liberalisation agenda.[136] The draft law would also increase urban mail tariffs by 66 per cent in 1998 – however these will still remain the lowest among EU countries – and define the services to be covered by the universal service provision, for which *Correos* will remain responsible.[137] The Government will continue to control the prices of this set of services, while other services currently provided by *Correos* will be gradually opened to competition. This reform should foster competition in intra-urban mail services and overnight delivery services – which were already opened to competition – and in the newly deregulated sector for inter-urban mail (weighing more than 350 grams) and parcels. Further steps to foster the efficiency and the competition of the sector would be to increase the accounting transparency of *Correos'* services so as to improve the social cost-benefit of subsidies and to allow for the private participation in mail services if the private sector proves to be cost-competitive. The draft legislation also envisages the creation of a compensation fund which would guarantee the financing of universal service.

Declining industries

Significant progress has been made in restructuring the largest loss making public enterprises under the AIE umbrella, with a 50 per cent reduction in employment over the last 10 years. Most of these firms' activities are concentrated in industries which have been greatly affected by technological progress and/or by competitors in other parts of the world. The main loss-making sectors have been coal mining, shipyards, steel and aluminium production, and military equipment manufacturing. Their restructuring is complicated by the fact that about three-quarters of the labour force in these sectors (about 35 000) are geographically concentrated in the northern part of Spain (Asturias, Galicia, and the País Vasco).

Coal

Spanish coal has become far too expensive relative to the price and quality of coal imports and alternative energy sources, while environmental considerations are also reducing demand. Purchasing Spanish publicly mined coal relative to imported coal represents a five-fold increase in cost to electricity companies, which consume 95 per cent of domestic coal production.[138] The high cost has resulted in coal subsidies amounting to nearly Ptas 250 billion in 1996 (about

0.3 per cent of GDP). Approximately, one half is financed through a charge on the electricity tariff (about 5 per cent), and the remainder is in the form of direct transfers from the state budget.[139] Rough estimates suggest that the coal sector has received approximately Ptas 1.6 trillion in subsidies during the period 1989-97 (approximately 3 per cent of 1997 GDP) not including the implicit subsidisation through a captive electricity sector.

Two large restructuring programmes have reduced employment by almost one-half and reduced production by nearly 10 per cent during 1989-97. Despite these efforts, the productivity in the publicly-owned mines is still half that of the private ones and below the EU average especially when the lower quality of Spanish coal is taken into account. Moreover, the cost per worker is second only to that of German miners and nearly four times that of British coal miners. A third restructuring plan was approved in July 1997. The July plan took the place of a more ambitious restructuring programme proposed by the Government but abandoned after the November coal miners' strikes. It will reduce both employment (through early retirement and voluntary departures) and production by around 30 per cent (to 18 000 and 13 million tonnes, respectively) during the period 1998-2005. Financial assistance to coal mines will decline in line with reduced production (some 4 per cent per year). The viability of the plan is in doubt as its time frame surpasses the 2002 year limit set by the EC after which no further aid can be provided to the coal sector. To move towards the EC targets, an agreement was reached in January 1998 with the two large public coal mines, Hunosa and Minas de Figaredo, on a new restructuring plan for the period 1998-2001. This accord includes employment cuts (from 9 800 to 6 000), with early retirements to be made at 100 per cent of net salary, and a reduction of production (to no more than 1.8 million tons).

Reflecting the liberalisation of the electricity sector, the new 8-year *Plan de Carbon* permits the free negotiation of coal prices between the electricity companies and the mines, thus introducing a new framework whereby the financial aid is received by the mine and not the electricity company. At the same time, the electricity charge will be converted into an explicit tax from 1998, thus improving transparency by providing financial support for coal through the budget. Implicit subsidies through a captive market will also be reduced as the new electricity system guarantees only a minimum purchase of 15 per cent of total electricity production compared with 30 per cent currently. An important component of the programme is the containment of substantial resources for reactivation measures. The total cost of the 8 year programme is estimated to exceed Ptas 1 trillion (nearly 1½ per cent of 1997 GDP), with about one-half directed at staff reduction.

Shipyards

The Spanish shipyards suffer from inefficient production and an expensive labour force. Despite the reform plan agreed in 1995, which included, *inter alia*, plans for a 40 per cent reduction in the workforce by 1998, operating losses in the shipyards doubled in 1996 compared with the plan's target (Ptas 45 billion versus Ptas 20 billion). Absenteeism is considered a major problem and has been estimated to result in the loss of almost 20 per cent of working time. To reduce labour costs, functional, geographic and working time flexibility are considered imperative. In the event, the European Commission approved a final injection into Spanish shipyards amounting to Ptas 230 billion (0.3 per cent of GDP) in April 1997. The terms of the agreement were that production capacity would be reduced by 47 500 tonnes but that no individual yard would be closed and employment would not be reduced. However, yards that are still not profitable at end-1998 would not receive further assistance. This agreement was preceded by an agreement with unions to reduce absenteeism and accept *i)* more flexible labour contracts, *ii)* improved functional mobility, and *iii)* a reduction in wages in real terms. State assistance linked to ship production rather than to the sector may nevertheless be prolonged past the 1998 date if an October 1997 proposal by the EC is approved.[140] The process of privatising the shipyards was initiated with the sale of the *Hijos de J. Barreras* yard in December 1997. The major military manufacturer (*Empresa Nacional Bazan*) also builds military vessels. It has an outstanding order from the Spanish Government to build F-100 frigates which should be sufficient for its continued activity for 10 years.

Steel and aluminium

The restructuring and privatisation of *Corporacion Siderurgica Integral* (CSI) – the large state-owned steel firm – may become a good example for restructuring other loss making enterprises. Following a two-year restructuring program, which reduced employment by 50 per cent, and brought the firm back into a profitable situation, 35 per cent of CSI was sold to an international strategic investor in July 1997, Arbed of Luxembourg, and the remainder of the company had been offered for sale through a public offering. The joint group – Aceralia Arbed – has become the second largest steel maker in the EU behind British Steel, and provides the Spanish firm with international experience and know-how. The choice of Arbed resulted in lower immediate funds than other offers but the package included assurances for significant future investments and promises not to reduce the work force. Another successful operation involved the sale of the aluminium firm Inespal to the American firm Alcoa. The attractiveness of the Spanish firm was linked to the envisaged liberalisation of the electricity sector.

Quantification of the effects of liberalisation

This section provides estimates of the potential effects at the macroeconomic level of introducing competition into the five more dynamic sectors described above: telecommunications, airlines, and electricity, gas and fuel. The loss making sectors, especially coal, are excluded from the analysis as their role in the economy is expected to gradually diminish. The analysis consists of three stages, and is based on the methodology developed by the OECD for its regulatory reform project.[141]

In the first stage, the potential effects arising from improved competition and a well-functioning regulatory framework for the natural monopoly components are assessed. The quantification of these effects depends partly on benchmarking (*i.e.* the observed effects of the introduction of reforms in other countries) and partly on an assessment of the conditions currently existing in these sectors in Spain, as they have been described in the sections above. In all five sectors, sizeable gains are assumed in labour and capital productivity, as these previously publicly owned firms shed labour (Table 22). A large reduction in the price of intermediate inputs is assumed only in the energy sector where the price of coal is assumed to fall by 50 per cent. Reflecting the end of current large investment programmes, capital costs are assumed to drop significantly in the energy and telecommunication sectors. Competition should also result in a fall in profits in the energy and telecommunications sectors. Finally, innovation is expected to result in large price reductions for the telecommunication sector.

In the second stage, a demand-driven increase in each sector's output, arising from these potential price gains, is estimated and subsequently aggregated across the sectors to produce the direct effects on output and employment.[142] The

Table 22. **Assumptions and effects of sectoral deregulation**

	Electricity	Air transport	Gas and petrol	Telecom-munications	Total of sectors
Assumptions (% change):					
Costs of intermediate inputs	..	..	..	–10%	
Gas and petrol	–7%	–7%	–7%	n.a.	
Coal	–50%	n.a.	n.a.	n.a.	
Nuclear	0%	n.a.	n.a.	n.a.	
Electricity	–20%	–20%	–20%	n.a.	
Air transport	n.a.	–10%	n.a.	n.a.	
Labour costs:					
– Labour productivity	25%	20%	20%	35%	
– Wages	–3%	–15%	–10%	–15%	
Capital costs	–25%	–5%	–25%	–25%	
Profits	–15%	0%	–15%	–10%	
Innovation: effect on output	0%	5%	0%	30%	
Price elasticity of demand	–0.50	–1.50	–0.50	–0.50	
Sectoral effects (in %):					
– Direct price effect	–20.1	–10.0	–6.8	–22.4	
– Price-induced output effect	10.1	15.0	3.4	11.2	0.62
– Output effect, incl. innovation	10.1	20.8	3.4	44.6	1.31
– Employment effect[1]	–12.0	0.7	–13.8	7.1	
– Employment effect, excl. innovation[2]	–12.0	–4.1	–13.8	–17.6	
Effects on total economy (in %):					
Total employment:					
– Contribution of each sector	–0.05	0.00	–0.02	0.05	–0.02
– Contribution of each sector, excl. innovation	–0.05	–0.01	–0.02	–0.12	–0.20
Labour productivity:	0.65	0.07	0.47	0.70	1.89
Capital productivity:	0.65	0.02	0.59	0.50	1.76
Wages:	–0.01	–0.03	–0.02	–0.11	–0.16
Memorandum items:					
– Share in business sector GDP	2.60	0.36	2.34	2.01	7.31
– Share in business sector employment	0.40	0.18	0.17	0.70	1.45

1. Sectoral employment effects include impacts of productivity growth, price-induced output growth and the assumed effect of innovation-induced output growth, but ignores the possible impact of lower wage premia.
2. As (1), but excludes sectoral innovation effects.
Source: OECD calculations based on 1990 Input-Output Table of Spain.

aggregate effect is a 1½ per cent increase in output, while employment is broadly unchanged as labour shedding in some sectors is broadly offset by rising employment from the increase in output. With labour productivity increasing almost commensurably with output, and wages falling slightly, unit labour costs fall by about 1½ per cent. However, this static approximation of the effects of enhanced competition underestimates the impact on the economy since it does not take into account the dynamic interactions between sectors. Specifically, the first-round output effect is expected to increase the capital stock which subsequently has further repercussions on output. A more intuitive explanation arises from a demand side description of the multiplier effect. In essence, the lower prices in these critical sectors stimulate output in the other sectors of the economy that use the output of the sectors undertaking reform. In the third step, these second-round effects are estimated using the OECD Secretariat's INTERLINK model, and result in a cumulative increase in total output (direct and second-round effect) of the order of 4 to 5 per cent.[143] However, employment gains are negligible, reflecting the medium-term properties of the model: namely, that the gains in labour productivity are fully reflected in real wage increases rather than in employment gains. This result brings out the important policy conclusion that the sectoral reforms could lead to employment gains, if labour markets are sufficiently flexible. This assessment underlines that product market reform should go hand in hand with labour market reform.

Assessment

Important progress has been made over the recent period in restructuring and selling enterprises under the State's control. The Government's ambitious programme to make public enterprises financially self sufficient and to sell most of the remaining public enterprises by the turn of the century should greatly reduce what has been a heavy drain on past budgets. Over the past decade, public enterprises' total financing needs met from the state budget have been the source of a large percentage of the debt accumulated during this period; rough estimates suggest that public enterprises could account for about one quarter of the general government debt. In contrast to these developments, regional governments appear to be running the risk of repeating the costly mistakes made by the central government in the past regarding the management of public enterprises. Acknowledging that they are gradually taking on responsibilities formerly undertaken by the central government – which may require the creation of new institutions – this does not necessitate the creation of enterprises which absorb large resources from the public purse, nor enterprises which do not provide public services (*e.g.* industrial firms).

The progress to date as well as the culmination of this programme should put Spain ahead of many other continental European countries as regards the reform of the public enterprise sector. The Government's efforts to promote competition and efficiency in the sectors formerly dominated by public enterprises will now be the critical part of this reform effort, with any reduction of public debt from the privatisation proceeds an important, but secondary benefit. Receipts from privatisations during the period 1996-2000 could raise revenues equivalent to some 4 per cent of GDP. The experience of other OECD countries which have preceded Spain in liberalising similar sectors suggests that much emphasis must be placed on designing the pertinent regulatory framework. An appropriate design would generate sufficient competition so as to attain the full potential of the reform for the economy which could amount to an increase 4-5 per cent of GDP based on OECD estimates. The importance of this facet of the reform is accentuated by the fact that the sectors being liberalised provide key inputs to the economy (*e.g.* energy, telecommunications, and transport), and often contain natural monopoly components (*i.e.* network industries). A poor design which resulted in monopolistic or oligopolistic behaviour would effectively replace public monopolies by private ones, and not produce the potentially large price reductions that would stimulate output, and, with labour market flexibility, raise employment.

A speedy implementation of reforms will bring forward the gains and provide Spanish enterprises with a head start *vis-à-vis* their competitors in the EU and other global markets. In sectors which are potentially competitive, the Government can move quickly towards privatisation. Its recent privatisation of steel and aluminium firms are cases in point. Regarding sectors which the Government uses to offer important public service components, including train transportation services, television and mail delivery, the authorities should review whether parts cannot be operated by the private sector. Train transportation could follow the concession agreements currently used by the publicly owned but privately run inter-city buses. The social component of the service would be included in the terms of the concession. Competition could also be introduced for rail track construction through bids for build-operate-transfer or build-transfer projects, following the recent examples for highways and the high velocity train track, respectively. Regarding public television, private channels – whose rapid proliferation has cut into marketing revenues – may now be performing some of the initial objectives of public television and may have reduced the need for such an extensive public operation. Overall, the operation of enterprises providing social services will need to be looked at carefully so as to minimise the creation of incentives that distort behaviour (*e.g.* subsidisation of transportation) and increase budgetary costs. Declining industries, such as coal and shipyards, will probably need to be targeted to significantly smaller niche markets or reduce production drastically. The trade-off between a longer and shorter transition period should be re-evaluated. A longer transition will have a larger overall cost to the economy – but one which can be borne by the whole population – while a shorter transition period will inevitably lead to redundancies which will need to be accompanied by supporting adjustment policies for the affected workers, such as re-training services. Environmental concerns support a speedy closure of the coal mining industry, as does its distortionary effect on electricity production.

The network industries require difficult decisions regarding the design of an industry structure which spurs competition. In sectors built around capital intensive networks involving huge sunk costs, there are clear elements of natural monopoly. Economies of scope permitting, ownership of such networks should be separated from ownership of other parts of the sector, and be subjected to efficiency enhancing regulations. Where such separations are economically or political difficult, accounting separations should be introduced so as to ensure transparent and economically efficient access conditions. In addition to suitable vertical splits, horizontal separation, which creates several competing firms, as well as facilitates the use of yardstick regulation, should be used.

In all sectors, fair access must be guaranteed to the network component. In the electricity sector, the use of a market pricing mechanism (to which all generation must go except for direct contracting), the independent ownership of the high-tension grid and third-party access rules, appear sufficient to create a level playing field as far as the high-tension distribution system is concerned. In the gas and oil sectors, third party access and the access prices are problems that remain to be solved. The envisaged hydrocarbon law should widen third party access to the networks and make it more equitable. Nevertheless, an independent ownership of CLH and ENAGAS from the main refineries and Gas Natural, respectively, would go far in promoting competition in these sectors as vertical separation of the industries would promote much further transparent and equal access to the respective networks. In train transportation, the separation of operations, in addition to better financial accounting, should only be first steps towards the creation of opportunities for private operation of trains as well as private development and operation of infrastructure. In telecommunications, access to Telefonica's basic telephony network has been established for the second operator (Retevision), with the exception of customers without digital lines; however, the interconnection price appears high based on future long-term marginal costs. Moreover, a lower interconnection price – for a short predetermined period – could assist the development of competition to the dominant firm. Airline competition is frustrated by limited access to slots at the major airports. Consideration should be given to moving further than current EC directives and auctioning the slots historically belonging to individual airlines as concessions for fixed periods.

Horizontal competition requires the existence of several firms, as well as entry and exit opportunities (*i.e.* market contestability). In many sectors, the degree of concentration appears likely to be excessive and thus provide incentives for collusion or other non-competitive practices. One measure of market concentration frequently used is the Herfindal Hirschman Index (HHI).[144] An HHI of 1 800 – equivalent to the existence of between five and six equally sized firms – has been used in the United States as an indication that a market is highly concentrated.[145] In the case of the Spanish electricity generation, the HHI has risen from 1 200 in 1980 to 3 800 in 1996, equivalent to having approximately three firms with equal market shares.[146] In the other main sectors, the (former) public enterprises are still *de facto* monopolies (telecommunications and gas) or dominate a highly concentrated sector (aviation and oil); the HHIs in these latter two sectors are about 4 500, equivalent to between two and three firms with equal market shares.

The effects of the high degree of concentration could be mitigated by easy entry of new competitors or imports. However, in Spain, such new sources of competition may be limited in the short term due to technological factors in the electricity generation and gas distribution sectors, while in other sectors unfair access to the corresponding networks appear to constitute an important barrier to entry. Under these circumstances, consideration should be given to the lowering of entry barriers or the break-up of existing firms. The rationale that the maintenance of a small number of enterprises will safeguard against foreign take-over may not be correct and may, in fact, have the opposite result of attracting attention to their profitable position. In the electricity sector, excess capacity (especially base capacity) reduces the likelihood of profitable entry, while imports are constrained in the short-term by environmental considerations. Horizontal competition would be enhanced if the recent concentration in this sector was reversed by severing the recently made links between some of the generators. As for local distribution, this is a sector which seems ideally suited to an appropriate horizontal split designed to facilitate yardstick regulations. In the gas sector, entry is feasible through imports from France and the new hydrocarbon law should permit the introduction of a second operator to compete with Gas Natural in conjunction with fair access to the pipeline network. The major obstacle to the generation of more competition in the fuel refining sector appears to lie solely with constrained access to CLH's network. With fair access to the network, entry should be attractive in both the gas and oil sectors as the former is expected to experience strong demand growth while there is little excess capacity but a lot of obsolete capacity in the latter sector.

The telecommunication and aviation sectors are more susceptible to international competition, and barriers to entry are easier to overcome. Under EC guidelines both sectors are facing enhanced international competition. In the short term, the main impediment to entry in the telecommunication sector appears to be a high interconnection price. Similarly in the aviation sector, the major restrictions to further entry appear to be the availability of slots, access to airport infrastructure, and the reinforcement of a dominant position of Iberia by the provision of its own terminal.

Providing consumers the choice to select the supplier will also enhance competition. This process should be accelerated as it is not foreseen for small consumers before 10 years in the electricity sector and 15 years in the gas sector. In the gas and electricity sectors, competition may nevertheless continue to be limited in the downstream supply market, if switching and marketing costs are high, especially in the high margin small consumer market. The likelihood of this being the case reinforces the need for improving competition between gas importers and electricity generators, respectively. However, in the oil sector, downstream competition would require the existing long term fixed margin contracts between the wholesaler (dominated by the refineries) and the pump stations to be abolished.

In view of the relatively sparse number of players in these sectors, enhancing inter-modal competition will reinforce significantly the reform effort in any individual sector. Such a broad reform strategy will also serve to prevent distortions in one sector from slowing down liberalisation in another area. Areas where parallel reform would be most fruitful are the set of energy sectors (electricity, natural gas, and fuels) and the transportation sectors (aeroplane companies, railroads and bus companies). Wider reform is also important since the products in one sector are often critical inputs for other sectors; *e.g.* natural gas is an input into electricity generation and fuel is an input into transportation.

With competition unlikely to develop quickly in most of these sectors, price caps appear necessary to control excess profits. Their level is difficult to set and therefore periodic reviews should not be far apart. For example, successive reviews in the United Kingdom were able to set increasingly tighter price caps in the telecommunications sector. Benchmarking can guide the pricing process if there exists sufficient horizontal competition, while a pool price mechanism can be another valuable source of price information. In cases where prices pass on historical sunk costs to consumers, such as the stranded costs in the electricity sector, their value should not be pre-committed but re-examined periodically and the price cap adjusted accordingly. If reviews found that caps were insufficiently tight, the existence of claw-back provisions could provide the opportunity to recover excess profits. Nevertheless, the price cap reviews and the claw-back provisions must not be so onerous that they stifle the incentives of regulated firms to improve their efficiency. The appropriate design of a price cap can eliminate several distortions. For example, if the cap does not provide for full pass through of costs, it increases incentives to find more competitive suppliers. In the event of different markets within a sector, price caps should avoid the cross-subsidisation of industry by households, as is currently the case in the gas and electricity sector, or between more or less accessible regions.

The process of introducing competition by necessity must continue to evolve and react to sectoral developments. International experience supports the positive role of independent and promptly acting regulators in this regard. To enhance competitive practices, procedures which speed up the decision-making process undertaken by the *Tribunal de Defensa de la Competencia* and the *Servicio*, should be introduced, and the new regulator for the gas, oil and fuel sector should be given strong powers, similar to those provided to the telecommunications regulator (CMT).

V.   Entrepreneurship

Against the background of the recent improvements that have been made in Spain's economic policy framework and its overall economic performance, intensified entrepreneurial activity could play an important supporting role. The OECD *Jobs Study* (OECD, 1994a) argued that entrepreneurship is one of the keys to a buoyant economy, capable of adapting and adjusting to a changing economic environment. This chapter examines some aspects of the state of entrepreneurial activity in Spain, the institutional framework within which Spanish businesses operate and the programmes and policies of the Spanish Government aimed at stimulating different aspects of entrepreneurship.

The state of entrepreneurship in Spain

At its most general, entrepreneurship can be defined as the process of identifying economic opportunities and acting upon them by developing, producing and selling goods and services. As such it is central to the functioning of market economies. However, there are several more narrow definitions in common usage depending on the emphasis put on different aspects of entrepreneurial activity. Measuring the degree of entrepreneurship present in an economy is likewise very difficult and depends on the interpretation placed on a variety of imperfect indicators. These measurement problems would be exacerbated by any informal and non-recorded economic activity taking place, although it can be argued that informal activity is, in some sense, an entrepreneurial response to obstacles faced in the formal sector.

Small businesses and entrepreneurship

Entrepreneurship is often associated with the activity of small and medium size enterprises (SMEs), although a well-functioning and dynamic economy is likely to be associated with entrepreneurial behaviour in large as well as small firms. As in many other countries, Spanish SMEs have been a major source of employment creation in recent years. Spain has around 2.7 million enterprises, and 55 per cent of them are one-person businesses, a much higher proportion than elsewhere in Europe. Spain also has a very high proportion of very small enterprises or micro enterprises (with one to nine employees), compared with the rest of Europe, let alone the United States and Japan. These differences are most apparent in the services sector, especially trade, hotels and restaurants. For example, in Spain 45 per cent of employees in the trade, hotels and restaurants sector are employed in very small firms and another 28 per cent in small firms (with 10-49 employees). In Europe, only Italy and Portugal have a higher proportion of employment in very small enterprises in this sector.[147] In the United States, in contrast, almost half of the workforce of the sector is employed in 6 500 very large enterprises (500 or more employees, Eurostat, 1995). And in the Spanish transport sector, more than three-quarters of businesses are one person operations, in striking contrast to other OECD countries. To some extent these statistics may reflect a more extensive use of subcontracting arrangements, so as to circumvent tight job protection measures. However, the higher proportion of micro enterprises in some of these sectors where larger enterprises have tended to develop in many other countries and where some economies of scale and/or scope might be expected to exist, may be a signal that some barriers to expansion exist.

Entrepreneurship and firm turnover rates

One approach to the study of entrepreneurship emphasises firm start-ups and closures as an indicator of willingness to engage in risk-taking activity and capacity to innovate, and as an indicator of the ease with which resources are able to move quickly from one activity to another. The reported enterprise birth rate – the number of new firm registrations relative to the stock of existing firms – is estimated to be around 4 to 5 per cent in Spain, which is lower than other European countries. However the definitions used for firm births vary considerably from one country to another, making international comparisons very difficult. To facilitate cross-country comparisons, the European Observatory (ENSR) has produced estimates of birth rates, according to ''harmonised'' definitions. On these estimates, the firm start-up rate is one of the highest in Europe, although it also has the widest margin of uncertainty attached to it.[148] Given the uncertainties attached to the harmonised statistics and also the possibility that the unadjusted statistics may significantly understate the degree of turbulence,[149] the existing data on firm start-up rates do not provide a reliable indicator of the degree of entrepreneurship in the Spanish economy. However, one possible interpretation of the differences between the birth rates could be that opening a one-person business is less difficult than opening a larger one.

Regional dimensions of entrepreneurship

Indicators of the regional distribution of entrepreneurship show significant differences as in other OECD countries. In the period 1990-92 unadjusted start up rates exceeded 8 per cent in the regions of Madrid and Murcia and were below 5 per cent in regions such as Castilla-La Mancha, Canarias, Extremadura and Galicia (IMPI, 1996). However geographical variations would be more relevant and significant at sub-regional level as most industrial firms and related business services are concentrated within industrial districts or so called "local productive systems". More than 140 such clusters of firms have been identified (Celada, 1991). They are located in all regions, including within the main metropolitan areas, urban-industrial centres of intermediate size as well as in smaller urban nuclei with a strong local artisan or industrial tradition. They are heavily concentrated in Cataluña (23 clusters), the Valencia Region (23 clusters) and Andalucía (29 clusters). They are specialised in a variety of industries, ranging from software in Sabadell (Cataluña), machine tools (Bajo Deba) and aeronautical components (South Madrid) to toys (Ibi), ceramics (Castellon) and furniture (Urola). These industrial districts are an important source of industrial production and exports, whose strength is largely derived from a geographical concentration of specialised, flexible and co-operating firms, which permits them to take advantage of externalities and the minimisation of transaction costs.

According to one research study on a sample of firms (one from each of 23 selected local systems), a distinction should be made between two types of clusters. On the one hand, clusters of competing yet also co-operating small and medium size enterprises which develop complementary production activities often related to local resources. On the other hand, there are systems organised around a large and vertically-integrated firm which subcontract and outsource a large range of activities to smaller and highly flexible firms. The survey listed the positive externalities gained by both forms of collaboration. These comprised the following: First, the existence of a pool of well skilled, locally mobile and flexible labour force. Second, the practice of exchanging orders so as to smooth fluctuations in demand. Third, the rapid diffuse of incremental and adaptive innovation through informal communication, imitation and rivalry. Fourth, the use of common bodies for accounting, raw material procurement and product distribution, and, in some cases, the joint acquisition of shared equipment (Costa Campi, 1993). These attributes of clusters allow firms to operate in a more dynamic and entrepreneurial fashion.

Factors affecting entrepreneurship

Despite the strong macroeconomic performance and a number of recent structural reforms (see Chapter III), the Spanish economy has not yet fully overcome the strong corporatist philosophy and heavy regulation of economic activity from its past. Even after recent reforms, the overall business environment and the prevailing web of regulations and other institutional factors combine to generate what could be significant impediments to entrepreneurial activity. These features of the institutional framework could discourage risk-taking, either in establishing new ventures but more likely in the expansion of existing activities, and limit the scope for developing flexible and innovative working arrangements. Removing impediments to entrepreneurial activity and fostering a more favourable business environment should therefore form an important part of government efforts to stimulate growth. The rest of this section considers the main institutional factors that affect new businesses and/or act as constraints on expansion.

Product markets and competition

Competition in product markets can be expected to stimulate entrepreneurship, especially because innovation of processes or products can be rewarded by greater market share and increased returns. The European Single Market, by providing greater scope for competition from imports and opening up new markets, has played a positive role in stimulating entrepreneurial activity in Spain. However, competition in Spain has traditionally been severely limited in many sectors of the economy, especially, at the level of major enterprises where the public sector has dominated (see Chapter IV) as well as for some services normally provided by smaller and medium sized enterprises (especially those providing professional services).

The *Tribunal for the Defence of Competition* has made recommendations in a number of service sectors of the economy, where it has found effective competition lacking. Since several of their recommendations have recently been implemented, the shortcoming identified may have played a significant role in constraining entrepreneurship only in the past. For example, professional services were subject to a compulsory minimum fee structure and other constraints until 1996, and until 1996, funeral services were operating as local monopolies in a number of municipalities. However, some areas of road transport still need further liberalisation, including the removal of the quota system limiting the number of vehicles for discretionary passenger services and heavy freight vehicles. The rules governing installation and maintenance services were also found to be complex by the Tribunal and thus deleterious to competition. The Tribunal has also made recommendations in the areas of commercial distribution, petrol distribution, retail banking, ports, pharmacies and the film industry. Acknowledging the recent progress in many areas, further action seems necessary to promote product market competition, including from foreign sources which can contribute know-how in production and trading.

Opening or closing a business

Setting up a new business in Spain appeas to be a more cumbersome process than in other European countries. Irrespective of an entrepreneur's choice to incorporate, all new enterprises must undertake approximately 13 to 14 general steps prior to starting a business, and some additional steps apply in specific sectors.[150] Moreover, incorporation involves a minimum of five additional steps (only 12 per cent of enterprises are incorporated).[151] On average, each step requires four separate pieces of documentation, and involves a minimum of six different agencies, with the total time required to fulfill these legal requirements estimated to be between 19 and 28 weeks. In contrast, it takes around half a day to establish a new enterprise in the United States.

Closing a business is also a complicated and expensive process in Spain, especially because of the labour regulations. These make it difficult to reduce the workforce for economic reasons despite recent legislative attempts in this regard, which raises losses sustained when an uneconomic business does close (see below). Furthermore, only about one quarter of businesses that go bankrupt are covered by limited liability (ENSR, 1995), so that the cost to the owner of an unsuccessful business can be very high and this is likely to discourage people from taking the risk. An inter-ministerial Commission is currently reviewing the trade-off between the rights and obligations of debtors and creditors, in recognition of the adverse effects that current bankruptcy legislation has on risk-taking, and entrepreneurship more generally, while also taking into account the effect that reduced creditor protection may have for credit costs.

Finance

Obtaining finance has been difficult and costly for many Spanish businesses. As recently as late 1997, 43 per cent of Spanish firms surveyed in the European Business Survey cited the cost of finance as a main short-term constraint on expansion, while 32 per cent cited it as a long-term constraint (Figure 24). Difficult access to bank finance could be related to the high interest rates that

Figure 24. **COST OF FINANCE AS A CONSTRAINT ON BUSINESS**

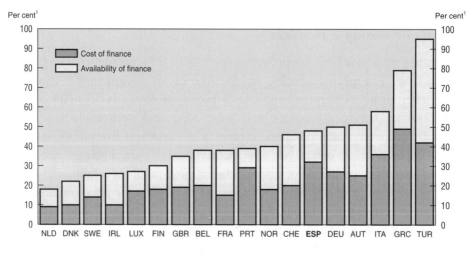

1. Sum of responses, given as percentage of respondents. Respondents were allowed to choose more than one constraint.
Source: Grant Thornton International Business Strategies Ltd., 1997.

existed in Spain until 1996-97 and, perhaps more importantly, to credit rationing by banks which have traditionally focused their activities on better-established and larger enterprises. Among smaller and medium-sized Spanish enterprises, only 47 per cent of those surveyed felt that they had sufficient access to finance to be able to carry out their plans over the next three years, compared with a European average of 55 per cent. At the other extreme, in Denmark and the Netherlands, around 70 per cent of such enterprises felt confident about their access to finance.[152]

Venture Capital

Venture capital is typically viewed as an important source of finance to potentially fast-growing companies and therefore plays an important role in a dynamic and entrepreneurial economy. The Spanish venture capital market remains relatively under-developed and to some extent still reflects a government dominated origin.[153] Despite the recent development of private providers, even as recently as in 1996, government agencies provided almost 20 per cent of new venture capital raised in Spain, compared with less than 3 per cent for Europe as a whole. Banks were the largest private sector provider, supplying 37 per cent of new venture capital raised in Spain, compared with 27 per cent for Europe generally.

In contrast, institutional investors (mainly insurance funds and pension funds) provided virtually no such funding in Spain, while playing a much larger role in many other countries, especially in the United States and the United Kingdom. In part, this reflects the relatively small total financial assets of institutional investors (only 40 per cent of GDP), with such investors' relatively limited size possibly linked to the generous nature of the public pension scheme which has discouraged recourse to private pension systems in the past (Table 23). Other factors limiting such funding are the existence of legal constraints that effectively prohibit insurance companies from holding unlisted shares[154] and private pension funds' (which were only established from 1987) concentration of their investments almost entirely in government paper.

Very little venture capital funding is flowing into early stage investments (Table 24). Instead, Spanish venture capitalists are far more active in financing expansion, and unlike other European countries, institutional buy-outs and replacement capital do not absorb any significant amount of venture capital in

Table 23. **Financial assets of institutional investors**

Per cent of GDP

	Insurance companies	Pension funds	Investment companies	Other	Total
United States	40.7	59.8	39.2	31.1	170.8
United Kingdom	71.8	68.8	21.7	0.0	162.3
Netherlands	52.5	88.7	17.2	0.0	158.4
Sweden	52.4	2.4	22.2	37.8	114.8
Canada	29.3	39.5	19.1	0.0	87.9
Japan	38.3	0.0	9.8	29.3	77.4
Australia	35.2	28.7	9.3	2.7	75.9
France	37.8	0.0	37.5	0.0	75.3
Denmark	45.6	17.5	3.7	0.0	66.8
Korea	23.4	3.1	31.2	0.0	57.7
Finland	12.4	0.0	0.9	36.7	50.0
Germany	28.1	2.7	15.3	0.0	46.1
Norway	31.3	6.4	4.9	0.0	42.6
Spain	**17.8**	**2.1**	**18.4**	**0.0**	**38.3**
Portugal	9.7	8.8	16.4	0.4	35.3
Austria	20.1	1.0	14.1	0.0	35.2
Greece	2.5	10.9	9.6	0.0	23.0
Italy	9.2	0.4	7.4	0.0	17.0
Hungary	3.3	0.1	1.1	0.0	4.5

Source: *Institutional Investor Statistical Yearbook 1997,* OECD.

Spain.[155] As Government involvement in venture capital has diminished, the percentage of early stage deals has fallen from 80 per cent in 1986 to only 26 per cent in 1996. Notwithstanding the increasing emphasis on later stage investments, which would generally be considered less risky than early stage investments, an analysis of 75 completed disinvestments showed that less than 10 per cent generated an annualised rate of return more than 25 per cent. Another 30 to 35 per cent generated returns between 0 and 25 per cent while the remaining disinvestments were loss making. While losses are to be expected, what seems to be missing are the spectacular successes associated with venture capital investment in other countries, such as the United States.

Venture capital investment may be constrained by exist difficulties, which have been cited as a problem in Spain. Most successful venture capital disinvestments have been realised through management buy-backs, and only 5 initial public offerings (IPOs) arising from venture capital backed investments took place in 1996 (although a number of successful non-venture capital backed IPOs

Table 24. **Venture capital in Europe and the United States, 1996**

Total investments, excluding institutional buy-outs

	Investments made, in million ECU	Number of deals	Investments made, as a per cent of GDP	Seed and start-up investment as a per cent of total investment
United States	7 892.4	1 502	0.13	34.8
Total Europe	3 744.7	4 081	0.05	11.8
United Kingdom	840.4	1 014	0.09	4.9
France	746.4	1 000	0.06	13.0
Germany	564.0	708	0.03	16.8
Netherlands	408.0	248	0.13	22.6
Italy	356.0	174	0.04	12.7
Sweden	236.3	158	0.12	2.3
Spain	**181.2**	**152**	**0.04**	**6.5**
Belgium	105.8	153	0.05	19.2
Norway	82.2	150	0.07	6.9
Switzerland	55.6	21	0.02	9.6
Ireland	35.5	62	0.07	8.5
Finland	35.1	101	0.03	25.9
Denmark	34.0	38	0.02	6.8
Greece	32.0	23	0.03	19.5
Portugal	30.5	71	0.04	3.8
Austria	1.0	4	0.00	25.8
Iceland	1.0	4	0.02	0.0

Source: EVCA (1997), *A survey of venture capital and private equity in Europe, 1997 Yearbook; Venture One (1997),* *National venture capital association, 1996 Annual Report.*

also took place). Perhaps reflecting administrative difficulties, several of these IPOs took place in the UK and US markets, rather than in Spain itself. Although there exist several second-tier markets operating in Spain, none of them seem to be particularly attractive to such companies. The recent introduction of the electronic trading system *mercado continuo,* could provide further opportunities for smaller companies to make IPOs.

Informal investors, known as "angels" have played a significant role in a number of other OECD countries in providing equity finance together with general guidance and/or specific business skills, especially to starting businesses.[156] Many such "angels" in other OECD countries have themselves been successful in business and want to invest their funds and expertise in new ventures. The very nature of this type of finance makes it hard to measure and no data are available for Spain. But the evidence from other countries suggests that there is a virtuous circle with angel investment: the more successful entrepreneurs that exist, the more potential angels there will be. In Spain, the strong presence of family businesses would almost certainly be linked to intra-family informal investment which may be a significant and particularly flexible and less costly source of finance, especially for young and small businesses.

Taxation

Overall taxation is low in Spain, and the average effective tax rate on capital is estimated at 19 per cent in 1993, compared with an unweighted OECD average of around 35 per cent (Table 25). However, while there are in principle few

Table 25.   **Average effective tax rates**

	Capital[1]			Labour[2]		
	1965-75	1975-85	1985-94	1965-75	1975-85	1985-94
United States	0.42	0.42	0.40[3]	0.17	0.21	0.23[3]
Japan	0.23	0.35	0.44	0.12	0.17	0.21
Germany	0.21	0.29	0.26	0.29	0.35	0.37
France	0.17	0.25	0.25	0.29	0.37	0.43
Italy	..	0.22	0.28	..	0.28	0.32
United Kingdom	0.50	0.60	0.52	0.24	0.25	0.21
Canada	0.41	0.38	0.44	0.17	0.22	0.28
Australia	0.34	0.42	0.45	0.13	0.18	0.19
Austria	0.17	0.20	0.21	0.33	0.38	0.41
Belgium	0.26	0.35	0.33	0.31	0.37	0.40
Denmark	..	0.42	0.42	..	0.35	0.41
Finland	0.22	0.32	0.41	0.23	0.31	0.38
Netherlands	..	0.30	0.31	..	0.43	0.46
Norway	0.25	0.38	0.37	0.33	0.34	0.35
Portugal	..	..	0.15	..	..	0.21
Spain	..	**0.12**	**0.19**[3]	..	**0.25**	**0.29**[3]
Sweden	..	0.45	0.58	..	0.46	0.48
Switzerland	0.17	0.24	0.25[3]	0.19	0.26	0.26[3]

1. Average effective tax rate on capital defined as household income taxes paid on operating surplus of private unincorporated enterprises and on household property and entrepreneurial income; plus tax on income, profit and capital gains of corporations.
2. Average effective tax rate on labour defined as household income tax paid on wages plus payroll or manpower taxes, divided by wages and salaries (including income of self-employed) plus employers' contributions to social security and to private pension.
3. Figure for 1993.
Source: Leibfritz *et al.* (1997).

differences in the treatment of incorporated and unincorporated businesses, in practice the differences can be significant. Most importantly, personal income tax rates are progressive from 25 to 56 per cent, with the highest tax rate applying from 182.4 per cent of the average income, compared with a flat corporate tax rate of 35 per cent. However, since 1992, small unincorporated businesses in Spain can avoid the higher personal income tax rates by choosing "standard forfaitaire flat rate" taxation in exchange for simplified accounting requirements.[157] Moreover, personal corporate taxation constrains a plethora of tax deductions applying to SMEs. The simplification of capital gains taxation in 1997, which made it into a flat rate of 20 per cent should encourage investment participation in SMEs.[158]

There are two specific tax provisions, however, that could deter entrepreneurship for incorporated enterprises. First, the treatment of losses is relatively strict under Spanish regulations. Losses can be carried forward and offset against future profits for only five years, compared with the United States and the Netherlands, for example, where losses can be carried forward for 15 years and indefinitely, respectively.[159] These limits penalise start-ups, in particular as these firms may sometimes make losses for several years before breaking even and then moving into profit. Second a tax of 1 per cent on all new equity capital issued, adds to the costs of incorporation or expansion and could be another deterrant. This tax also discourages the use of equity options as a way of sharing the risk with employees.

Labour markets

Labour markets could be more important in deterring entrepreneurial activity in Spain than in other countries. In Spain, the labour market remains relatively inflexible, despite the recent developments discussed in Chapter III. Employment protection legislation is among the strictest in the OECD, and has led to the widespread use of fixed-term contracts which are not subject to high dismissal costs. Thus, fixed-term contracts provide opportunities for greater flexibility and are particularly used by smaller firms. If the much lower prevalence of fixed-term contracts in larger firms reflects the need for more stable employment relationships as a means for firm development, then the dual labour market may be an evidence of constraints to firms' ability to grow past being small. Another obstacle to firm expansion could be collective agreements which also apply more frequently to larger firms and establish rigid job demarcation of the tasks and responsibilities that can be carried out by different employees. Of course the cost of restructuring for well-established larger firms is also high, discouraging these firms from becoming more entrepreneurial. One possible impact of these labour market rigidities could be to push activity into the informal sector, although by its very nature it is difficult to estimate the extent to which this has taken place.

High unemployment in Spain may also have two particular implications for entrepreneurship. The profile of the typical entrepreneur in other countries is someone aged 35 to 45 with significant experience gained by working two or three years in medium or large enterprises. This typical entrepreneur generally starts a business that builds on that experience. However, adding to the risk that a new business will not survive, there is a risk in Spain of staying unemployed after the termination of an entrepreneurial venture. Combined with comprehensive protection for workers who have permanent contracts, and the significant insurance and security this entails, a potential entrepreneur could be discouraged. High youth unemployment may exacerbate the situation, because the formative years of experience would be harder to gain, and time previously spent in unemployment would be likely to further discourage someone from subsequently quitting a good job.

Administrative and compliance burden

An examination of the ongoing regulatory and administrative requirements on Spanish businesses would suggest that the administrative burden is high. Surprisingly, however, when surveyed in 1996, established small and medium-sized enterprises in Spain reported fewer constraints due to regulation and associated administrative burden than in any other European country (Figure 25). There are two possible explanations for this: first, there is an inherent self-selection bias in the survey, because only existing firms are surveyed and these have learnt to deal adequately with these constraints. The lengthy process of starting a business, outlined earlier, may have discouraged firms unable to deal effectively with administrative requirements from ever starting up. The other possible explanation is that enforcement is weak, so compliance is not considered important by firms.

Evidence, albeit partial, suggests that the legal framework for business, as in other countries, could be improved. However, the overall judicial system has been rated as less efficient than in many OECD countries (Figure 26) and the risk

144

Figure 25. **REGULATION AND ADMINISTRATIVE BURDENS**

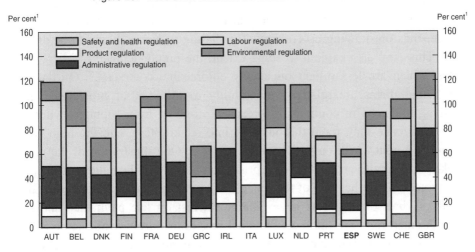

Per cent[1]

Safety and health regulation
Product regulation
Administrative regulation
Labour regulation
Environmental regulation

AUT BEL DNK FIN FRA DEU GRC IRL ITA LUX NLD PRT **ESP** SWE CHE GBR

1. Sum of responses, given as percentage of respondents. Respondents were allowed to choose more than one constraint.
Source: Grant Thornton International Business Strategies Ltd., 1997.

Figure 26. **EFFICIENCY OF JUDICIAL SYSTEMS**[1]

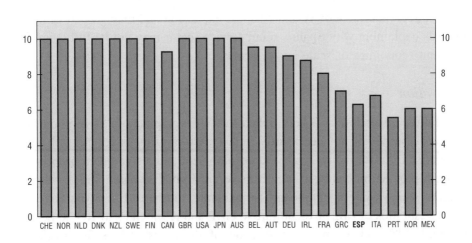

CHE NOR NLD DNK NZL SWE FIN CAN GBR USA JPN AUS BEL AUT DEU IRL FRA GRC **ESP** ITA PRT KOR MEX

1. Each item is scaled from zero to ten, with the higher score indicated higher confidence in the system.
Source: La Porta, *et al.*, "Law and finance", NBER Working Paper 5661, 1996.

of government modifications to contracts is judged higher. If legal enforcement of contracts through the courts is more difficult to obtain, entrepreneurial activity that depends on drawing up contracts for sharing of risk is likely to be discouraged. This may also explain to some extent, the preponderance of micro enterprises, which are less reliant on legally enforceable contracts.[160] On the other hand, small firms are relative vulnerability to the lack of protection against abusive provisions in contracts,[161] breach of contract by a supplier (where one such occurrence may force the business into bankruptcy), and the high cost of enforcing a contract through the judicial system. One illustration of the relative weakness of small versus large enterprises can be seen in the pattern of payments for invoices. Spain has one of the longest average payment periods in the OECD (73 days), half of the firms never charge interest on late payments, and small Spanish enterprises are the most punctual payers in Europe while large Spanish enterprises on average have longer payment periods than anywhere else in Europe.

One specific aspect of the administrative burden which may particularly discourage entrepreneurial activity is the administration of land development. The obstacles to land development have resulted in an artificial scarcity of land and high land prices with developers facing a long and involved administrative process to get the necessary permission, and significant costs (see Chapter III). Such restrictions on land development may be particularly inhibiting to larger-scale entrepreneurial activity and business expansion and may go part of the way towards explaining why Spain's retail service sector may not be fully exploiting apparent economies of scale and/or scope.

Innovation

Entrepreneurship is closely linked to the development of new products and processes, although not necessarily high-technology intensive. Not all innovations arise from formal research and development and a significant proportion of Spanish production has been in sectors where formal research and development (R&D) is anyway less significant (for example, tourism). But Spain has among the lowest ratios of R&D expenditure to GDP and researchers to 10 000 people in the OECD,[162] and a smaller proportion of these researchers are working in enterprises (Table 26), which suggests that Spain's capacity for generating or adapting new ideas is more limited in this narrow sense than in many other

Table 26. **Researchers by sector of employment**[1]

	Business enterprise	Government	Higher Education	Total researchers per 10 000 labour force
		Percentage		
United States[2]	79	6	13	74
Japan	70	6	22	81
Germany[2]	56	15	29	58
France	45	18	35	59
Italy	37	18	45	33
United Kingdom[3]	57	10	29	51
Canada[2]	46	10	43	52
Australia[3]	26	15	57	64
Austria[2]	55	7	38	34
Belgium[4]	48	4	46	43
Czech Republic	41	36	23	26
Denmark[2]	43	22	34	47
Finland[2]	36	23	40	61
Greece[2]	16	24	59	20
Hungary	28	34	39	28
Iceland	34	39	25	58
Ireland	40	5	52	52
Mexico	10	31	58	5
Netherlands	38	22	38	48
New Zealand[2]	24	27	49	37
Norway[2]	48	20	32	69
Poland	22	23	55	28
Portugal[5]	8	24	46	16
Spain	**23**	**16**	**60**	**30**
Sweden[2]	52	8	40	68
Switzerland[6]	54	4	43	46
Turkey	14	12	74	7

1. Data for researchers by sector refer to 1995 unless otherwise noted. Data for number of researchers refer to 1994 unless otherwise noted.
2. Data refer to 1993.
3. Data refer to 1994.
4. Data refer to 1991.
5. Data for number of researchers refers to 1992.
6. Data for researchers by sector refer to 1991; data for number of researchers refer to 1992.
Source: OECD (1997), *Main Science and Technology indicators.*

OECD countries. Reinforcing this view, the inventiveness coefficient (resident patent applications per head of population) is lower in Spain than in many other OECD countries and fewer Spanish patent applications per head of population were registered with the European Patent Office in 1996 than for almost any other European country (Table 27). Although direct data on the overall amount of

Table 27. **Inventiveness coefficient**[1]

Resident patent applications per 10 000 population

Switzerland	4.7
Australia	4.7
Sweden	4.6
Germany	4.6
Finland	4.6
United States	4.1
New Zealand	3.6
United Kingdom	3.2
Austria	2.5
Denmark	2.5
Norway	2.4
Ireland	2.3
France	2.2
Luxembourg	1.4
Netherlands	1.2
Canada	0.9
Belgium	0.9
Iceland	0.8
Spain	**0.6**
Portugal	0.1
Turkey	0.0

1.   Data refer to 1994.
Source: OECD (1997), *Main Science and Technology Indicators.*

innovation taking place are difficult to obtain, in manufacturing, only 11 per cent of firms were recorded as having developed or introduced innovations in products or processes during the period 1992 to 1994 (National Statistical Institute). Around 80 per cent of manufacturing SMEs have no R&D activities and only 9 per cent have financed internal R&D projects.

Some industrial districts provide good examples of strong interaction between firms, and in a few cases (such as Valencia,) between a technological centre (IMPIVA) and enterprises. The research mentioned above (Costa Campi, 1993) shows that 80 per cent of firms surveyed within these selected districts have introduced product innovation and 70 per cent have introduced process innovation during the last three years, mostly through co-operation with more advanced local firms or through sub-contracting and association. More than 80 per cent of the technical information acquired by the enterprises comes from the local market, through the informal interchange of knowledge between entrepreneurs, technicians and workers. In addition, half of these firms have established formal agreements in the R&D field. Such innovation and close linkages have created more opportunities for start-ups.

There are a number of explanations for the relatively mediocre innovation performance in Spain. One panel of 75 experts concluded that main factors impeding consideration towards innovation was due to culture (87 per cent of experts), and the lack of financial and human resources for innovation (82 per cent), followed by the poor ability of public research institutions to promote technological development and deficient public finance institutions to finance innovation. (Fundacion COTEC, 1997*b*.) And in a survey of enterprises, finance and lack of know-how were considered the most significant obstacles to innovation in Spain. But for each of the possible barriers to innovation, a higher percentage of Spanish firms found it very important than other European enterprises (Figure 27). Protection of intellectual property does not seem to feature as an issue, although little research on the effectiveness of patent protection in Spain is available.

Management skills and the role of the education system

Robust development and expansion of enterprises require strong management skills. Though the degree to which these are obtained from secondary education is an issue, amongst very small enterprises, only one third of owners/ managers have completed secondary education, and even for firms with more than 50 employees, some 20 per cent of managers have not completed secondary education. More importantly, management training efforts are not only limited but they are highly concentrated in some industrial regions and cities and need to be not only spread more widely but also intensified, according to FORCEM. Supporting the importance of an open economy, in some export-oriented industrial districts, there are signs that management skills have improved with EU membership due to structural changes related to a new competitive environment and the pressure to innovate. Improvements in business training have been actively supported by employers' organisations chambers and the network of technological institutes, often located close to these districts. But universities seem particularly inactive in this field and do not seem to be much involved in promoting a new entrepreneurial spirit and management skills (except for the few business schools and those institutions involved in relevant European programmes).

149

Figure 27. **BARRIERS TO INNOVATION**

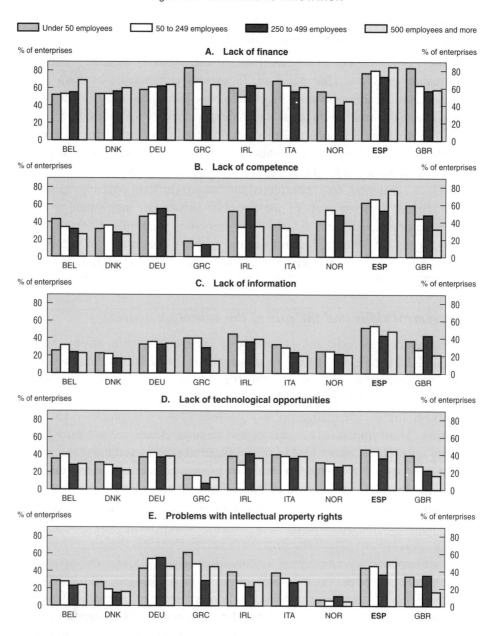

Source: Green paper on innovation, Bulletin of the European Union.

Policies and programmes to promote entrepreneurship

Policies for SMEs

The Spanish government earlier this year announced a new strategy for SME (and by extension, the promotion of entrepreneurship). This strategy has five main planks: institutional change, administrative simplification, taxation issues, enterprise promotion and economic promotion. The institutional changes, primarily a shift of responsibilities for SME policy from the Ministry of Industry to the Ministry of Economy, reflects a broadening of SME policies from their earlier focus on the manufacturing sector and a recognition of the importance of linking policies in this area with the broader economic framework.

Administrative simplification is recognised as an ongoing process, but two particular channels have been set up to facilitate the process. The first is the establishment of a Working Group on SME policies under the Government Commission for Economic Affairs, to take stock of measures affecting SMEs, examine ways of getting simplified and better co-ordinated administrative procedures and develop a common policy for study of SMEs. The second is the establishment of the Observatory of SMEs to provide a permanent dialogue with SMEs and a vehicle for identifying problems and solutions. Information on firms, technology and markets, as well as promoting co-operation between firms (as a means to improve competitiveness, transfer of technology and access to export markets), are also new priorities. An "information area" has been set up (with around 250 information requests a month) and the design of a national network – based on few regional bodies that already exist – has been planned.

An inter-ministerial commission has recently reported on a number of tax issues and a number of changes were announced in the 1998 budget. For SMEs, corporate tax will apply at the rate of 30 per cent instead of 35 per cent on the first 15 million pesetas of profit. The rate will also apply to equity increases arising from the sale of assets related to the company's activities. The limits for calculating tax according to the standard flat rate method have been raised to Ptas 100 million and the forfaitaire system will be integrated into the standard flat rate method without requiring increased accounting obligations.

Innovation

Both national and regional governments have taken a number of initiatives in order to improve diffusion and transfer of innovation to firms, with significant funding also coming from the EU. The initiatives include information training and advice on product design[163] as well as technological development projects.[164] In addition, the 12 technological parks which have been set up during the last decade host 400 high technology, small and medium-sized firms. A large amount of public money (EU in particular, national and regional) has been allocated in the past to financing industrial land development, with very mixed – and diverging – appreciation of their impacts and benefits. In 1995, half of the Ptas 5.7 billions budget was allocated to the funding of projects to establish enterprise support agencies or structures[165] and more than a quarter to "industrial product development" projects submitted by firms.[166] At the regional level, publicly-funded networks of around 230 enterprise agencies supporting innovation have been set up and especially among these, a network of regional technology agencies which, in addition to technological advice, provide a large range of services such as information and training as well as testing, certification and standardisation.

Only a few national and regional innovation programmes have been assessed, and these according to quite narrow criteria. For example, an evaluation of the programme on product design shows that such support increased employment in around half of the firms concerned and export capacity by around 30 per cent. And the evaluation of the Madrid regional government support scheme to technological innovation, *Programa de Modernizacion Industrial*, PMI, showed that two thirds of participating enterprises increased their sales and improved the quality of their products.[167] However, the programme had a poor impact on the level of training and skills of employees. (Fonfria Mesa A, 1996). These results for the firm are not surprising, (not least because they may reflect selection bias) but they give no indication of the economy-wide impact nor whether these schemes provided value for money.

Entrepreneurial development programme

An important new support programme on "entrepreneurial development", with several different objectives and targeted on SMEs, has been launched for the years 1997-99 with 50 per cent co-financed by EU funds (and up to 70 per cent in developing areas). This programme puts more emphasis on information and advice (intangible supports). The Ptas 13 billion budget for 1997 includes several sub-programmes: co-operation among firms; information; support to design and innovation; financing support (mostly guarantees) and aids to supporting business institutions and services (the so-called intermediary organisations). An additional aim is to rationalise, better co-ordinate and integrate the large range of dispersed support provided to firms by central and regional governments, including EU funding.

Concluding remarks

An assessment of the extent to which entrepreneurial activity is actually occurring in Spain is not altogether straightforward as it relies on imperfect indicators, which may be unable to detect some of the more entrepreneurial aspects of the Spanish economy. Nevertheless, there are signs that entrepreneurial activity could be strengthened through efforts to improve the institutional framework within which economic activity takes place. Major efforts have already been made over recent years to improve the institutional framework and these efforts have been rewarded with recent strong performance of SMEs. But some aspects still require further reform especially in addressing the rigidities that discourage firm expansion. In particular, further efforts to increase labour market flexibility and improve product market competition would provide more scope for entrepreneurial activity. Making it easier to start up and close a business would also be positive steps. Improvements in the range and quality of data and further research and analysis of different aspects of entrepreneurship in Spain would also help the authorities to better determine the most effective combination of policy settings for entrepreneurship.

Notes

1. The *Prever* plan, launched in April 1997, reduces registration fees by up to Ptas 80 000 for new car buyers who simultaneously withdraw from circulation their previous car, if it is more than 10 years old. Contrary to the earlier *Renove* plan, the *Prever* plan is of indefinite duration.

2. Owner-occupied houses represent 80 per cent of the housing market in Spain. Equity prices have increased by 89 per cent from year-end 1995 to November 1997.

3. In the Spanish national accounts, stockbuilding also contains some statistical adjustments.

4. In 1996, agriculture accounted for a large part of total output growth (about one third). Good weather conditions, after several years of severe drought, permitted a 20 per cent growth in agricultural output in 1996.

5. On the supply side, the recovery is becoming more broadly based following the 1996 agricultural bonanza. The service sector, due to its large size, continues to be a significant source of growth and its pace remained relatively stable during 1996, and picked up in 1997.

6. This estimate corrects for the upward bias currently existing in Spanish employment statistics. The labour force survey data have been biased upwards by the gradual incorporation of the results of the 1991 census between the first quarter of 1995 and the second quarter of 1996. Similarly, social security registration data which in the past have provided reliable indicators of employment developments appear to be biased upwards by registration reflecting a shift of workers from the informal to the formal sector.

7. The composition of the number of unemployed remained broadly unchanged with the share of youth and long-term unemployed at 43 per cent and 55 per cent, respectively, in mid-1997.

8. The large share of fixed-term contracts is a reaction by firms to the high firing costs in Spain.

9. Specifically, among new indefinite contracts over the period from June to December 1997, about one-half resulted from the conversion of previously fixed-term contracts and one-third from contracts designed for so-called priority groups – the long-term unemployed, workers between the age of 18 and 25 and over the age of 45. These new contracts benefit from a partial exemption of social security payments for a 2 year period and lower firing costs (see Chapter III).

10. The male share of part time employment does not differ significantly from other OECD countries; however, the female share is far below the corresponding OECD average.

11. Part of the service sector inflation could reflect Spain's process of catching up to the income levels of its European partners.

12. The share of Spain's exports to Latin America, Asia and the United States were 6.0 per cent, 5.2 per cent and 4.2 per cent respectively in 1996, and grew by 25, 29 and 27 per cent respectively in the 12 months to October 1997.

13. The fifth balance of payment manuel classifies capital transfers in a separate account outside the current account (in the capital account). Capital transactions are classified in the financial account.

14. The Maastricht target is the average inflation rate – according to a harmonised price index – of the three EMU countries with the lowest average inflation in 1997 plus a spread of 1.5 percentage point. Spain has complied with this limit since July 1997 when average inflation over the 12-month period fell to 2.6 per cent and equalled the Maastricht limit. As the lower inflation attained by Spain during 1997 progressively enters into the calculation of the average price index, the degree of compliance is likely to increase. The interest rate limit consists of the average long-term interest rate of the three countries comprising the inflation criterion plus a spread of 2 percentage points. Spain has been below this limit since early 1997.

15. This transaction comprised borrowing resources at lower cost from abroad and investing them in Spanish fixed-rate instruments whose value was expected to increase as Spanish interest rates converged towards those prevailing in their prospective EMU partners.

16. The financial conditions indicator contains the weighted average of the short and long-term interest rates in real terms and the real effective exchange rate (based on unit labour costs in manufacturing). The interest rate variable has a unitary coefficient while the coefficient of the exchange rate variable is the ratio of exports to GDP.

17. ALP comprises M3 plus other liquid assets in the hands of the public, mainly short-term government securities.

18. The external accounts have not provided liquidity in 1996 and absorbed liquidity in 1997. Though Spain experienced capital inflows during 1996 and 1997, the net foreign assets of the banking system were constant in 1996 and declined in 1997 as banks increased their recourse to foreign borrowing.

19. Base money in real terms has picked up throughout the 1996-97 period, though it is growing below the pace of the monetary aggregates. The growth of base money was contained by the Government's build up of a large cushion in its current account at the central bank in late 1996 (Ptas 1 trillion) and its reversal in late 1997 was sterilised by open market operations. On the asset side of the central bank balance sheet, credit to banks has fallen dramatically during the past two years, as they have turned to foreign borrowing. The banks' reaction reflects, *inter alia*, the scarcity of domestic time deposits, banks' participation in convergence transactions, and a competition induced narrowing of intermediation margins (from approximately 5 per cent at the beginning of 1996 to about $3^1/_2$ per cent in mid-1997). However, banks' foreign borrowing has subsequently been converted into domestic resources and thus contributed to the build up of international reserves of the central bank. Thus, the overall effect of banks' foreign borrowing has been broadly neutral for base money.

20. An evaluation of the 1996 outcome is complicated by several factors. First, the 1996 draft budget was rejected by Parliament and fiscal policy was based on the prorogation of the 1995 budget and the use of Royal Decrees to obtain additional fiscal adjustment. Second,

unrecorded and unpaid expenditure from the 1995 (and prior) budget exercises was detected in 1996. This unexpected expenditure raised the 1995 deficit on a national accounts basis by 0.8 per cent of GDP. This spending related mostly to investment and capital transfers. Third, in line with Eurostat regulations, the fiscal accounts (national accounts basis) were revised to record social security contributions on an accrual basis, while previously they had been recorded on a cash basis.

21. The Government announced a large package of measures in July 1996, several of which had a fiscal component. Their implementation is largely from 1997 onwards and the main ones are considered in the description of the 1997 Budget. The Government had also announced expenditure cuts (mostly in investment) of Ptas 200 billion (0.3 per cent of GDP) in mid-1996.

22. The recovery in wages appears to have pushed up social security contributions (0.3 per cent of GDP). The excise tax hike raised indirect taxes (0.2 per cent of GDP), while non-tax revenues were supported by higher dividends by public enterprises and the Bank of Spain (0.2 per cent of GDP).

23. The residual increase in the debt is accounted for by the payments for the above-mentioned uncovered expenditure (0.8 per cent of GDP), the extension of credits (0.5 per cent of GDP) and the counterpart between market value and face value on Government securities, debt assumptions and valuation effects (totalling 1 per cent of GDP).

24. The anti-fraud measures applied to the following areas: contributory benefits (temporary incapacity, invalidity pensions, survivors' pension, family benefits and the minimum pension complement), non-payment of contributions and non-contributory benefits. In the area of payment arrears, measures have introduced a registrar and closer co-operation with the income tax authorities. These actions were taken in July 1996.

25. The wage freeze applied to the cost of living increase only; wages could increase for other reasons such as seniority. The strict replacement norm for retirees did not apply to the armed forces, and justice and educational personnel.

26. A set of expenditure control reforms were passed in order to avoid a repetition of the 1996 developments when large amounts of unplanned expenditures were uncovered. The main measures are: i) the credits that could be automatically enlarged were limited, ii) credit transfers from capital to current operations were prohibited, and iii) the carry forward of expenditures to future budgets was severely curtailed. These measures were accompanied by stricter monitoring, especially of the development of obligations.

27. The change in the withholding tax would bring forward from 1998 to 1997, 14 per cent of a firm's estimated tax liabilities. Regarding the revaluation option, the incentive for the firm is the larger depreciation deductions that can be applied to future tax liabilities.

28. In addition, the number of tax brackets was reduced significantly, and brought down from 18 to 10.

29. Comparison of expenditure data with 1996 are complicated by the distortionary effects of the uncovered expenditures and the 1996 elections.

30. The reduction in government assets would more than offset the increase in the liabilities from asset transactions. Asset transactions are projected by the authorities to amount to Ptas 700 billion, and comprise the capitalisation of the new entities such as GIF, and credits to the Government's bank ICO.

31. As part of the process of widening the demand for government securities, two new instruments were introduced in 1997: an 18 month treasury bill aimed at mutual funds and strips. The rapid development of the domestic government bond market has reduced the share of bonds held by non-residents from nearly 50 per cent in 1993 to below 24 per cent in 1997.

32. The operation reduces future interest payments but has an estimated cost of Ptas 150 billion, part of which could be booked under ESA methodology as an asset transaction below the line in the budget. Specifically, Ptas 70 billion would comprise a financial transaction, Ptas 37 billion would be added to interest payments and Ptas 47 billion will be paid in fees at the time of the new debt's maturity.

33. The programme has been judged realistic in an assessment made by the European Commission. *Convergence Programme of Spain – An assessment,* DG II, Brussels, April 18, 1997.

34. Personal income tax revenue should not suffer much from the increase in the Budget of a whole set of deductions oriented to the family (*e.g.* for the number of children and for family help) and the deductions for private pensions as these will apply to the 1999 returns.

35. The price of tobacco was raised by an average of 20 per cent and is expected to raise approximately Ptas 80 billion. Indirect taxes are biased upwards by the transformation of the charge on electricity prices to subsidise the coal sector by a tax. The new tax will raise Ptas 100 billion but will have a broadly neutral effect on the budget as transfers to coal mines also increase (*i.e.* the net impact is envisaged to be a budgetary improvement of Ptas 40 billion).

36. The measures to combat fraud are envisaged to provide savings of the order of Ptas 200 billion (0.2 per cent of GDP).

37. The agreement reached after the finalisation of the 1998 Budget contains a commitment to maintain the growth of health expenditure financed by the budget in line with nominal GDP but only from 1999 onwards. To contain health expenditure in 1998 to some Ptas 175 billion above the increase implied by the growth of nominal GDP, the agreement reduces the number of drugs eligible for reimbursement by social security and lowers the cost of a range of drugs through an accord with the pharmaceutical industry. Nevertheless, these measures are not sufficient to fully cover the cost of the increase in health expenditure in 1998, with the residual financing (Ptas 90 billion) coming from the state budget and savings obtained through the reform of temporary disability payments (see Chapter III). During 1994-97, a similar agreement was relatively successful in containing the growth of health expenditure financed from the central budget equal to that of nominal GDP.

38. The primary balance and the cyclically adjusted primary balance are almost of equal magnitude since the output gap is projected to be broadly closed by 1999.

39. The Stability and Growth Pact provides for large fines for members whose deficit exceeds 3 per cent of GDP in any one year. The fines are waived in "exceptional circumstances", of which one case is a 2 per cent or more decline in GDP during the year of the fiscal slippage.

40. The moderate growth scenario of the 1998-2000 convergence programme contains a much milder slowdown in activity, which does not draw out the precariousness of the budget in the longer run. Annual GDP growth slows to an average of 2.6 per cent, and as a result the general government deficit is projected to fall to 2.4 per cent of GDP in 2000.

41. If Spanish output is growing at its potential, estimated to be 2.7 per cent, fines would be paid up to a nearly 5 per cent drop in output growth with larger drops triggering the above-mentioned exceptional circumstances clause. If the budget elasticity is 0.6, then the structural deficit would need to provide room equivalent to 2.8 per cent of GDP.

42. For a detailed analysis of the Spanish health and pension systems, see the *OECD Economic Survey of Spain* (1996).

43. The Spanish courts ruled that the Government should provide compensation of some Ptas 500 billion (0.6 per cent of 1997 GDP) to victims who had purchased in 1981 what subsequently proved to be toxic colza oil.

44. Before the 1994 reform, firms were required, in practice, to incur losses for two years before layoff proceedings could begin.

45. Eight out of every 10 dismissals are the result of an agreement between the worker and the employer, with one out of every 10 resulting from a labour court decision and the remainder resulting from mediation. The average dismissal cost is more than twice as large for dismissals arising from mutual agreements than those resulting from the courts' decision. Moreover, almost ¾ of judges' decisions were for the employee (this ratio excludes cases pending or cases where conciliation was reached). A new arbitration mechanism (approved in January 1996) could be useful in reducing the cost of dismissal procedures.

46. These financial incentives replace broadly equivalent ones, with the exception that the new ones are also extended to the case of a conversion from a fixed-term contract for males below age 45. The previously existing financial incentives mainly consisted of lump sum payments to firms in the event a worker was hired under an indefinite contract and were targeted to workers above age 45, the long-term unemployed, women under-represented in their profession, the youth under training contracts and handicapped persons. At the same time, the employers' social contribution rate for individuals unemployed under certain fixed-term contracts (*contratos temporales de fomento de empleo*) and either above age 45 or long-term unemployed were also reduced.

47. Specifically, fixed-term contracts permitted for "determined work or service" can henceforth be limited by collective agreements, and fixed-term contracts for "eventualities of production" are limited to 6 months out of every 12 months, though collective agreements can raise this limit to three-quarters of a 18 month period. Previously such fixed-term contracts could be renewed for 3 years.

48. The 1997 reform filled the gaps in workers' contracts arising from the suppression of the *Ordenanzas laborales*. The *Ordenanzas laborales* are a series of rules and regulations which limit the responsibilities and tasks which members of different trades and guilds are allowed to perform. These rules have been progressively abolished. The 1994 reform provided the option to introduce contract terms previously covered by the *Ordenanzas laborales* by agreements reached in the context of collective bargaining.

49. A review of collective bargaining agreements signed since 1994 indicates that clauses on geographical and functional mobility have doubled, as have clauses specifying commitments to training. However, there has also been increased recourse to stimuli to early retirement and wage indexation.

50. Temporary disability benefits, which amounted to around 0.8 per cent of GDP in 1996, are reportedly used fraudulently in many instances. This scheme often gives rise to higher benefits than the unemployment insurance and allows the duration of benefits to be lengthened. The 1998 budget law introduced the possibility for doctors from the social security administration (INSS) and mutual insurance companies to review the health situation of the beneficiaries.

51. The Toledo Pact is a set of recommendations for the reform of the pension system presented by a Parliamentary commission in March 1995 (*OECD Economic Survey of Spain,* 1996)

52. The calculation assumes that wages, adjusted for inflation, increase by $1^1/_2$ per cent per year. The report accompanying the draft law to Parliament (*Memoria Economica del Anteproyecto del Ley*) estimates a $3^1/_2$ per cent reduction in the average pension based on the historical development in wages.

53. There exist 11 separate ceilings for contributions depending on the classification of work. Unifying the contributions ceiling is estimated by the authorities to affect only about 5 per cent of total contributors.

54. Specifically, eligibility for a pension will henceforth require having contributed to social security for two out of the last 15 years prior to the receipt of a pension. Previously the regulations specified 2 years out of the last 10 years. Early retirement provisions are extended to all workers with 40 years of contributions with the annual reduction in pension reduced to 7 per cent per year compared with 8 per cent for other eligible candidates (previously only workers who were in the system prior to 1967 could retire before the age of 65) as well as to special cases of workers including those affected by enterprise restructuring agreements.

55. The estimated impact on the state budget is about 1.3 per cent of GDP (based on the 1997 Budget), though this magnitude will partly depend on the definition of non-contributory pensions. The legislation provides clarifications but leaves open the issue of how the supplement to a minimum pension will be classified.

56. If no new taxes are raised, *ceteris paribus,* on a consolidated general government basis, budgetary imbalances would net out (a surplus on the contributory scheme would offset borrowing to finance the non-contributory scheme). The introduction of new taxes to finance the non-contributory schemes would have a positive impact on the general government deficit. However, a build up of a reserve fund for the contributory scheme may delay essential reforms to this not yet mature but generous pension system.

57. In the recent past, indexation has been in line with inflation (adjusted *ex post* for the excess of realised inflation above target). In 1997, however, inflation was lower than expected and the benefit of the overperformance relative to the initial target (the difference between 2.6 per cent and 2 per cent, the 12 month inflation rate in December) will be compensated by providing for a less-than-full pension indexation to projected 1998 inflation. This decision reflects the fact that the law was not yet applicable in 1997.

159

58. The 1996 *OECD Economic Survey of Spain* contains a detailed analysis of the pension system.

59. The maturation of the system will be somewhat mitigated by 1967 legislation which provides retirees until 2010 a bonus inversely related to their years of contributions.

60. Until the recent reform, individuals registered with the system from 1967 had the right to retire prior to age 65 with a reduced pension (the reduction is 8 per cent for every year before the age of 65). For the individuals who entered the system after 1967, a pension cannot be received until the age of 65 unless retirement is not voluntary but due to special labour market conditions, such as a firm closure (see footnote 54).

61. Approximately 60 per cent of invalidity pensions are granted to individuals age 50-65. Their generosity is due to the fact that invalidity pensions provide 70-100 per cent of the final wage depending on the degree of invalidity and, in contrast with old-age pensions, are free of income tax.

62. The September 1997 reform which limits exemptions on contributions should provide similar short-term benefits. Specifically, exemptions from social security contributions are limited to 20 per cent of the minimum wage. Previously, exemptions amounted to an estimated 14 per cent of wages.

63. Minimum pension supplements are means tested but their abuse is reportedly widespread. Approximately one in three pensioners receive such supplements, which amount to 10 per cent of pension expenditures.

64. The Toledo pact also contained recommendations for regulations across regimes to be made more uniform, especially as concerns their contribution rates. The current reform has not addressed this issue.

65. The OECD simulations covering the period to 2070 – undertaken prior to the 1997 reform – indicate that pension expenditures would accelerate rapidly from the beginning of the next century and a gap of the order of 9 per cent of GDP would eventually open up between expenditures and revenues by 2050. The magnitude of the disequilibrium is significantly higher after the contributions of the unemployed provided from the Budget (through the employment agency, INEM) are deducted from total contributions, as they originate from general taxation resources.

66. This simple condition is derived from the equation setting total expenditures equal to total receipts.

67. Three of the 17 regions did not approve the new financing model and thus continue to be ruled under the previous 1991-96 agreement. These are: Andalucia, Castilla la Mancha and Extremadura. In addition, there are two regions, Navarra and the Basque country, that had more economic and political responsibilities transferred much earlier. In particular, they have powers over the collection of a number of taxes and over setting their rates.

68. The regional authorities were also made responsible for their investment decisions on infrastructure development, regional police and some welfare services.

69. For example, the current maximum marginal rate of 56 per cent is divided into the component kept and controlled by the State – 85 per cent (*i.e.* 47.6 per cent) – and the component which the regional government keeps – 15 per cent (*i.e.* 8.4 per cent) which can be increased by a maximum of 20 per cent to 10.08 or reduced by up to 20 per cent to 6.72 per cent.

70. See Ezquiaga I. and F. Garcia (1997), "Una evaluacion del sistema de financiacion autonomica para el quinquenio 1997-2001" in Cuadernos de Informacion Economica, No. 120-121, March-April 1997.

71. The set of three guarantees are the following:

    i) if a region's personal income tax revenues grow more slowly than the national income, the central government will compensate through transfers up to 90 per cent of the rate of growth of the State personal income tax collection;

    ii) if the growth of a region's total revenues is inferior to 90 per cent of that of the other regions, the Government will make up the difference;

    iii) if the level of financing per capita falls below 90 per cent of the national average over the 5 year period, the government will make up the difference, up to 90 per cent of the national average.

72. Its main recipients are less developed regions, *i.e.* those with an income per head below 75 per cent of the EU average.

73. Among the existing constraints on the regions' borrowing is the possibility for the central government to deny permission to issue new bonds or borrow in foreign currencies to regions that had exceeded a ratio between debt service and current revenues of 25 per cent.

74. Seven regional governments out of 17 have accepted responsibility for their health care system.

75. See *1996 OECD Economic Survey of Spain.*

76. In 1993, wholesale prices had been reduced by 3 per cent and retail margins were cut through an accord reached between representatives of the pharmaceutical industry and INSALUD.

77. *Plan de garantía por demora quirúrgica.*

78. The growth in health expenditure in any region can exceed that of GDP, however the excess has to be financed from regional resources.

79. The liberalisation of professional services basically entailed the elimination of required minimum professional fees and introduced the requirement for a single national membership in place of regional ones.

80. During the past 10 years the price of urban land has increased, on average, by 250 per cent compared with an increase of 170 per cent increase in the CPI. The price of land in the large cities has increased by much more, with Madrid's real estate prices having increased by over 400 per cent over the same period.

81. There are three types of land: land which can not be urbanised, land which can be urbanised, and urban land (with the respective share of total land being 88 per cent, 6 per cent and 6 per cent). The decision for the transformation to land which can be urbanised rests with the regional governments (following a recent constitutional court decision), while authority for urban planing and individual licensing rests with local government. The percentage of total land classified for urban use is low compared with other countries (*e.g.* 14 per cent in the Netherlands).

82. The 1985 Water Act categorised the use of water and established an order of preference: *i)* town supply; *ii)* irrigation and other agricultural uses; *iii)* electricity production; *iv)* other

industrial uses; *v)* aquaculture; *vi)* recreational uses; *vii)* water transportation; and *viii)* others. For further details, see OECD (1997*a*), *Environmental performance review of Spain.*

83. An enterprise is considered public by the Spanish authorities when: *i)* the general government holds directly or indirectly at least a 50 per cent share, or *ii)* the general government does not hold a majority stake but it has an effective control on the operation of the enterprise. The analysis of public enterprises covers the enterprises that have been so-defined until their privatisation during the past couple of years.

84. The database used is the Bank of Spain's survey of Spanish enterprises, which covers a representative sample of the larger private enterprises and most of the public enterprises (the private and public enterprises surveyed comprise, respectively, 19 per cent and 10 per cent of total non-financial enterprise value added at factor cost).

85. The sample's implicit estimate for private sector compensation is likely biased upwards by its focus on large firms. Another indication of the sample bias is the fact that only 15 per cent of the workers in the sample have fixed term contracts compared with an economy-wide ratio of approximately one in three.

86. Sources: Spain, EPA survey; France, INSEE, "Répertoire des entreprises contrôlées majoritairement par l'État", 1995 data; UK: Office for National Statistics, *Economic trends,* Annual supplement, 1995 data.

87. Calculated from the Banco de España's database (Central de Balances).

88. Estimates from *La Negociación Colectiva en las Grandes Empresas*, various issues.

89. A more complete measure of the burden on the deficit, though one which is difficult to construct, would include dividends from profitable enterprises and compare the net flow from a firm's balance sheet (dividends minus transfers) against a benchmark rate of return.

90. These include the debt of the AIE (Ptas 1 000 billion), of a previous grouping of enterprises, INI, (Ptas 200 billion), the train monopoly RENFE (Ptas 400 billion) and the public television station RTVE (Ptas 600 billion).

91. *Comisión de Seguimiento de la Negociación Colectiva de las Empresas Publicas.*

92. In the 1997 State budget, transfers to public enterprises (operating subsidies and capital transfers) amounted to Ptas 525 billion compared with a estimated Ptas 935 billion in 1996. The 1998 budget projects a cut in transfers to public enterprises and entities to Ptas 517 billion.

93. Partly as a result, total new borrowing guaranteed by the State increased to Ptas 525 billion in 1997 (0.7 per cent of GDP) and Ptas 345 billion in 1998 (0.4 per cent of GDP). The AIE was allowed to borrow Ptas 275 billion from the SEPI (money coming from privatisation proceeds and SEPI's projected operating profits) or to borrow under State guarantee.

94. The former AIE's losses were projected to be Ptas 180 billion in 1997 ($^1/_4$ per cent of GDP). The accumulated liabilities of the AIE and INI amount to about 2 per cent of GDP.

95. For a complete description, see Ballesteros Pinto (1997).

96. For profit making enterprises, wages are to increase in line with the official projection for inflation as measured by the CPI (forecast at 2.1 per cent in 1998). For loss-makers, wage increases in nominal terms are allowed if they reflect productivity gains but should in any case remain lower than the official inflation projection.

97. The publicly controlled bank Argentaria – whose full privatisation will be undertaken in 1998 – has significant holdings in telecommunications and electricity.

98. Recently, Caja de Madrid purchased 5 per cent of Telefonica and Caja de Cataluña 3 per cent of Repsol.

99. Recent changes to accounting and tax legislation reduced equity participation limits – for consolidating revenues from shareholdings and eliminating the double imposition of dividends – to 3 per cent and 5 per cent, respectively.

100. For example, though conclusions are obviously difficult to draw, some studies have shown that profitability is lower in the French enterprises which form part of the "noyaux durs".

101. The authorities hold "golden shares" in Telefonica, Repsol and Argentaria. Their duration is 10 years in the case of Telefonica and Repsol and a maximum of four years for Argentaria. A golden share is also envisaged for Tabacalera.

102. The Endesa group refers to Endesa and the electricity companies it controls; among other companies Fecsa and Sevillana, in which Endesa bought controlling shares in late 1996. The Endesa group accounts for almost half of the electricity generation and about 40 per cent of distribution in Spain. The corresponding figures for Iberdrola are 36 per cent of generation and 39 per cent of distribution.

103. Total capacity is much higher – about 170 per cent – but hydro plants are intermittent and not necessarily available at peak demand.

104. In 1996, the structure of installed capacity was divided between energy sources as follows: hydro (35 per cent), nuclear (16 per cent), coal (23 per cent), gas (17 per cent), imports (1 per cent) and autoproducers/co-generators (7 per cent). Production shares reflect costs (*i.e.* cheaper base capacity is used more often): hydro (22 per cent), nuclear (34 per cent), coal (32 per cent), gas (1 per cent), imports (2 per cent) and autoproduction (9 per cent).

105. OECD (1997*b*), International Energy Agency, *Energy Prices and Taxes*, Paris. These calculations are adjusted using purchasing power parity exchange rates and are based on average prices (total payments divided by output). Eurostat data are based on listed prices and rank Spanish electricity prices in the middle of the OECD. The IEA data implicitly takes account of seasonal discounts, specific contracts and discounts for interruption and are thus considered a more appropriate basis for an international comparison.

106. The construction of five nuclear plants was stopped in 1982, which resulted in a cost of Ptas 729 billion (about 1 per cent of 1996 GDP).

107. About one-half of coal sector subsidies is financed from the electricity tariff. This charge adds about Ptas 0.75 per kWh to the final price (5 per cent). The Ministry of Industry decides each year the percentage to be added to the tariff. It is collected by OFICO (*Oficina de Compensaciones de la Energia Electrica*) and distributed by the National Energy Commission.

108. There exists a complicated compensation system which results in large intercompany payments in order to compensate for the large differences in the fuel mix of electricity companies. For example, Endesa has a much larger than average share of coal generation while Iberdrola's generation mix is more heavily invested in hydroelectric production.

109. The main elements of the EC directive ("Council and Parliament Directive EC 96/92 of 19 December 1996 concerning common rules for the internal market in electricity") applies to the authorisation of new generators, third-party access to the grid network, and the liberalisation of the consumer market (in 1999, to purchasers with annual consumption greater than 40 Gwh, with this floor falling in 2000 to 20 Gwh and in 2003 to 9 Gwh).

110. The price reductions are far more rapid for the industrial sector than for small consumers, with the former declining almost twice as fast as the latter.

111. The commercial side of the pool will be run by a power exchange and will be separate from the technical side, (*e.g.* dispatch) to be run by an independent system operator.

112. There is obviously a high degree of uncertainty surrounding the calculation of the stranded costs. In the case of Spain, these were calculated as the difference between the actual value of investments and the value of investment if more efficient technology were to be used. The assumed switch in technology is estimated to permit generation costs to fall from Ptas 9 per kWh to Ptas 6 per kWh, which implies a reduction in final prices of the order of 20 per cent. The distribution of the stranded costs between firms is a complicated calculation based (*prorata*) on the distribution formula for standard costs under the existing legislation (*Marco Legal Estable*). *Inter alia*, this formula takes account of inter-firm differences in generating technology. As a result, the Endesa Group and Iberdrola could receive, respectively, 60 per cent and 30 per cent of the fixed component of the stranded costs. The value of the stranded costs will be reviewed in 2002.

113. Almost all gas is imported, with an increasingly large share coming through the pipeline connection with Maghreb countries, which became operational in November 1996. The large infrastructure investment over recent years has resulted in a large accumulation of debt by the Gas Natural/Enagas monopoly.

114. OECD (1997*b*), International Energy Agency, *Energy Prices and Taxes*, Paris.

115. The price of natural gas is freely negotiable for certain industrial sectors; *e.g.* electricity generation and the production of primary materials.

116. See Armstrong, Cowan, and Vickers, "Regulatory Reform: Economic Analysis and British Experience".

117. Legislation permitting the placement of pumps at retail outlets has led to large price reductions, but these have been of a temporary nature and linked to purchases from the outlet stores.

118. In addition, following the truckers strike at end 1996, the trucker's association was promised the possibility to negotiate diesel prices directly with wholesalers.

119. See OECD 1997*c* for further details.

120. Total wages per mainline remained lower than the OECD average in 1995. See OECD (1997*c*).

121. In May 1997, Telefonica launched a new voluntary early retirement plan for employees aged 55 or more. It aims to cut employment by 20 000 by 2001. This reduction would add to a 15 per cent cut in the workforce during the past four years.

122. A majority share of Retevison (70 per cent) was sold in July 1997 to Endesa and the Italian communications company STET.

123. Telefonica shares were sold in four tranches over a long period dating back to the mid-1980s. In February 1997, the State offered its remaining 21 per cent of the capital. The State nevertheless, kept a "golden share" which imposes for a 10 year period prior government approval with respect to a limited number of fundamental transactions, including the acquisition of 10 per cent of the company's stock and the sale of material assets.

124. Specifically, prices will be proposed by Telefonica, examined by both the Government (General Directorate for Economic Policy) and the regulatory authorities, and approved by the CMT.

125. In March 1997, Telefonica asked for a reorganisation of its tariffs which was approved by the Government and will be effective in 1998. Local communications prices and the telephone monthly service fee will increase by 12 per cent and 200 Ptas respectively (local calls amount for 80 per cent of telephone call charges).

126. To reduce the employment consequences on handling staff employed by Iberia, new handling operators were required to absorb part of Iberia's employees at prevailing conditions.

127. The 1992 capital injection was accompanied by a complete programme of restructuring and investment. The second package also forced Iberia to divest from some of its large Latin American investments (Aerolinas Argentinas and Austral).

128. A recent McKinsey survey stressed that certain categories of personnel in Iberia were paid above their international counterparts. A cost analysis established by Iberia also pointed that the cost per available seat kilometre was more than 40 per cent lower in private Spanish companies.

129. Under Spanish law, a company must experience profits for three years before it can go public. However, a 10 per cent share is expected to be sold to British Airways and American Airline (5 per cent each) under their strategic agreement.

130. Any licensed EU carrier now has access to the routes between all airports in the EU regardless of destination or point of departure, but access is dependent on slot availability. Earlier, Member States regulated the sharing of capacity on each route and prices were fixed bilaterally.

131. See OECD (1997d). In Gatwick and Heathrow in the United Kingdom, tariffs vary by time of day and by season and are based upon a flat rate irrespective of aircraft size. Athens also initiated differential landing charges in 1991 with an additional 25 per cent charge during the period June to September for landings between 11.00 and 17.00.

132. There also exists a separate national narrow gauge railway company, FEVE, though it is much smaller in terms of market shares and State transfers received.

133. Preston John and Chris Nash, *European Railway Comparisons and the Future of RENFE*, FEDEA, Madrid, June 1994.

134. The European Commission Directive 91/440 requires that infrastructure be separated from operations in rail services, at least by separate accounting. European Conference of Ministries of Transport (1997) outlines policies in different countries.

135. Similarly in Mexico, the three main railroad sections have recently been opened to concession auctioning (see the *1998 OECD Economic Survey* of Mexico).

136. In December 1996, EU countries decided to delay the full deregulation of postal services up to 2003 and established common rules for the development of postal services. The only segment of the market which will remain protected until then will be items of domestic and international correspondence weighing less than 350 grams and/or costing less than five times the basic tariff. The size of the protected sector will be reviewed in the year 2000.

137. The protected activities include inter-urban letters weighing less than 350 grams, international mail, the issuance of stamps and mail money orders.

138. Specifically, coal produced in publicly owned mines (Hunosa and Figaredo) costs between Ptas 29 500 and 41 600 per tonne compared with an average of Ptas 12 500 for privately owned Spanish mines and Ptas 5 100 per tonne for imported coal (c.i.f.). The all inclusive price of imported coal for electricity firms ranges from Ptas 6 200 to 8 400.

139. In accordance with EU decisions on coal subsidies, the price of coal will gradually be reduced to the market level. The price of Spanish coal is based on the international price plus electricity companies' avoided investment costs from burning Spanish coal rather than imported coal.

140. The EU proposal would extend shipbuilding assistance from 1 January 1999 to 31 December 2000. It would permit aid up to 9 per cent of the value of the contract, while aid for research development would not be limited. The EU proposal has been prompted by the continuing delay in the final approval of the 1994 OECD agreement on shipbuilding by the United States.

141. OECD (1997e), *The OECD Report on Regulatory Reform.*

142. The weights applied to the various components of price and the aggregation across sectors are based on the latest available input-output matrix for Spain (1990).

143. The coefficients for the second-round multiplier effects are based on those of the larger OECD countries' estimates and thus produce a multiplier of a similar order of magnitude with these countries. This assumption is not expected to greatly influence the estimated outcome.

144. The index is derived from the sum of the squares of the market shares.

145. Under the 1992 Horizontal Merger guidelines used in the United States by the Federal Trade Commission, the Department of Justice and the Federal Energy Regulatory Commission, a market is highly concentrated if the HHI is above 1 800 (which corresponds to between five and six firms with equal market share. Frankena, Mark, *Market Power in the Spanish Electricity Power Industry*, March 1997.

146. CNSE and *Tribunal de Defensa de la Competencia.*

147. Sectoral data is not available for Greece.

148. The main adjustment for Spain is the inclusion of the self-employed in the harmonised estimates.

149. Turbulence would include data on firm closure rates. Very little is known about the true firm closure rates (*i.e.* the percentage of firms who cease trading each year) and the only study of firm survival rates, suggested a survival rate of 70 per cent after the first three years (ENSR 1995). Because of the arithmetic link between start-up, closure and survival rates, such a high survival rate could only be consistent with a low start-up rate.

150. These steps are set out in detail on the website of the Ministry of Economics, http://www.mcx.es/pyme/.

151. The percentage of businesses that are incorporated varies from almost 10 per cent in the United States and Germany to just under 50 per cent in Japan and the Netherlands (OECD, 1994*b*).

152. Of responding firms, 19 per cent had 1-10 employees, 36 per cent had 11-25 employees and 20 per cent had 26 to 50 employees.

153. Venture capital in Spain was originally developed as a government tool for allocating money for regional development. Reflecting these origins in 1986, 18 out of the 22 venture capital investment bodies were primarily funded by central or regional governments.

154. The lifting of similar restrictions in the United States in the early 1970s led to a major inflow of funds into venture capital (see US survey). Overall, Spanish institutional investors held only 6 per cent of their portfolios in (listed) shares in 1996.

155. Most venture capital is being invested in industrial products and services, agriculture/fishing, leisure and other non-financial services (but not transportation). (Marti, 1997).

156. In the United States, for example, such investment capital is estimated to be at least twice as important as formal venture capital and in the Netherlands and Australia it is estimated to be around the same size as the formal market.

157. The forfaitaire system (taxation based on observable physical characteristics) can be chosen by unincorporated businesses with less than two staff and turnover less than Ptas 7.9 million. The standard flat rate applies to unincorporated businesses with less than 12 staff and turnover less than Ptas 50 million. Under the standard flat rate, unincorporated businesses can deduct wages and a flat rate to cover general expenses (which varies between sectors).

158. Previously, capital gains tax applied to investments, where the assets had been held for at least one year, and the capital gains paid were reduced for each subsequent year that the assets are held, although they were indexed to inflation.

159. Losses can also be carried backwards for up to 3 years in the United States and the Netherlands.

160. It is often argued that micro-enterprises rely to a significant extent on factors such as reputation and local networking for enforcing contracts, rather than relying on recourse through the judicial process.

161. Under Spanish civil law, protection against abusive contract provisions for businesses relies on the provisions embodied in the 100 year old civil code.

162. More than half of these R&D activities are located within the regions of Madrid (40 per cent) and Cataluña (27 per cent).

163. The *Sociedad para el Desarrollo del Diseño y la Innovacion* (DDI), whose aim is to improve the quality, the image, the design and the competitiveness of products, has financed around 1 000 projects since its creation in 1992.

164. The *Plan de Actuacion Tecnologico Industrial* managed by the Ministry of Industry supported 637 projects in 1995 at a cost of Ptas 11.6 billion and the *Centro para el Desarrollo Tecnologico* co-financed 271 technological development projects in 1995.

165. Projects were funded up to 75 per cent.

166. Projects were funded up to 50 per cent.

167. While a similar proportion improved their relations with their clients; the subsidy/investment ratio was 1 to 6.7; the proportion of participating firms which regard their commercial position as ''better than their competitors'' increased from 16 to 38 per cent while firms that consider they have been able to improve their technological position have risen from 5 to 36 per cent.

Glossary of acronyms

ACESA	Aguas de la Cuenca del Ebro (Public entity responsible for water work)
AENOR	Asociacion Española de Normalizacion y Certificacion
AIE	Agencia Industrial del Estado (Public holding controlling loss-making industrial public enterprises up to 1997)
ALP	Activos Liquidos en manos del Publico (M3 plus other liquid assets)
ALPF	Broad monetary aggregate (ALP plus mutual funds)
BBV	Banco Bilboa Vizcaya
BCH	Banco Central Hispano
CASA	Defence company controlled by the State
CCAA	Regional Government (Comunidad Autonoma)
CLH	Compania Logistica de Hidrocarburos (Company controlling oil storage capacities and the pipeline)
CMT	Comisión del Mercado de las Telecomunicaciones (Regulatory body for telecommunications)
CNSE	Comisión Nacional del Sistema Electrico (Regulatory body for electricity)
CSI	Corporacion Siderurgica Integral (Steel company)
DGPE	Direccion General del Patrimonio del Estado
GIF	Gestor de Infraestructuras Ferroviarias (Public entity responsible for several new railway works)
HHI	Herfindal Hirschamn Index
HUNOSA	Coal mine entreprises controlled by the State
INEM	Instituto Nacional de Empleo
INE	Instituto Nacional de Estadística
INI	Instituto Nacional de Industria (Public holding which controlled industrial public enterprises up to 1995)
OFICO	Oficina de Compensaciones de la Energia Electrica
PMI	Programa de Modernizacion Industrial
Repsol	Oil Company
RENFE	National Train Company

RTVE	National Radio and Television Company
SEPI	Sociedad Estatal de Participaciones Industriales (Public holding controlling industrial public enterprises)
SEPPA	Sociedad Estatal de Participaciones Patrimoniales (agent for privatising firms controlled by DGPE)
TISA	Telefonica Internacional S.A. (International call subsidiary of Telefonica)

Bibliography

AENOR (1997), Asociación Española de Normalizacion y Certificacion, Survey quoted in *La Vanguardia,* 15 September.

Armstrong, Mark, Simon Cowan and John Vickers (1994), ''Regulatory Reform: Economic Analysis and British Experience'', MIT Press, Cambridge, Massachussetts.

Ballesteros Pinto, J.F. (1997), ''La politica de infraestructuras en los PGE-97'', *Boletín Económico de ICE,* No. 2527, 16-22 December 1996.

Bank of Spain (1997), *Inflation Report.*

Buesa, Mikel and Jose Molero (1997), ''Evaluacion del plan de promocion de diseño industrial'', *Universidad Compultense de Madrid.*

Casado, Juan and Fernando (1996), ''Estrategia y resultados de la empresa familiar en España'', in *Economia Industrial,* No. 310, 1996/IV, Ministerio de Industria y Energia, Madrid.

CB, Consulting survey, quoted in *Cinco Dias,* ''Informatica para Empresas'', 18 September 1997.

Celada, F. (1991), ''Los sistemas productivos locales de caracter industrial'', *Area y Sistema,* Madrid.

Centre Européen des Entreprises à Participation Publique, CEEP (1994), ''Les entreprises à participation publique dans l'Union européenne'', *Annales du CEEP 1994.*

Costa Campi, Maria Teresa *et al.* (1993), ''Cooperation entre empresas y systemas productivas locales en España'', IMPI, Ministero de Industria.

Cuervo Garcia, Alvaro (1997), ''Las privatizaciones en España'', *Cuadernos de información económica,* No. 119.

ENSR (1995), ''The European Observatory for SMEs'', *Third Annual Report.*

Esquiaga, I. and F. Garcia (1997), ''Una evaluacion del sistema de financiacion autonomica para el quinquenio 1997-2001'', *Cuadernos de Informacion Economica,* No. 120-121, March-April 1997.

European Commission (1995), *Green Paper on Innovation,* Bulletin of the European Union Supplement 5/95, Brussels.

European Commission (1997), *Convergence Programme of Spain – An assessment,* DG II, Brussels, April 18.

European Conference of Ministers of Transport (1997), ''The separation of Operations from Infrastructure in the Provision of Railway Services'', Round Table 103.

Eurostat (1995), ''Enterprises in Europe'', *Fourth Report,* Luxembourg.

Ferreras Diez, Pedro (1997), "Antecedentes y lineas estrategicas del plan de privatizationes", *Cuadernos de informacion economica*, No. 119.

Fonfria Mesa (1996), "Factores organisativos en el desarollo tecnologico de las PYMES", *Economia Industrial*, No. 310, 1996/IV, p. 163.

Frankena, Mark (1997), "Market power in the Spanish Electricity Power Industry".

Fundacion COTEC (1997*a*), "Informe COTEC, Tecnologia y innovation en España", Chapter VI, Madrid.

Fundacion COTEC (1997*b*), "Documento para el debate sobre el Sistema de Innovacion", Libro verde, Madrid.

García, J., P.J. Hernández, A. López (1997), "Differencias salariales entre sector publico y sector privado en España", *Papeles de Economia Española*, No. 72.

Grant Thornthon International Business Strategies Ltd. (1996), *European Business Survey*, May, United Kingdom.

Ibarra, Josep-Antoni (1995), "La informalidad en España: un viaje hacia la institucionalizacion de la economia oculta", *Boletín de Estudios Económicos*, Vol. L, No. 155, pp. 263-278, August.

IGAE, *Cuentas de las empresas publicas*, 1993-94.

IMPI (1996), "La pequena y mediana empresa en España 1995", *Informe annual*, Madrid.

INE (1997*a*), *Encuesta sobre innovacion tecnologica en las empresas*, 1994, Madrid.

INE (1997*b*), *Encuesta de Población activa, Resultados detallados*, Primer trimestre.

La Porta, Rafael, Florencio Lopez-de Silane, Andrei Shleifer and W. Robert (1996), "Law and Finance", NBER Working Paper, 5661.

López López, Teresa and Alfonso Utrilla de la Hoz (1997), "La configuracion del sector publico empresarial en España", *Cuadernos de información economica*, No. 119.

Marti Pellon, José (1997), "El capital Inversion en España : Estudios y Monografias" Editorial Civitas, Madrid.

Martin, P. John (1996), "Measures of replacement rates for the purpose of international comparisons: a note", *OECD Economic Studies,* No. 26, pp. 99-115.

Ministerio de Economía y Hacienda, *La negociacíon colectiva en las grandes empresas*, various issues.

OECD (1994*a*), *The Jobs Study*, Paris.

OECD (1994*b*), *Taxation and Small Business*.

OECD (1996), *Economic Survey of Spain*.

OECD (1997*a*), *Environmental performance review of Spain*.

OECD (1997*b*), International Energy Agency, *Energy Prices and Taxes*, various issues.

OECD (1997*c*), *Communications Outlook*.

OECD (1997*d*), *The Future of International Air Transport Policy: Responding to Global Change.*

OECD (1997*e*), *The OECD Report on Regulatory Reform.*

OECD (1997*f*), *Privatisation: recent trends*, Financial Market Trends, No. 66, March.

OECD (1998), *Economic Survey of Mexico.*

Pampillón Olmedo, R. (1997), ''Concurrencia y transparencia en las privatizaciones en España'', *Boletín económico de ICE*, No. 2546.

Preston, J. and C. Nash (1994), ''European Railway Comparisons and the Future of RENFE'', Documento de Trabajo 94-09, FEDEA.

Tribunal for the Defence of Competition (1995), *Competition in Spain: Appraisal of Progress to date and some new recommendations 1995,* Madrid.

Viñals, J. and Juan F. Jimeno (1997), ''El mercado de trabajo español y la unión económica y monetaria europea'', *Banco de España*, Servicio de Estudios, Documento de Trabajo No. 9717.

Yarrow, G. (1995), ''Airline Deregulation and privatisation in the UK'', *The Economic Analysis*, No. 143, December.

Annex I

Equilibrium in a pay-as-you-go pension system

The condition necessary for a pay-as-you-go system to be in equilibrium (receipts equal to payments) at any moment in time, is:

(1) $C \times W \times E = B \times W \times P$

where C is the effective contribution rate,

W is the average wage,

E is the number of contributors,

B is the effective replacement rate for an old-age pension in the general regime,*
and P is the number of old-age pensioners.

Equation (1) can be re-written as:

(2) $C/B = d$ where d is the ratio of old-age pensioners to contributors.

Based on this simple equation, several important inferences can be made concerning the Spanish pension system:

- With the ratio of old-age pensions to contributors currently standing at about 55 per cent (a ratio which is much higher than the old-age dependency ratio due to the large number of early retirees), and the effective contribution rate and effective old-age replacement rate are estimated to be 25 per cent and 35 per cent, respectively, the equilibrium condition is consistent with the fact that the pay-as-you-go system is in surplus (25/35 > 0.55).
- However, the demographics are projected to deteriorate, with the dependency ratio projected to rise from 25 per cent currently to 67 per cent by 2050 (according to World Bank population projections which indicate that the population will decline by an average of $^2/_3$ per cent per year over the next half century). In this situation, the replacement rates would have to fall over time to maintain equilibrium, and by 2050 it would have to fall to the obviously untenable rate of 17 per cent. The adjustment would have to be greater to the extent that the system matures.

---

* The effective replacement rate is derived from the ratio of the average pension to the average wage. When pensions are indexed to wages, the effective replacement rate is equal to the replacement rate defined as the ratio of the value of the pension at the time of retirement to the last wage.

This result reflects the fundamental drawback of a pure pay-as-you-go system; *i.e.*, the potential for large inter-generational transfers when the population growth declines or turns negative. Until now, favourable demographics permitted the pay-as-you-go system to be in surplus. However, the current ageing of the Spanish population will put pressure on the pay-as-you-go-system. Further financial pressure will arise from the maturing of a generous pension system – with a larger share of individuals qualifying for pensions and many with higher replacement rates. Unlike a funded system, a pure pay-as-you-go system accumulates no savings which could be used when the demographics deteriorate. In many other countries in similar circumstances, the pay-as-you-go systems have accumulated a significant (though usually insufficient) amount of savings in anticipation of the population's ageing – in essence acting as a partially funded system. However in the case of Spain, accumulated savings do not exist as the system's surpluses have been used to cover the cost of the public health system. To the extent that adjustments to the system's regulations focus on the current contributors – rather than current pensioners – the younger generations would in essence be paying for two pensions; their own as well as that of the previous (older) generation.

Annex II

Calendar of main economic events

1995

November

Parliament rejects the Government's budget bill. The 1995 Budget Act is extended to 1996.

December

The Bank of Spain cuts its intervention rate by a quarter percentage point to 9 per cent.

The Government approves a series of budget measures supplementing the extension of the 1995 Budget Act to 1996.

1996

January

Entry into force of the new Corporate Tax Act which, *inter alia*, eliminates international double taxation of profits.

The registration tax for small motor vehicles is cut from 12 per cent to 7 per cent.

Entry into force of the new Commerce Act which, *inter alia*, gives regions (Autonomous Communities) the right to regulate the hours of businesses operating within their jurisdiction.

The Bank of Spain cuts its intervention rate by a quarter percentage point to 8.75 per cent.

Agreement between trade unions and employers on an out-of-court settlement of labour disputes. The agreement calls for compulsory mediation prior to strikes over proposed collective redundancies, geographical relocation of labour, substantial changes in working conditions or breaches of contract.

March

Legislative elections (on 3 March) give a relative majority to the *Partido Popular*.

The Bank of Spain cuts its intervention rate by half a percentage point to 8.25 per cent.

April

The Bank of Spain cuts its intervention rate by half a percentage point to 7.75 per cent.

The Government announces a Ptas 165 billion cut in government spending, including Ptas 140 billion in investment outlays.

May

The Bank of Spain cuts its intervention rate by a quarter percentage point to 7.50 per cent.

June

Announcement of a package of measures which amend the tax system and promote competition. Subsequently, Royal Decrees were adopted which, *inter alia*, permitted the voluntary revaluation of corporate balance sheets (along with a 3 per cent tax on the appreciation of book assets), eliminated the domestic double taxation of profits, simplified the individual income tax treatment of financial capital gains and liberalised many sectors (including telecommunications, land use, professional services and funeral services).

The Government presents a programme to modernise public enterprises.

July

The Government approves a plan to fight tax and social security fraud.

The Government approves Ptas 721 billion in additional appropriations to cover non-budgeted expenditure relating to prior financial years.

Increase in the excise tax on alcoholic beverages and tobacco.

August

Agreement between pharmaceutical laboratories and the Ministry of Health under which the laboratories pledge to surrender a portion of their profits to the State if drug consumption increases by more than 2.6 per cent.

September

Presentation of the draft State Budget for 1997.

Adoption of a new financing model for the Autonomous Communities, covering the period 1997-2001.

October

The Bank of Spain cuts its intervention rate by half a percentage point from 7.25 per cent to 6.75 per cent.

The Government and trade unions sign an agreement reforming the public pension system for the period 1997-2000.

The Council of Ministers approves a set of tax and administrative measures, including a reduction in the number of income tax brackets (from 15 to 10) applicable to 1997 taxes (payable in 1998), with 15 per cent of the revenue redistributed to the Autonomous Communities; introduction of administrative mechanisms to encourage private participation in the financing of infrastructure.

Amendment of the Water Act, *inter alia* to extend concessions for the construction, maintenance and operation of hydraulic facilities to 75 years.

Adoption of a decree on medicinal drug prices, to enter into force in March 1997, calling for a nearly 4 per cent decrease in those prices (reduction of the margins of pharmacists and wholesalers, reduction of the tax on drugs).

The Government transfers collection of special taxes on tobacco, alcohol and fuel to the Basque Country.

The Government announces a plan to combat social security and unemployment benefit fraud in 1997.

November

The Navarre General Council approves a cut in the corporate tax rate to 32.5 per cent (identical to the rate adopted by the three Basque Country General Councils), along with a number of tax deductions (to convert temporary jobs to permanent ones, for capital investment, etc.).

December

The Government announces a reduction in the profit tax for small and medium-sized enterprises.

The Bank of Spain cuts its intervention rate by half a percentage point from 6.75 per cent to 6.25 per cent.

Partial privatisation (3.81 per cent of the share capital) of Gas Natural.

The Government approves an average 3 per cent decrease in electricity prices for 1997.

Creation of a tax on insurance premiums.

1997

January

The Bank of Spain cuts its intervention rate by a quarter of a percentage point from 6.25 per cent to 6.00 per cent.

Launch of the partial privatisation (20.9 per cent of the share capital) of Telefónica via a public sale offer.

February

Adoption of a law encouraging development of generic drugs.

The Government approves a liberalisation plan covering, *inter alia*, telecommunications, land use and urban housing, energy and tobacco. A new system of incentives for private sector participation in infrastructure projects is also proposed.

The Government announces a reduction in the price of international telephone calls.

The Government accepts the principle of a transfer of administrative control over unemployment benefits to Catalonia.

March

The Bank of Spain cuts its intervention rate by a quarter of a percentage point from 6.00 per cent to 5.75 per cent.

April

The Government authorises Telefónica to reorganise telecommunications prices.

Launch of a new plan to encourage new car purchases (PREVER), through the use of a subsidy for scrapping old cars.

The Bank of Spain cuts its intervention rate by a quarter of a percentage point from 5.75 per cent to 5.50 per cent.

Employers and trade unions agree on a labour market reform which would encourage the creation of indefinite-term jobs. *Inter alia*, it calls for the introduction of a new type of indefinite-term contract with reduced redundancy costs for certain groups of workers, a new definition of the grounds for economic redundancies and proposals for improving the collective bargaining process.

Launch of the privatisation of Repsol via a public sale offer.

The Government approves the convergence programme for the Spanish economy for the period 1997-2000.

May

The Bank of Spain cuts its intervention rate by a quarter of a percentage point from 5.50 per cent to 5.25 per cent.

The Government approves as law the agreement on labour market reform between trade unions and employers, as well as a reform of financial incentives associated with new work contracts. It also introduces a set of income tax reductions for small and medium-sized enterprises.

June

Parliament adopts legislation for gradual reform of government pension schemes by the year 2000.

July

The Treasury creates stripped government debt issues.

September

The Government approves the tobacco price increase proposed by Tabacalera (a public enterprise).

The Government announces the dissolution of the holding company *Agencia Industrial del Estado* (AIE) and transfers former AIE firms, their employees and their debts to another holding company controlling public industrial enterprises – SEPI.

Launch of a public sale offer for Endesa.

Presentation of a draft State Budget for 1998.

October

The Bank of Spain cuts its intervention rate by a quarter of a percentage point from 5.25 per cent to 5.00 per cent.

Parliament approves the Electric Protocol, calling for major changes in the way competition in the sector is regulated.

November

The Government announces that it is taking a number of drugs, deemed of little therapeutic value, off the list of medicines reimbursed by the social security system, with a view to decrease wholesale drug prices.

December

Privatisation of a shipyard, Hijos de Barreras.

STATISTICAL ANNEX AND STRUCTURAL INDICATORS

Table A. **Main aggregates of national accounts**

Billion pesetas

	Current prices					1986 prices				
	1992	1993	1994	1995	1996[1]	1992	1993	1994	1995	1996[1]
I. Expenditure										
1. Private consumption	37 277	38 475	40 675	43 224	45 654	26 122	25 540	25 760	26 154	26 660
2. Government consumption	10 093	10 701	10 963	11 591	11 943	6 808	6 972	6 948	7 041	7 038
3. Gross fixed capital formation	12 889	12 092	12 767	14 402	14 712	9 618	8 601	8 753	9 474	9 540
4. Changes in stocks	488	6	190	299	429	405	5	148	228	314
5. Exports of goods and services	10 420	11 841	14 438	16 510	18 764	8 828	9 580	11 178	12 093	13 345
6. *less:* Imports of goods and services	12 063	12 180	14 333	16 246	17 840	11 605	11 001	12 250	13 327	14 328
7. Gross Domestic Product at market prices	59 104	60 935	64 700	69 780	73 662	40 176	39 697	40 537	41 663	42 569
II. Value added by sector										
1. Agriculture, forestry and fishing	2 071	2 161	2 146	2 041	2 583	1 979	1 971	1 772	1 537	1 888
2. Industry	14 353	14 339	15 332	16 828	17 468	11 065	10 717	11 203	11 737	11 821
3. Construction	5 054	4 957	5 150	5 736	5 720	3 059	2 891	2 938	3 134	3 045
4. Services	33 757	36 013	38 206	41 116	43 505	21 598	21 778	22 263	22 865	23 337
5. Net indirect taxes	3 871	3 464	3 865	4 057	4 385	2 476	2 340	2 363	2 391	2 477
III. National income										
1. Compensation of employees	28 982	30 065	30 563	32 055	33 936					
2. Gross operating surplus	25 027	26 430	29 121	32 439	33 846					
Households and private non profit institutions	14 990	16 221	17 442	18 959	20 016					
Corporate and quasi-corporate enterprises	9 420	9 525	10 929	12 656	12 982					
General government	617	684	750	824	848					
3. *less:* Consumption of fixed capital	6 452	6 974	7 425	7 952	8 629					
4. Net national income at factor cost	47 557	49 521	52 259	56 542	59 153					

1. Provisional data.

Source: National Institute of Statistics, *Contabilidad Nacional* (1997) and Bank of Spain, *Cuentas financieras* (1997).

Table B. **Income and outlay transactions of households**

Billion pesetas

	1989	1990	1991	1992	1993	1994	1995	1996[1]
1. Compensation of employees	20 942	24 012	26 827	28 982	30 065	30 563	32 055	33 936
2. Property and entrepreneurial income, gross	11 522	12 802	14 016	14 990	16 221	17 442	18 959	20 016
3. Other income from property	1 697	1 822	2 020	2 158	2 436	2 156	2 862	3 052
4. Current transfers	7 853	8 980	10 287	11 665	12 698	12 879	13 413	14 145
of which: Social security and social assistance benefits	6 617	7 723	8 966	10 229	11 314	11 446	11 768	12 401
5. Change in the actuarial reserves for pensions	262	267	337	170	203	95	115	144
6. Current receipts	42 276	47 883	53 487	57 965	61 623	63 135	67 404	71 293
7. Final consumption expenditure	28 367	31 303	34 269	37 277	38 475	40 675	43 224	45 654
8. Direct taxes on income and property	3 860	4 297	4 963	5 751	5 741	6 032	6 398	6 763
9. Current transfers	7 373	8 469	9 545	10 712	11 567	11 615	11 620	12 456
of which: Social security and social assistance contributions	5 637	6 457	7 249	8 198	8 670	8 979	8 931	9 668
10. Current disbursements	39 600	44 069	48 777	53 740	55 783	58 322	61 242	64 873
11. Disposable income (6-8-9)	31 043	35 117	38 979	41 502	44 315	45 488	49 386	52 074
12. Gross saving (11-7)	2 677	3 814	4 710	4 225	5 840	4 813	6 162	6 420
13. Saving rate, per cent (12/11)	8.6	10.9	12.1	10.2	13.2	10.6	12.5	12.3

1. Provisional data.
Source: National Institute of Statistics, *Contabilidad Nacional* (1997) and Bank of Spain, *Cuentas financieras* (1997).

Table C. **Public sector accounts**

Billion pesetas

	1991	1992	1993	1994	1995	1996[1]
	1. General government[2]					

	1991	1992	1993	1994	1995	1996[1]
Current account						
Receipts	21 423	24 164	24 905	25 595	26 608	28 617
Property income receivable	722	911	1 385	877	765	951
Indirect taxes	5 400	6 093	5 841	6 564	6 976	7 420
Direct taxes	6 604	7 344	7 280	7 413	7 978	8 534
Actual social contributions	7 033	8 041	8 501	8 824	8 780	9 519
Imputed social contributions	472	571	595	614	644	685
Miscellaneous current transfers	1 192	1 204	1 303	1 303	1 465	1 508
Disbursements	21 331	24 047	26 558	27 505	28 956	30 140
Final consumption expenditure	8 882	10 093	10 701	10 963	11 591	11 943
Property income payable	2 159	2 470	3 171	3 311	3 743	3 928
Subsidies	992	1 030	1 282	1 292	1 327	1 261
Social security benefits	8 370	9 509	10 294	10 663	11 014	11 604
Miscellaneous current transfers	928	945	1 110	1 276	1 281	1 404
Gross saving	663	734	−969	−1 160	−1 524	−675
Gross operating surplus	571	617	684	750	824	848
Net saving	92	117	−1 653	−1 910	−2 348	−1 523
Capital account						
Receipts	427	486	504	655	810	883
Capital transfers	320	357	354	468	634	697
Capital taxes	107	129	150	187	176	186
Disbursements	3 526	3 324	3 667	3 594	3 906	3 497
Gross fixed capital formation	2 645	2 389	2 477	2 538	2 494	2 197
Capital transfers	819	878	1 063	955	1 310	1 216
Net purchases of land and intangible assets	62	57	127	101	102	84
Balance	−3 099	−2 838	−3 163	−2 939	−3 096	−2 614
Net lending (+)						
or net borrowing (−)	−2 436	−2 104	−4 132	−4 099	−4 620	−3 289
(per cent of GDP)	(-4.4)	(-3.6)	(-6.8)	(-6.3)	(-6.6)	(-4.5)

1. Provisional data.
2. Central plus territorial government.
Source: National Institute of Statistics, *Contabilidad Nacional* (1997) and Bank of Spain, *Cuentas financieras* (1997).

Table C. **Public sector accounts** *(cont.)*

Billion pesetas

	1991	1992	1993	1994	1995	1996[1]
			2.	**Central government**		
Current account						
Receipts	11 791	13 285	13 470	13 750	14 625	15 792
Tax revenue	9 632	10 813	10 350	11 082	11 946	12 815
Property and entrepreneurial income (gross)	557	775	1 264	790	658	845
Current transfers	1 602	1 697	1 856	1 878	2 021	2 132
Disbursements	11 823	13 278	15 357	15 996	17 059	17 391
Purchase of goods and services	3 392	3 681	3 992	3 956	4 284	4 175
Current transfers	6 176	7 192	8 204	8 684	9 043	9 440
Subsidies	509	481	635	663	661	557
Other	1 746	1 924	2 526	2 693	3 071	3 219
Gross saving	261	312	–1 558	–1 896	–2 058	–1 222
Gross operating surplus	293	305	329	350	376	377
Net saving	–32	7	–1 887	–2 246	–2 434	–1 599
Capital account						
Receipts	164	129	129	160	348	290
Capital transfers	163	127	129	160	348	290
Capital taxes	1	2	0	0	0	0
Disbursements	1 790	1 792	2 266	1 587	2 072	1 547
Gross fixed capital formation	854	716	796	776	916	611
Capital transfers	896	1 050	1 381	739	1 095	894
Net purchases of land and intangible assets	40	26	89	72	61	42
Balance	–1 626	–1 663	–2 137	–1 427	–1 724	–1 257
Overall financial surplus (+) **or deficit (–)**	–1 365	–1 351	–3 695	–3 323	–3 782	–2 479

1.   Provisional data.
Source: National Institute of Statistics, *Contabilidad Nacional* (1997) and Bank of Spain, *Cuentas financieras* (1997).

Table C. **Public sector accounts** *(cont.)*

Billion pesetas

	1991	1992	1993	1994	1995	1996[1]
	3. Territorial government[2]					
Current account						
Receipts	5 099	5 777	6 117	6 365	6 721	7 222
Tax revenue	2 372	2 623	2 771	2 896	3 009	3 139
Property and entrepreneurial income (gross)	129	88	95	68	73	88
Current transfers	2 598	3 066	3 251	3 401	3 639	3 995
Disbursements	4 818	5 379	5 734	5 822	6 268	6 671
Purchase of goods and services	3 272	3 698	3 861	4 024	4 317	4 594
Current transfers	739	697	708	682	724	777
Other	807	984	1 165	1 116	1 227	1 300
Gross saving	488	631	650	847	795	912
Gross operating surplus	207	233	267	304	342	361
Net saving	281	398	383	543	453	551
Capital account						
Receipts	656	704	660	738	709	767
Capital transfers	550	577	510	551	533	582
Capital taxes	106	127	150	187	176	185
Disbursements	2 042	2 013	2 075	2 208	2 022	2 130
Gross fixed capital formation	1 628	1 531	1 531	1 635	1 439	1 455
Capital transfers	392	451	506	544	542	633
Net purchases of land and intangible assets	22	31	38	29	41	42
Balance	−1 386	−1 309	−1 415	−1 470	−1 313	−1 363
Overall financial surplus (+) **or deficit (−)**	−898	−678	−765	−623	−518	−451

1. Provisional data.
2. Regional and local government.
Source: National Institute of Statistics, *Contabilidad Nacional* (1997) and Bank of Spain, *Cuentas financieras* (1997).

Table C. **Public sector accounts** *(cont.)*

Billion pesetas

	1991	1992	1993	1994	1995	1996[1]
	4. Social security institutions[2]					
Current account						
Receipts	9 759	11 152	12 251	12 750	12 917	13 570
Social security contributions	6 964	7 967	8 417	8 741	8 683	9 420
Transfers	2 633	3 010	3 678	3 893	4 053	3 995
Other current receipts	162	175	156	116	181	155
Disbursements	9 917	11 439	12 400	12 956	13 287	14 047
Purchase of goods and services	2 218	2 714	2 847	2 982	2 990	3 174
Social security benefits	7 527	8 525	9 316	9 700	10 046	10 601
Current subsidies and transfers	172	200	237	274	251	272
Gross saving	–86	–209	–61	–110	–264	–367
Gross operating surplus	72	78	88	96	106	110
Net saving	–158	–287	–149	–206	–370	–477
Capital account						
Receipts[3]	88	290	554	95	92	149
Disbursements	176	157	167	138	152	144
Gross fixed capital formation	163	143	151	127	139	131
Capital transfers	13	14	16	11	13	13
Balance	–88	133	387	–43	–60	5
Overall financial surplus (+) **or deficit (–)**	–174	–76	326	–153	–324	–362

1. Provisional data.
2. Included in central government.
3. Capital transfers.
Source: National Institute of Statistics, *Contabilidad Nacional* (1997) and Bank of Spain, *Cuentas financieras* (1997).

Table D. **Labour market**[1]

	1990	1991	1992	1993	1994	1995	1996
	Thousands						
Labour force[2]	15 020	15 073	15 155	15 319	15 468	15 625	15 936
Employment[2]	12 579	12 609	12 366	11 838	11 730	12 042	12 396
Agriculture	1 485	1 345	1 253	1 198	1 151	1 106	1 076
Industry	2 978	2 890	2 804	2 540	2 474	2 486	2 500
Construction	1 220	1 273	1 196	1 088	1 059	1 135	1 176
Services	6 895	7 101	7 113	7 011	7 047	7 315	7 644
Employees, total	9 273	9 373	9 076	8 686	8 626	8 943	9 284
Unemployment	2 441	2 464	2 789	3 481	3 738	3 584	3 540
	Per cent						
Participation rate[2]							
Total (all age groups)	49.4	49.1	48.9	49.0	49.0	49.0	49.6
Men	66.7	65.8	64.7	64.3	63.3	62.7	63.1
Women	33.4	33.6	34.2	34.8	35.6	36.2	37.0
Structure of the labour force by level of education							
Illiterate or without studies	11.1	10.4	9.9	9.1	8.1	7.6	6.9
Primary	37.7	36.8	35.3	33.3	31.6	30.1	28.0
Secondary	35.7	36.7	38.1	39.9	41.2	42.1	43.2
Professional training and other post secondary	9.8	10.2	10.7	11.7	12.3	13.0	14.1
University degree	5.6	5.9	6.0	6.1	6.7	7.2	7.8
Employment structure[3]							
Agriculture	11.8	10.7	10.1	10.1	9.8	9.2	8.7
Industry	23.7	22.9	22.7	21.5	21.1	20.6	20.2
Construction	9.7	10.1	9.7	9.2	9.0	9.4	9.5
Services	54.8	56.3	57.5	59.2	60.1	60.7	61.7
Unemployment[4]							
Total	16.3	16.3	18.4	22.7	24.2	22.9	22.2
Two years or more	5.7	5.2	5.3	6.5	8.1	8.6	8.1
Male	12.0	12.3	14.3	19.0	19.8	18.2	17.6
Female	24.2	23.8	25.6	29.2	31.4	30.6	29.6
Less than 25 years old	32.3	31.1	34.5	43.2	45.1	42.5	42.0
Age 25-54	13.1	13.7	15.7	19.4	20.9	20.0	19.3
Age 55 and over	7.6	8.0	9.0	10.8	11.6	11.4	10.9

1. The data do not take into account the upward bias resulting from the gradual incorporation of the results of the 1991 census.
2. Excluding those who are on compulsory military service.
3. Per cent of total employment.
4. Per cent of total labour force.
Source: Ministry of Economy and Finance, *Síntesis Mensual de Indicadores Económicos* (1997) and Ministry of Labour and Social Affairs, *Boletín de Estadísticas Laborales* (1997).

Table E. **Price and wage trends**

Percentage change at annual rate

	1990	1991	1992	1993	1994	1995	1996
	Prices						
Consumer prices	6.7	5.9	5.9	4.6	4.7	4.7	3.6
Food	6.5	3.5	3.7	1.1	5.7	5.3	3.7
Non-food	6.8	7.2	7.1	6.2	4.3	4.4	3.5
Energy	8.2	7.6	6.7	7.5	3.6	3.5	3.7
Non-energy	6.6	5.8	5.9	4.4	4.9	4.7	3.6
Non-food and non-energy[1]	6.5	6.4	6.8	5.6	4.6	4.9	3.6
Industrial prices	2.2	1.5	1.4	2.4	4.3	6.4	1.7
Food	1.3	1.4	2.8	5.3	6.9	5.7	5.2
Non-food	3.6	4.6	3.3	1.8	1.6	4.6	2.2
Energy	5.4	3.4	2.2	3.6	3.1	2.0	3.0
Non-energy	1.8	1.1	1.4	2.2	4.4	6.9	1.5
Consumer goods	3.1	3.5	2.9	3.4	4.4	5.0	3.9
Investment goods	4.1	3.5	2.3	1.3	1.8	4.2	2.4
Intermediate goods	0.9	−0.7	−0.2	1.8	4.8	8.3	−0.5
of which: Non-energy	−1.3	−1.8	−0.3	1.1	5.5	10.4	−1.6
Unit value							
Exports	−1.8	−0.9	1.1	5.1	4.2	6.3	1.9
Imports	−3.4	−2.7	−1.2	5.2	5.8	4.4	2.2
of which: Non-energy	−4.7	−2.8	−0.1	4.5	6.2	4.4	1.0
	Wages						
Average increase in contractual wages	8.1	7.9	7.2	5.4	3.4	3.7	3.8
Monthly earnings per employee	8.5	7.6	7.5	6.4	4.7	4.5	4.5
of which: Industry	8.5	8.8	8.0	6.5	4.7	4.9	5.5
Daily pay in agriculture	11.5	9.2	9.8	5.4	6.2	6.0	4.1
Salary cost per head in construction (including social security contributions)	10.5	8.8	6.8	7.1	4.6	5.1	4.2

1. Seasonal food and energy excluded.

Source: Ministry of Economy and Finance, *Síntesis Mensual de Indicadores Económicos* (1997) and Bank of Spain, *Boletín Estadístico* (1997).

Table F. **Money and credit**

Billion pesetas

	1990	1993	1994	1995	1996	Oct 1996	Oct 1997
	1. Monetary indicators *(end of period, levels)*						
ALP	**50 793**	**65 429**	**70 046**	**76 479**	**82 119**	**79 150**	**82 930**
M1	14 163	16 181	17 338	17 888	19 116	17 957	20 193
Currency in circulation	4 533	6 509	7 164	7 535	7 941	7 650	8 072
Sight deposits	9 630	9 672	10 173	10 353	11 175	10 308	12 121
M2	23 037	26 967	28 753	29 638	31 718	29 879	33 204
of which: Saving deposits	8 874	10 786	11 416	11 750	12 601	11 922	13 011
M3	46 686	59 261	63 676	70 439	73 820	71 765	74 045
of which: Time deposits	13 868	20 620	22 181	24 749	24 227	24 861	21 702
Other liquid assets in the hands of the public	13 888	17 842	19 112	22 092	26 174	24 410	28 024
Non-monetary liabilities	4 518	4 328	4 230	4 508	4 829	4 422	5 017
General government	2 700	3 080	2 932	3 158	3 291	2 984	3 529
Private sector	1 818	1 248	1 298	1 350	1 538	1 438	1 488
	2. Credit aggregates *(end of period, levels)*						
Internal credit	56 911	66 672	74 419	79 560	86 687	83 739	91 214
Credit to general government	18 207	19 579	25 795	27 773	30 980	29 201	29 578
Bank credits	3 560	3 534	5 555	6 392	6 094	5 777	5 420
Securities	12 485	11 740	15 659	17 321	18 363	17 723	17 381
Money market credits	2 132	5 092	5 533	5 040	7 147	6 318	7 377
Other	30	– 787	– 952	– 980	– 624	– 617	– 600
Credit to private sector	38 705	47 094	48 623	51 787	55 707	54 537	61 636
Bank credits	36 295	44 026	45 445	48 241	51 828	50 515	57 351
Securities	2 405	2 964	3 008	3 166	3 565	3 698	3 907
Money market credits	205	197	250	380	315	324	377
Other	– 200	– 93	– 80	0	– 1	0	1
Credit to foreign sector	2 541	10 298	7 006	8 844	8 642	8 350	6060

Source: Bank of Spain, *Boletín Estadístico* (1997).

Table G. **Balance of payments**[1]

Million dollars

	1989	1990	1991	1992	1993	1994	1995	1996
Current account	-10 926	-18 033	-19 807	-21 098	-5 464	-6 809	1 126	1 767
Trade balance	-25 462	-29 073	-30 398	-30 160	-14 906	-14 681	-17 600	-14 889
Merchandise exports	44 861	55 484	59 891	65 990	61 901	73 821	90 986	102 106
Merchandise imports	70 322	84 557	90 288	96 150	76 807	88 502	108 587	116 995
Non-factor services, net	12 690	11 777	12 052	12 346	11 282	14 566	17 841	20 033
Non-factor services, credit	24 673	27 748	29 315	33 695	30 954	33 938	39 970	44 390
Non-factor services, debit	11 982	15 971	17 263	21 349	19 673	19 371	22 129	24 357
Factor income, net	-2 771	-3 523	-4 281	-5 737	-3 518	-8 171	-3 872	-5 936
Factor income, credit	3 764	7 762	10 898	14 087	11 828	8 676	13 655	14 112
Factor income, debit	6 535	11 285	15 179	19 824	15 346	16 848	17 527	20 048
Official transfers, net	1 446	160	869	-16	88	-240	-3 332	-4 775
Private transfers, net	3 171	2 626	1 950	2 470	1 591	1 717	8 089	7 334
Capital account	-9	1 440	3 176	3 500	3 031	2 590	6 256	6 367
Financial account	13 389	15 654	17 622	23 545	4 127	5 484	-1 254	-4 574
Direct investment abroad	-1 470	-3 441	-4 424	-2 170	-2 648	-3 899	-3 593	-4 629
Portfolio investment, assets	-168	-1 352	-2 379	-2 720	-6 840	-1 889	-577	-3 768
Other investment, assets	-109	-13 077	-7 000	-40 126	-73 890	9 892	-37 519	1 407
Direct investment in reporting countries	8 433	13 838	12 445	13 350	8 072	9 424	6 133	6 405
Portfolio investment, liabilities	8 237	10 045	21 901	12 265	55 140	-19 543	20 716	2 476
Other investment, liabilities	3 491	16 604	11 405	25 584	19 782	11 444	6 799	17 783
Reserve assets, net	-5 025	-6 963	-14 329	17 363	4 509	54	6 786	-24 246
Errors and omissions, net	-2 454	938	-991	-5 946	-1 695	-1 262	-6 128	-3 558

1. On a transactions basis.
Source: OECD Secretariat.

Table H.   **Foreign trade**[1]
1.   By commodity

Billion pesetas

	1990	1991	1992	1993	1994	1995	1996[2]
			1. Imports, cif				
1. Live animals and related products	372.0	433.8	461.4	500.9	599.6	632.0	638.7
2. Vegetables	289.6	330.8	342.2	393.3	497.2	667.9	602.0
3. Oils and fats	28.9	43.2	44.8	45.2	75.3	109.9	87.6
4. Food products, beverages and tobacco	311.3	376.1	431.7	473.3	563.1	639.6	645.7
5. Mineral products	1 172.3	1 185.4	1 157.4	1 228.7	1 340.0	1 385.1	1 623.1
6. Chemicals and related products	704.8	779.2	861.2	927.3	1 193.2	1 395.4	1 467.7
7. Plastic materials	355.1	377.0	412.1	420.8	562.0	757.4	778.2
8. Leather, leather manufactures	94.6	101.9	104.3	90.0	133.5	134.9	147.0
9. Cork and wood products	130.3	123.6	130.5	107.5	141.2	175.2	168.1
10. Paper, articles of paper pulp	268.3	288.8	302.3	297.7	381.6	504.9	450.6
11. Textile and related products	403.4	513.9	600.2	509.3	660.7	720.9	789.0
12. Footwear, hat-making	31.9	47.2	56.3	51.4	62.4	66.8	81.2
13. Mineral manufactures, plaster, glass	107.3	120.4	124.5	102.8	127.0	158.3	163.3
14. Pearls, precious stones, jewellery	63.5	74.8	73.1	54.7	78.1	91.2	92.0
15. Manufactures of metal	642.4	663.0	669.3	617.4	853.3	1 164.5	1 121.2
16. Machinery and electrical machinery	2 208.2	2 351.9	2 341.7	2 164.6	2 624.1	3 144.6	3 449.3
17. Transport equipment	1 210.4	1 316.0	1 498.8	1 462.2	1 772.0	1 957.8	2 317.6
18. Optical instruments, photographic apparatus, sound equipment	359.0	350.4	359.4	347.4	402.4	435.9	473.5
19. Arms and ammunition	4.5	4.6	3.4	8.5	9.8	10.4	5.7
20. Furniture, toys, sporting goods	131.7	170.9	214.1	181.4	205.7	221.3	236.7
21. Works of art, antiques	25.2	19.4	16.2	74.4	66.6	15.6	97.7
Total	8 914.7	9 672.1	10 205.0	10 058.9	12 348.7	14 389.3	15 435.7

1. By commodity

Billion pesetas

	1990	1991	1992	1993	1994	1995	1996[2]
			2. Exports, fob				
1. Live animals and related products	113.3	108.3	121.3	152.4	225.5	279.0	350.8
2. Vegetables	418.2	489.0	543.1	649.9	781.4	886.5	936.6
3. Oils and fats	92.5	118.4	60.4	91.7	124.6	120.7	162.0
4. Food products, beverages and tobacco	232.7	272.0	304.7	352.3	457.6	533.5	602.6
5. Mineral products	320.0	321.4	247.2	274.9	283.6	276.4	422.9
6. Chemicals and related products	343.1	360.7	390.7	498.4	662.9	786.0	841.3
7. Plastic materials	256.7	262.8	277.8	342.0	459.1	595.8	623.5
8. Leather, leather manufactures	72.7	64.6	72.2	84.4	111.4	117.7	142.3
9. Cork and wood products	51.8	50.1	55.1	60.6	75.0	90.9	95.9
10. Paper, articles of paper pulp	161.5	167.4	188.4	202.5	268.8	362.4	350.5
11. Textile and related products	228.5	240.1	253.6	303.8	391.6	507.0	573.9
12. Footwear, hat-making	157.0	141.8	135.4	162.2	234.3	251.9	270.7
13. Mineral manufactures, plaster, glass	171.3	185.1	216.9	259.2	340.0	393.6	422.8
14. Pearls, precious stones, jewellery	28.6	35.8	33.2	40.2	61.6	59.6	58.6
15. Manufactures of metal	539.7	572.7	565.6	698.4	839.3	974.6	1 046.2
16. Machinery and electrical machinery	868.1	978.3	1 070.8	1 219.2	1 540.2	1 852.3	2 097.5
17. Transport equipment	1 320.5	1 575.4	1 775.7	1 979.2	2 577.4	2 963.9	3 357.4
18. Optical instruments, photographic apparatus, sound equipment	53.1	62.4	78.5	98.3	124.2	118.4	158.7
19. Arms and ammunition	7.9	7.8	6.8	13.6	13.1	13.2	10.3
20. Furniture, toys, sporting goods	124.0	127.4	135.0	156.1	197.0	262.0	308.0
21. Works of art, antiques	81.9	83.9	73.4	40.3	27.6	30.5	98.6
Total	5 642.8	6 225.7	6 605.7	7 679.6	9 796.3	11 475.8	12 931.0

1.   Customs clearance basis.
2.   Provisional figures.
Source: Ministry of Economy and Finance.

Table H. **Foreign trade**[1] *(cont.)*
2. By geographical area
Billion pesetas

		1990	1991	1992	1993	1994	1995	1996[2]
				1. Imports, cif				
Total		8 914.7	9 672.1	10 205.0	10 131.0	12 348.7	14 318.3	15 435.7
OECD		7 158.6	7 753.8	8 203.4	8 000.2	9 779.9	11 364.6	12 255.6
of which:	United States	744.8	770.5	755.0	739.2	901.0	919.1	977.7
	Japan	395.2	451.5	475.6	434.5	440.0	472.7	436.3
	Canada	44.4	46.2	58.3	50.1	54.4	80.3	71.0
EU		5 602.2	6 091.6	6 485.7	6 308.0	7 915.4	9 362.5	10 226.9
of which:	United Kingdom	638.1	728.2	745.0	753.5	969.2	1 120.0	1 278.0
	France	1 307.3	1 467.7	1 619.3	1 700.1	2 155.7	2 454.9	2 754.7
	Germany	1 463.0	1 565.5	1 673.7	1 514.9	1 803.7	2 189.6	2 284.8
	Italy	905.6	971.7	1 003.1	856.4	1 104.5	1 310.0	1 471.8
	Portugal	222.8	263.3	275.8	268.7	343.2	421.6	452.6
Non OECD countries		1 756.1	1 918.3	2 001.6	2 130.8	2 568.9	2 953.6	3 180.1
	Ex-COMECON	189.9	127.4	152.5	200.6	261.2	370.6	346.8
	OPEC	630.4	679.3	586.2	590.9	738.8	789.1	963.9
	Latin America[3]	414.7	440.3	445.3	454.7	542.3	619.3	638.8
	Other	521.0	671.2	817.6	884.5	1 026.5	1 174.6	1 230.5
				2. Exports, fob				
Total		5 642.8	6 225.7	6 605.7	7 754.6	9 796.3	11 423.1	12 931.0
OECD		4 690.4	5 179.8	5 535.5	6 230.7	8 019.2	9 350.4	10 434.4
of which:	United States	328.9	305.8	315.3	372.7	481.9	472.2	544.0
	Japan	64.3	61.4	61.6	71.9	131.7	157.1	155.1
	Canada	35.8	38.2	34.7	45.6	56.5	55.7	56.0
EU		4 028.6	4 548.7	4 845.9	5 348.1	6 917.2	8 264.6	9 238.1
of which:	United Kingdom	507.2	477.9	505.7	638.1	804.6	915.9	1 098.9
	France	1 173.1	1 244.4	1 335.0	1 465.6	1 971.2	2 345.8	2 600.9
	Germany	756.0	992.6	1 036.5	1 132.6	1 390.4	1 760.1	1 879.1
	Italy	603.8	706.7	719.4	704.4	902.2	1 045.3	1 129.8
	Portugal	341.7	410.4	496.5	563.2	762.6	951.1	1 112.5
Non OECD countries		952.4	1 045.8	1 070.2	1 523.9	1 777.1	2 072.7	2 496.6
	Ex-COMECON	66.8	85.2	84.8	120.2	165.7	195.9	284.0
	OPEC	192.1	215.4	231.9	307.0	305.5	338.0	350.8
	Latin America[3]	221.3	235.7	315.4	482.0	610.4	642.8	782.9
	Other	472.2	509.5	438.0	614.7	695.6	896.1	1 079.0

1. Customs clearance basis.
2. Provisional data.
3. Central and South America excluding Ecuador, Venezuela, Cuba and Mexico.
Source: Ministry of Economy and Finance.

Table I. Foreign assets and liabilities

Billion pesetas, end of period

	1991	1992	1993	1994	1995	1996[1]
Liabilities	23 774.2	29 490.2	42 020.9	42 248.2	45 675.0	49 898.0
Monetary institutions	9 400.0	11 808.7	15 140.1	16 404.2	16 714.0	20 047.0
Bank of Spain	46.7	52.4	65.8	67.9	67.0	129.0
Banking system	9 353.3	11 756.3	15 074.3	16 336.3	16 647.0	19 918.0
Government	3 125.0	3 870.0	10 227.0	7 874.0	9 915.0	10 391.0
Private sector	11 249.2	13 811.5	16 653.8	17 970.0	19 046.0	19 460.0
Assets	15 902.7	19 591.4	30 925.8	30 034.7	33 494.0	38 679.0
Monetary institutions	12 064.2	14 587.6	24 582.3	22 376.9	24 388.0	27 591.0
Bank of Spain	6 731.3	5 604.1	6 151.7	5 796.1	4 567.0	7 960.0
Banking system	5 332.9	8 983.5	18 430.6	16 580.8	19 821.0	19 631.0
Government	119.7	127.9	135.8	135.8	136.0	136.0
Private sector	3 718.8	4 875.9	6 207.7	7 522.0	8 970.0	10 952.0

1. Provisional data.
Source: Bank of Spain, *Cuentas financieras* (1997).

197

Table J. **Public sector**

	1985	1990	1993	1994	1995	1996[1]
	Per cent of GDP					
Structure of general government expenditure and tax receipts						
Expenditure, total	41.2	42.0	47.6	45.8	44.8	43.6
Current consumption	14.7	15.6	17.6	16.9	16.7	16.5
Transfers to households	16.0	15.9	18.7	18.4	17.5	17.6
Subsidies	2.4	1.9	2.1	2.0	1.9	1.8
Fixed investment	3.7	5.0	4.3	4.1	3.8	3.2
Other	4.3	3.5	4.9	4.4	4.9	4.5
Tax receipts, total	31.2	35.3	36.4	36.1	35.1	35.7
Income tax	8.5	12.0	11.9	11.4	11.5	11.6
Personal income	6.5	8.6	9.4	9.3	9.2	9.2
Corporate profits	2.0	3.4	2.5	2.1	2.3	2.4
Social security contributions	13.2	13.4	14.9	14.6	13.6	13.9
Taxes on goods and services	9.5	9.9	9.6	10.1	10.0	10.2
Memorandum item:						
Net lending	−6.8	−3.8	−6.8	−6.3	−6.5	− 4.5
	Per cent					
Taxation						
Personal income tax						
Lowest marginal rate	8	25	20	20	20	20
Highest marginal rate	66	56	56	56	56	56
Number of brackets	(34)	(16)	(17)	(17)	(17)	(17)
Marginal rate[2]	33	27	24.5	24.5	24.5	24.5
Average rate[2]	10.4	10.9	12.3	12.9	13.2	13.5
Social security contributions[3]						
Marginal rate[2]	36.6	36.2	37.7	38.2	37.2	37.2
Employees' contribution rate	6.0	6.0	6.1	6.6	6.4	6.4
Employers' contribution rate	30.6	30.2	31.6	31.6	30.8	30.8
VAT standard rate	..	12.0	15.0	15.0	16.0	16.0

1. Provisional data.
2. The average bracket for a single production worker.
3. Including unemployment, social security and other obligatory contributions.
Source: OECD, *National Accounts* (1997) and *The Tax/Benefit Position of employees* (1997).

Table K. **Production structure and performance indicators**

Per cent of total

	1985	1990	1993	1994	1995	1996[1]
Production structure						
Factor cost, current prices						
Agriculture	6.2	4.9	3.8	3.5	3.1	3.7
Industry	30.2	27.5	25.0	25.2	25.6	25.2
Construction	6.7	9.7	8.6	8.5	8.7	8.3
Services	56.9	57.8	62.7	62.8	62.6	62.8
Production structure						
Factor cost, 1986 prices						
Agriculture	6.8	5.5	5.3	4.6	3.9	4.7
Industry	30.4	29.8	28.7	29.3	29.9	29.5
Construction	6.7	8.6	7.7	7.7	8.0	7.6
Services	56.1	56.2	58.3	58.3	58.2	58.2
Productivity growth[2]						
Agriculture	5.2	10.9	4.2	− 6.4	− 9.7	26.2
Industry	6.8	− 0.7	6.9	7.3	4.2	0.1
Construction	7.4	2.4	3.9	4.5	− 0.5	− 6.2
Services	0.8	− 0.1	2.3	1.7	− 1.1	− 2.3
Sectoral distribution of foreign						
direct investment projects						
Manufacturing and mining	62.2	35.0	..	..	..	..
Trade and tourism	14.0	9.5	..	..	..	..
Financial sector	17.8	46.5	..	..	..	..
Other	6.0	9.0	..	..	..	..
Sectoral distribution of industrial						
employment						
Food, beverages and tobacco	16.0	14.7	15.8	15.9	15.7	16.2
Textiles and clothing	18.0	16.9	15.3	15.6	15.6	14.5
Chemicals and refining	6.9	6.3	5.8	6.0	5.8	6.1
Metal products	13.9	14.0	13.3	12.7	13.2	12.7
Electrical and mechanical machinery	8.1	9.0	8.7	9.0	9.2	9.7
Electronic machinery and equipment	3.0	3.4	3.2	3.0	2.8	2.7
Transport equipment	9.5	9.3	9.8	9.7	9.5	9.7
Other	24.7	26.5	28.2	28.1	28.3	28.3

1. Provisional data.
2. Sectoral production/sectoral employment.
Source: Bank of Spain, *Cuentas financieras* (1997), National Institute of Statistics and Ministry of Economy and Finance.

BASIC STATISTICS:

INTERNATIONAL COMPARISONS

	Units	Reference period [1]	Australia	Austria
Population				
Total	Thousands	1995	18 054	8 047
Inhabitants per sq. km	Number	1995	2	96
Net average annual increase over previous 10 years	%	1995	1.4	0.6
Employment				
Total civilian employment (TCE)[2]	Thousands	1994	7 943	3 737
of which: Agriculture	% of TCE	1994	5.1	7.2
Industry	% of TCE	1994	23.5	33.2
Services	% of TCE	1994	71.4	59.6
Gross domestic product (GDP)				
At current prices and current exchange rates	Bill. US$	1995	360.3	233.3
Per capita	US$	1995	19 957	28 997
At current prices using current PPPs[3]	Bill. US$	1995	349.4	167.2
Per capita	US$	1995	19 354	20 773
Average annual volume growth over previous 5 years	%	1995	3.3	2
Gross fixed capital formation (GFCF)	% of GDP	1995	20.1	24.7
of which: Machinery and equipment	% of GDP	1995	10.5 (94)	9 (
Residential construction	% of GDP	1995	5.6 (94)	6.4 (
Average annual volume growth over previous 5 years	%	1995	3	3
Gross saving ratio[4]	% of GDP	1995	16.9	24.9
General government				
Current expenditure on goods and services	% of GDP	1995	17.2	18.9
Current disbursements[5]	% of GDP	1994	36.2	47.8
Current receipts	% of GDP	1994	34.2	47.3
Net official development assistance	% of GNP	1994	0.33	0.33
Indicators of living standards				
Private consumption per capita using current PPPs[3]	US$	1995	12 090	11 477
Passenger cars, per 1 000 inhabitants	Number	1993	438	418
Telephones, per 1 000 inhabitants	Number	1993	482	451
Television sets, per 1 000 inhabitants	Number	1992	482	480
Doctors, per 1 000 inhabitants	Number	1994	2.2 (91)	2.4
Infant mortality per 1 000 live births	Number	1994	5.9	6.3
Wages and prices (average annual increase over previous 5 years)				
Wages (earnings or rates according to availability)	%	1995	2	5
Consumer prices	%	1995	2.5	3.2
Foreign trade				
Exports of goods, fob*	Mill. US$	1995	53 092	57 200
As % of GDP	%	1995	14.7	24.5
Average annual increase over previous 5 years	%	1995	6	6.9
Imports of goods, cif*	Mill. US$	1995	57 406	65 293
As % of GDP	%	1995	15.9	28
Average annual increase over previous 5 years	%	1995	8.1	5.9
Total official reserves[6]	Mill. SDRs	1995	8 003	12 600
As ratio of average monthly imports of goods	Ratio	1995	1.7	2.3

* At current prices and exchange rates.
1. Unless otherwise stated.
2. According to the definitions used in OECD *Labour Force Statistics.*
3. PPPs = Purchasing Power Parities.
4. Gross saving = Gross national disposable income minus private and government consumption.
5. Current disbursements = Current expenditure on goods and services plus current transfers and payments of property income.
6. Gold included in reserves is valued at 35 SDRs per ounce. End of year.

EMPLOYMENT OPPORTUNITIES

Economics Department, OECD

The Economics Department of the OECD offers challenging and rewarding opportunities to economists interested in applied policy analysis in an international environment. The Department's concerns extend across the entire field of economic policy analysis, both macro-economic and microeconomic. Its main task is to provide, for discussion by committees of senior officials from Member countries, documents and papers dealing with current policy concerns. Within this programme of work, three major responsibilities are:

- to prepare regular surveys of the economies of individual Member countries;
- to issue full twice-yearly reviews of the economic situation and prospects of the OECD countries in the context of world economic trends;
- to analyse specific policy issues in a medium-term context for the OECD as a whole, and to a lesser extent for the non-OECD countries.

The documents prepared for these purposes, together with much of the Department's other economic work, appear in published form in the *OECD Economic Outlook, OECD Economic Surveys, OECD Economic Studies* and the Department's *Working Papers* series.

The Department maintains a world econometric model, INTERLINK, which plays an important role in the preparation of the policy analyses and twice-yearly projections. The availability of extensive cross-country data bases and good computer resources facilitates comparative empirical analysis, much of which is incorporated into the model.

The Department is made up of about 80 professional economists from a variety of backgrounds and Member countries. Most projects are carried out by small teams and last from four to eighteen months. Within the Department, ideas and points of view are widely discussed; there is a lively professional interchange, and all professional staff have the opportunity to contribute actively to the programme of work.

Skills the Economics Department is looking for:

a) Solid competence in using the tools of both microeconomic and macroeconomic theory to answer policy questions. Experience indicates that this normally requires the equivalent of a Ph.D. in economics or substantial relevant professional experience to compensate for a lower degree.

b) Solid knowledge of economic statistics and quantitative methods; this includes how to identify data, estimate structural relationships, apply basic techniques of time series analysis, and test hypotheses. It is essential to be able to interpret results sensibly in an economic policy context.

c) A keen interest in and extensive knowledge of policy issues, economic developments and their political/social contexts.

d) Interest and experience in analysing questions posed by policy-makers and presenting the results to them effectively and judiciously. Thus, work experience in government agencies or policy research institutions is an advantage.

e) The ability to write clearly, effectively, and to the point. The OECD is a bilingual organisation with French and English as the official languages. Candidates must have excellent knowledge of one of these languages, and some knowledge of the other. Knowledge of other languages might also be an advantage for certain posts.

f) For some posts, expertise in a particular area may be important, but a successful candidate is expected to be able to work on a broader range of topics relevant to the work of the Department. Thus, except in rare cases, the Department does not recruit narrow specialists.

g) The Department works on a tight time schedule with strict deadlines. Moreover, much of the work in the Department is carried out in small groups. Thus, the ability to work with other economists from a variety of cultural and professional backgrounds, to supervise junior staff, and to produce work on time is important.

General information

The salary for recruits depends on educational and professional background. Positions carry a basic salary from FF 305 700 or FF 377 208 for Administrators (economists) and from FF 438 348 for Principal Administrators (senior economists). This may be supplemented by expatriation and/or family allowances, depending on nationality, residence and family situation. Initial appointments are for a fixed term of two to three years.

Vacancies are open to candidates from OECD Member countries. The Organisation seeks to maintain an appropriate balance between female and male staff and among nationals from Member countries.

For further information on employment opportunities in the Economics Department, contact:

Administrative Unit
Economics Department
OECD
2, rue André-Pascal
75775 PARIS CEDEX 16
FRANCE

E-Mail: compte.esadmin@oecd.org

Applications citing "ECSUR", together with a detailed *curriculum vitae* in English or French, should be sent to the Head of Personnel at the above address.

OECD PUBLICATIONS, 2, rue André-Pascal, 75775 PARIS CEDEX 16
PRINTED IN FRANCE
(10 98 24 1 P) ISBN 92-64-15988-6 – No. 50025 1998
ISSN 0376-6438